Growing Up Protestant

Growing Up Protestant

Parents, Children, and Mainline Churches

MARGARET LAMBERTS BENDROTH

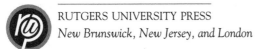

RUTGERS UNIVERSITY PRESS
New Brunswick, New Jersey, and London

Library of Congress Cataloging-in-Publication Data

Bendroth, Margaret Lamberts, 1954-
    Growing up Protestant : parents, children, and mainline churches / Margaret
Lamberts Bendroth.
        p. cm.
    Includes bibliographical references and index.
    ISBN 0–8135–3013-X (cloth: alk. paper) — ISBN 0–8135–3014–8 (pbk. : alk. paper)
    1. Family—Religious life. 2. Protestant churches—United States. I. Title

BV4526.2 .B44 2002
261.8'3585'0973—dc21   2001019841

British Cataloging-in-Publication data for this book is available from the British Library.

Manufactured in the United States of America

To Nathan

Contents

Acknowledgments

THIS BOOK BEGAN as part of a Lilly Endowment project on the Education and Formation of People in Faith, led by Dorothy Bass at Valparaiso University. The final product owes much to her long-term encouragement and practical support, for which I'm deeply grateful. Other members of this project—Scott Appleby, Jon Pahl, and Virginia Brereton—also helped to push my thinking forward in numerous directions. I'm also grateful to Don Browning and the members of the Family, Religion, and Culture project at the University of Chicago for my first introduction to the complexities of family-related issues past and present. Marcia Bunge's invitation to participate in her working group on the Child in Christian Thought, another Lilly project based at Valparaiso University, also introduced me to an insightful group of scholars who prodded me forward on some thorny theological issues I'd have otherwise avoided. In more ways than I could count, the ideas in this book as well as the decision to set them into writing reflect the influence of this growing network of religion scholars, historians, and theologians.

A summer stipend from the Louisville Institute provided invaluable funds for research travel and a quiet place to write, and I am much indebted to James Lewis and the institute for this kind help as well as to the other summer stipend and dissertation fellows for their constructive suggestions at our January meeting. Calvin College also awarded me a Calvin Research Fellowship for the fall of 2000, allowing the necessary course releases to complete this book with reasonable equanimity. The interlibrary loan staff at Calvin provided patient and invaluable assistance, as did Kenneth Ross and the librarians at the Presbyterian Historical Society in Philadelphia.

Kind friends and colleagues—Virginia Brereton, Ellen Ezorsky, James Bratt,

and Dorothy Bass—have read all or parts of this manuscript. Suzanne Bratt, Deirdre King Hainsworth, and Sarah Best Castricum, my student assistants, also provided invaluable help along the way. I am grateful to David Myers, my editor at Rutgers University Press, for his ongoing support and enthusiasm for this project, even when it was still in the rogue proposal stage.

My parents, who raised me with a clear sense of identity within a religious tradition, have perhaps the most long-term investment in this book, and I owe them a deep debt of thanks. It is also customary for authors to thank their spouses and children for their support and encouragement, and I do this happily, adding a special word of appreciation to the enthusiastic border collie who oversaw, and impeded, much of the writing process. Of course, the fundamental irony of writing a book about families is that it requires forced absences from the company of spouse and children. I thank Norman, Nathan, and Anna for their mostly gracious attitudes about this and for providing the busy human background for my reading and writing about ideal Christian families. Our years together have kept me humble and deeply contented.

Growing Up Protestant

Introduction

Mainline Protestant Churches and American Families

Home and family are key, yet relatively unexplored, dimensions of religion in the United States, especially for the past one hundred years. American cultural lore is replete with images of nineteenth-century domestic piety, of saintly Victorian mothers and their Bible-reading children—but what of their grandchildren and great grandchildren? As families changed in composition and function and as the content of belief shifted under the stresses of modernity, where did religion fit? What might modern parents say to their children about Christianity? These are some of the questions this book seeks to answer. Put simply, its goal is to summarize and reflect upon a long discussion about Christian child rearing, the role of godly parents, and the meaning of religion in modern life.

The subjects of this study are white, middle-class mainline Protestants, here principally northern Presbyterians, Baptists, Methodists, and Congregationalists, generally moderate to liberal in theology.[1] They are hardly an exotic group; even in the highly sensitive atmosphere of our time, they seem to have evaded any specific social location. Mainline Protestants are, in many ways, the neutral backing to the ethnic crazy quilt of American diversity, the mythical standard by which everyone else becomes an "other."

This symbolic role is both a handicap and a privilege. The right to be ethnically invisible comes at a cost, including the assumption that people who in some sense represent normality have no stories worth telling. This book, then, is an attempt not to investigate an unfamiliar realm of American religious experience but to explore some more-traveled regions. The purpose is not to reestablish mainline churches at the center of American religion nor to simply excoriate them for perceived failures. This study analyzes the evolving meaning of the "Christian family" in middle-class culture, as a means of making concrete some of the unspoken assumptions about domestic piety that have circulated for the past century and a half within mainline churches.

Scholars have paid scant attention to the religious dimensions of modern family life. It is not hard to gather the impression from historical accounts that religion simply disappeared from homes at the close of the Victorian era.[2] Although domestic piety changed between the nineteenth and twentieth centuries, it has certainly survived and left behind a paper trail large enough to require some fairly arbitrary limitations in my approach to the topic. I do not, for example, deal with church directives regarding marriage, easily the subject of another book, nor do I attempt to reconstruct in any systematic way the psychological experience of children in Protestant homes or an ethnography of religious practices or holiday observances. I have highlighted certain gender issues, especially as they are reflected in the changing role of mothers, but I do not differentiate much between directives for boys and girls. My emphases have, as much as possible, followed those in my sources, which focus on changing Protestant conceptions about the relative roles of parents and children, especially the very young. Because so much theological concern has centered on the problem of original sin, infant damnation, and the nature of childhood faith, teenagers and young adults do not make much of an appearance until the final chapters.

Not surprisingly perhaps, much of the material in this book speaks to the controversies over family values in the present day. Mainline Protestants have been bit players in many of these debates but not necessarily for political or theological reasons. One could say that family-related issues have riveted the attention of mainline churches but mostly as a progression of hotly contested debates in sexual ethics and church polity, beginning with divorce and remarriage in the late 1950s, premarital sex in the 1960s and 1970s, and abortion and homosexuality in the 1980s and 1990s.

In the meantime *family values* has become associated with conservative evangelical organizations. Parlayed from bumper stickers to presidential debates, the phrase suggests nostalgia for a better, earlier time when family life was more harmonious and less secular, when government was less intrusive and churches and parents exercised real spiritual authority. *Family values* has become so strongly tied to evangelical causes that many moderate and liberal Protestants have shied away from the phrase, reinforcing the assumption that only theologically and politically conservative Protestants are pro-family.

But the history of religion and the family, at least until the past few decades, suggests otherwise. For one thing, conservative Protestants have embraced family issues only very recently. Over its long history the American evangelical tradition has been deeply suspicious of domestic entanglements; its individualistic piety has at times sounded almost antifamily, taking very seriously Christ's call to leave everything and serve him alone. Indeed, as this book argues, the identification of erstwhile fundamentalists as pro-family is one of the ironies of recent history.

In contrast, mainline Protestants have diligently pursued family issues for most of the twentieth century. In researching this book, I read scores of books, pamphlets, and periodical articles describing the ins and outs of Christian child rearing, church programs for educating parents, and self-administered tests for determining whether a home was indeed Christian. I read a multitude of denominational resources for sustaining the family altar as well as many spiritual biographies detailing this practice remembered from childhood. And I found meticulously gathered surveys and interviews conducted by church-based researchers attempting to measure the presence of religion in Protestant families. I did not come anywhere close to exhausting these resources—if gauged only by the number of forests slain in behalf of the written word, mainline churches could easily support a claim to be family advocates.

A Paradoxical Legacy

Historic Christianity has, of course, embraced family values only inconsistently. Indeed, as the opening chapter describes, nineteenth-century Protestant domesticity ran up against a long tradition of theological ambivalence. Christ himself never married, and he called men away from their wives and children to become disciples. "Anyone who loves his father or mother more than me is not worthy of me," he commanded; likewise, "anyone who loves his son or daughter more than me is not worthy of me" (MT 10:37).

But Christ also used familial metaphors in a positive sense: "Whoever does the will of my Father in heaven is my brother and sister and mother" (MT 12:50). The New Testament church, organized around households in the Mediterranean world, followed a similar course, using family metaphors to denote their supernatural unity and commitment to one another, as "brothers" and "sisters" in Christ.[3] Still, the persistent ascetic strain within Christian thought fostered regular suspicion of untoward earthly allegiances; during the Middle Ages Mary was

said to be a model of motherhood because she willingly relinquished her beloved son, Jesus, to a violent death on the cross.[4]

Nineteenth-century American Protestant attitudes toward the family owe
much to Martin Luther's humanist rejection of Roman Catholic asceticism, specifically its rules on clerical celibacy. Luther's stance brought a new spiritual importance to domestic life, to marriage and to the raising of Christian children.
During the Protestant Reformation the school of the church was no longer a
monastery but a loving family, parents and children bonded by their common
allegiance to God and to the head of the household. The Protestant Reformers
admonished fathers to take responsibility for teaching their children about the
faith and wrote catechisms for their use.[5]

The English and American Puritan tradition, another important precedent
of American Protestantism, further elevated family religion. Hugh Latimer, for
example, argued that Christian homes should be distinguished from all others
by specific behaviors—honesty, fairness, kindness, and obedience—and serve as
schools of godly conduct.[6] Early Massachusetts laws required the head of each
household to catechize his children and servants at least weekly and to instruct
them in the Scriptures.[7] Indeed, following the Reformation tradition, the New
England divines viewed the home as a "little church," with the father acting as
priest to his wife and children. Psalm singing, as well as regular times of prayer—
at daybreak, before meals, and in the evening—reinforced the necessity of family piety as a means of grace. "Would any man or woman know whether they
have received a spirit of grace and prayer or no?" John Cotton asked. "Why aske
thine own heart, dost thou pray with thy Family?"[8]

Yet, despite the importance of domestic ritual, neither the Reformers nor
the American Puritans viewed the family as itself a source of divine grace. The
Protestant tradition certainly allowed that domestic relationships might well
impart indirect blessing to individuals; although Protestants no longer elevated
marriage to the level of a sacrament, they did understand it as an institution
ordained by God, designed for the spiritual benefit of the human race. But the
very notion of the home as somehow redemptive was, for cultural as well as theological reasons, conceptually impossible for seventeenth-century people to grasp.
For Puritan women and men home was a place where they alternately worked
and rested. A sense of hominess—as a private location defined by its intangible
personal comforts—would not begin to emerge, at least among the middle classes,
until the early nineteenth century.[9] And that changing sensibility would become
fundamental to American Protestant notions of Christian domesticity.

In the early nineteenth century, within American middle-class Protestant culture, the Rousseauian ideal of innocent, untrammeled childhood took on a profoundly religious cast. The middle-class family emerged from the industrial revolution as a powerful Protestant symbol, the wild innocence of Emile transformed into the wan purity of Little Eva. The Christian nurture theology of Horace Bushnell further cemented this connection, emphasizing the salvific potential of parental love and the domestic environment. Thus, loving actions might be a means of divine grace and child rearing, no longer merely an economic or social responsibility but a godly task with eternal consequences.

Models of Protestant Domesticity

Subsequent Protestant generations have variously interpreted this semi-mythic paradigm. Even the nature of the child, for example, has taken on a variety of theological and cultural meanings, beginning with debates in the early nineteenth century over childhood sinfulness. After Bushnell, American Protestants tended to describe children with relatively passive metaphors—as miniature adults, empty vessels, or reflecting mirrors—that took a fairly optimistic view of adult influence. But ambivalence about the child's nature remained as the optimism faded. Twentieth-century Protestants often referred to children as seedlings, relatively complete and requiring only the right kind of encouragement; yet, mindful of the totalitarian thrust of world events, they also worried that children were too psychologically vulnerable to resist the authoritarian schemes of adults. To a degree, the often contradictory understandings of children in modern-day American culture—as deeply impressionable beings or as dangerously immune to adult influence—are rooted in the layered complexity of Protestant thought about the nature of childhood.

Protestant domesticity has also entertained various notions about motherhood. Although the praying mothers of Bushnell's day had little in common with the activist social housekeepers of the turn of the century, they shared a conviction that, as women, they were naturally equipped to act as moral guides to children. The more egalitarian ethos of the twentieth century, and the rising prestige of "expert" scientific knowledge, chastened this confidence. Mothers still played a primary role in promoting home religion but increasingly as intermediaries, often behind the wheel of a car. By the mid-twentieth century mother was the one who escorted children to institutions staffed by religious professionals—people who were specifically trained in tasks that had once belonged to women simply by virtue of their sex.

Even the Protestant understanding of domesticity itself has changed over time. Nineteenth-century Protestants, for example, were more apt to talk about the virtues of the "Christian home," while by the turn of the century the more usual term was "Christian family." This shift from an institutional to a relational word is emblematic of the transition from Victorian to modern American culture. Once envisioned as a quiet refuge from the outside world, the model twentieth-century family was becoming yet another center of human activity in an increasingly centrifugal society. Today even Christian family sounds impossibly quaint. If the nineteenth-century paradigm of domestic life was the Victorian patriarch at prayer with his wife and children, a century later the dominant image of middle-class family life is a heavily annotated kitchen bulletin board next to a busy telephone.

These cultural changes held important but largely unarticulated theological consequences for Protestant parents. It was one thing for Victorians to raise godly children in a relatively static, sheltered institutional setting, with the prospect of daily reinforcement from school and church. But what of parents who competed with schools, sports teams, television sets, and toy manufacturers for their children's time and attention?

It is not difficult to interpret the story of mainline Protestants and the family as one of failure and decline—a classic narrative of secularization. And, certainly, from some perspectives it is. The regularly gathered statistics of denominational boards and committees have charted a slow but steady dropping off of normative indicators of domestic piety—the family altar and grace before meals—as well as general levels of religious literacy. A variety of impressionistic evidence suggests some kind of tipping point in the 1930s, a rising incidence of parents unable or unwilling to provide religious socialization for their children.[10]

But the story is hardly that simple. The Christian family ideal has never known a "golden age" when religious nurture worked without fail. For at least the past two hundred years parents have worried about their children's spiritual welfare, children have proven to be disobedient, and church leaders have excoriated parents for their permissiveness and religious illiteracy. Even the 1950s, that mythic era of family religion when unprecedented numbers of parents and children prayed and played together, was hardly so. In a longer historical perspective that 1950s family was not the apotheosis of the Protestant domestic ideal but its gasping conclusion. By the late 1950s a growing number of Protestant leaders suspected what most of their lay people already knew—that the middle-class family was not well suited to be an instrument of divine grace.

Each cultural setting has posed a different set of risks and challenges. Nineteenth-century Protestant domesticity, for example, reflected the impact of the market economy on women's roles and issues around the formation of middle-class identity. The turn-of-the-century Christian family was in part a creation of an emerging consumer economy of desire and an intellectual landscape increasingly dominated by the social sciences. The fabled 1950s suburban Protestant family was the end result of vigorous church programming as well as a potent mixture of wartime civil religion, postwar prosperity, and cold war anxieties.

The present tendency to see the family as a conservative icon—or in fact a progressive one—overlooks a great deal of historical complexity. In many respects Protestant domesticity was thoroughly conventional, easily confused with middle-class socialization. By the early twentieth century the distinguishing features of a Christian upbringing were not specifically religious beliefs or practices but a happy, cooperative, "wholesome," and "well-adjusted" personality—a circumstance that suggests some of the historical reasons why American religion tends to produce so many marketing strategists and so few Old Testament–style prophets. As a mark of middle-class respectability, the Christian home also lent itself to the support of secular patriotic ideals. In the late-nineteenth century, missionaries aided in nation building by "domesticating" freed slaves and Native Americans in the arts of Christian housekeeping. During World War II, upon the federal government's urging, Christian home life became a major conduit of American civil religion, exemplifying all that was best about the national character.

But at the same time Christian domesticity was the vehicle by which many Protestant laywomen gained access to the public world. Leaders of the great women's movements of the late nineteenth century—temperance, missions, and suffrage—used the language of Christian motherhood to challenge restrictive gender roles. The task of "home protection," they argued, demanded a new ordering of society with women at its moral, and perhaps even political, center. The language of self-realization and personal fulfillment, though muted in nineteenth-century women's movements, remained an important theme in Protestant child rearing throughout the twentieth century. The godly homes featured in countless articles in denominational magazines and Sunday school curricula

were never rule bound or hierarchical; anchored by love, they nurtured individual differences, allowing each child to grow up a Christian in his or her own
way.

Still, in many ways the Christian family paradigm is a frustrating legacy. It
is not hard to imagine that Christian nurture theology left a legacy of parental
guilt at least equal to its record of success. Families have all too rarely lived up
to the expectation Bushnell created, that they could chart a child's path to salvation. As the stories of many biblical families, from Adam and Eve to David
and Solomon, could amply testify, passing on a genuine faith across generational
lines has always been a tricky business.

Yet the ideal persists, perhaps because parenthood itself is so fraught with
daily theological challenges. My children regularly punctuated trips to the gro-
cery store and bedtime story readings with questions about what heaven will
look like and how soon I thought I was going to die. Now that they are older,
the issues are different but equally thorny: learning to be an ethical consumer,
deciding whether life is a glass half-empty or half-full.

And, despite the identification of family values with conservative evangelicalism, recent studies suggest that the "Golden Rule Christians" of the mainline are still deeply committed to a family-based religiosity. Mainline churches
contain higher proportions of intact marriages and nuclear families than evangelical ones; like baby boomers in general, these people continue to evidence
deep concerns about passing on some form of religious faith to their children.[11]

Not surprisingly perhaps, the last decade has seen renewed attention among
moderate to liberal Protestants toward family-related church programs and public
policy measures. Traditional denominational structures have been slow to respond; the new concern has bubbled up from individual congregations, issuing
in family ministry programs in a growing number of mainline Protestant seminaries. The other wing of conversation is among academics. For example, the
Family, Religion, and Culture project, based at the University of Chicago, has
built networks of discussion by sponsoring an array of historical, theological, and
practical studies. In many ways this new interest reflects a general social alarm
over a "family crisis" as well as a changing academic climate. The family sociologists of the 1960s and 1970s resisted problematizing rising rates of divorce or
out-of-wedlock pregnancy, arguing that the numbers indicated change rather
than decline in the family as an institution. A subsequent generation of
neoliberal scholars and activists has been less optimistic, citing the long-term

negative consequences of divorce on women and children and the economically and socially beneficial effects of two-parent, intact families.[12]

With the present and future state of families the focus of careful thought, the time seems right for mainline Protestant churches to revisit their own historical tradition of care for children and parents—and to begin to reflect upon its distinctive features. The rising sense of social urgency about the plight of American families has led some mainliners simply to emulate successful models from other traditions, without recognizing that they may be theologically inappropriate. The other temptation is to reuse the tried and true, even though some good ideas from the past may not be worth reinstituting. The family altar and the parent education class—always far more popular with church officials than with the lay people for whom they were intended—may well be a case in point.

At its best a mainline tradition includes three distinctive emphases. First, following the Christian nurture theology of Horace Bushnell, it defines parents as positive agents of grace in the lives of their children, assuming an authentic spiritual connection across generations. Bushnell was sharply critical of American individualism, especially as he saw it eroding the religious dimensions of the parent-child bond. Arguing that parents were not just didactic instructors in religious ideas or passive models of moral virtue, Bushnell believed that a child could directly benefit from a parent's spiritual vitality—or be permanently disadvantaged by its absence. Intergenerational spiritual connection has been a persistent theme in mainline Protestant discussions about child rearing, from Bushnell's theory of parental influence to the Progressive educators' insistence that morals are "caught not taught" and the 1950s celebration of family togetherness. This assumption is so fundamental that over time it has reinforced a tendency among mainline parents to present Christianity as a nonspecific set of socially desirable behaviors; by the early twentieth century religious language had all but disappeared from mainline discourse about families. Parents today can hardly be as sanguine as Bushnell about intergenerational communication, but they might welcome a renewed theological understanding of parenthood as a spiritual vocation, one that imagines its more mundane social functions within the larger context of spiritual responsibilities and privileges.

Mainline Protestant child rearing has also emphasized the importance of a congruent moral environment. Bushnell envisioned Christian nurture taking place primarily inside the home but within a network of reinforcing social institutions: in nineteenth-century Protestant culture schools and churches were the home's natural allies, fundamental elements of a civic culture designed to uphold the common good. This interconnected world did not survive long within the pluralistic centrifuge of American society and the inward turning of the middle-class psyche across the span of the twentieth century. Bushnell's tidy New England moral community is no doubt beyond recovery, but its intent was periodically evident in the language of home protection among nineteenth-century temperance reformers and in the civil rights rhetoric of the 1950s. In it survives the persistent conviction that Christian parents are not just psychological mentors to their children but also social activists whose concern for a livable society is fundamental to their task.

The mainline Protestant tradition has also emphasized respect for the separate world of children. Bushnell saw them not as undeveloped adults but as people capable of spiritual understanding appropriate to their age and experience. His Christian nurture theology helped launch a new awareness of childhood faith that continued into the twentieth century, reinforced by the religious education movements of the Progressive Era and the curriculum reforms of the 1940s and 1950s. Mainline churches have, of course, sometimes been child oriented to a fault; the many critiques of post–World War II "familism" were, without question, well deserved. But, when mainline churches resist the temptation to sentimentalize or to condescend to children, they reflect Bushnell's original emphasis, particularly his insistence on the separate integrity of each child's religious growth and development.

Even at its best, of course, no one tradition holds the key to understanding all the mysteries and challenges of family life. With that awareness I offer in the final chapter two evocative counterexamples to the mainline Protestant story, the Roman Catholic Christian Family Movement and the African American extended community. Although in some ways these stories echo mainline Protestant concerns, they pursue them in entirely different directions. These counterexamples clarify the limitations of mainline Protestant thinking about parents and children and suggest some possible new directions.

Certainly, the story in these pages could be told many other ways. The Christian home has been a powerful symbol in American Protestant culture and in American society more generally. Even in our present pluralistic age its attraction continues, witnessed by the burgeoning of evangelical parachurch organizations such as Focus on the Family, fatherhood initiatives such as the Promise Keepers, and a myriad of new family programs. But domestic religion hardly belongs to any one group on the Protestant spectrum. The mutual work of parents and children is essential to the survival of every religious tradition. Understanding the changing meaning and future prospects of families of all types and various descriptions can—and should be—the diverse work of many thoughtful people.

Chapter 1

Christian Nurture and Victorian Domesticity

"THE CHRISTIAN FAMILY," Presbyterian minister Joseph Collier declared in 1859, "is, or should be, the very type of heaven." A house was not just a place to eat or sleep and a family not only a set of blood relationships; Collier envisioned home as sacred space and religion as fundamental to a trouble-free domestic life. Indeed, he enthused, Christianity "makes better parents, more dutiful children, more faithful husbands and wives, more kind and affectionate brothers and sisters."[1]

Such an ambitious claim provoked little disagreement by the mid nineteenth century. Collier's treatise, which received a prize of $175 from the Presbyterian Board of Publication, was one of many hundreds of other books, poems, devotionals, and hymns endorsing domestic religion in the antebellum era. The enshrinement of "Home, Sweet Home"—a popular nineteenth-century song described by one Methodist author as "a Christian anthem"—is such a dominant feature of this era that it is tempting to merely note its existence without really analyzing the reasons it arose in the first place.[2]

But this would mean ignoring an important shift in religious thinking and social practice. The Victorian model of redemptive domesticity stands out against the broad flow of Christian belief. Although many types of Protestants emphasized the special covenantal nature of family relationships—the Puritans fondly described the home as a "little church"—they never accorded them redemptive power. For Christians through the ages salvation has typically been a province of the divine, often mysterious and beyond direct human control. But by the end of the nineteenth century many American Protestants found it difficult to conceive of salvation outside of the middle-class family or the middle-class family outside the realm of Protestant Christianity. Indeed, as Methodist author H. A. Boardman wrote in a popular guidebook of "hints on domestic happiness," "every view of [home] is radically defective, which excludes the ideas of God and heaven and eternity."[3]

The purpose of this chapter is to chart the convergence of Christian nurture and Victorian domesticity in the early nineteenth century. Only here can we begin to account for the power and durability of this ideal as it has developed in American Protestant culture. Although it has certainly altered over time, the conviction that the particular arrangements of family life could have eternal consequences has been a hard one for Protestants to shake. Indeed, dismissing the Victorian model of domestic Christianity as merely "sentimental" does not do justice to its importance, especially as an ongoing tradition within mainstream Protestantism. The Christian home was a powerful cultural construction, one with deep social and theological relevance, eminently useful in ordering middle-class lives and in routinizing access to the eternal realm beyond.

The Domestic Transformation

The redemptive family ideal emerged in the two decades before the Civil War, a key period in the development of the domestic ideal among the Protestant middle class. Within the shifting realities of an urbanizing, industrializing society, the ability to demonstrate proper standards of deportment became central to the sometimes hazy definition of *middle class* in the early nineteenth century. Facility with a three-pronged fork or proper use of a calling card could offer telling indicators of a decent upbringing. But, beyond that, specific norms of behavior and emotional affect—codified in conduct manuals and thoroughly imbued with Protestant piety—separated the rowdy poor and the stuffy rich from the solidly middle class. An emerging strain within Protestant Christianity, as this chapter will argue, became central to the internal dynamics of middle-class life, intertwining a system of theological assumptions with an evolving set of social practices.

This was not, of course, a simple process. By the early nineteenth century, in the wake of the Industrial Revolution, Western domestic life had undergone a complex series of transformations. Home was no longer a place where husbands, wives, and children tended cattle and grew crops alongside one another; the household of the new industrial era emphasized privacy, intimacy, and physical comfort. While European and white North American families remained basically nuclear throughout this period of transition—that is, composed around a single married couple—they grew smaller in size and in function. No longer large socially embedded households with varieties of kin relationships, nineteenth-century families became more self-contained units, joined together "for the sake of each other's well-being and development."[4]

Changes in family structure coincided with the economic transformation of the United States in the decades following the War of 1812. Widespread new construction of canals, roads, and steam power enabled a transportation revolution which, in turn, connected a myriad of local economies into an increasingly complex national market of supply and demand. The lure of manufactured goods drew farming households out of a subsistence economy into the interconnected world of U.S. industrial capitalism; rising demand for finished goods helped fuel industrialization as well as the nexus of middle-class occupations in finance and marketing that supported it. The market revolution, and its commercialization of both rural and urban life, deeply challenged the patterns of traditional society, including those around family life. It removed women from direct participation in economic production, shifting their role from producers to consumers of goods and services, and refashioned families themselves into units of consumption, less economically dependent on neighbors and relatives and increasingly caught in an individual struggle, led by a breadwinner father, for financial survival.[5]

Perhaps the most distinctive feature of this new middle-class family was its expectation of privacy.[6] For centuries people in the West had lived in single-room dwellings, slept in front of communal fireplaces, and found themselves at work the moment they emerged from bed. Even the very wealthy in early modern Europe did not expect freedom from prying eyes. Indeed, if eighteenth-century etiquette books are any indication, Westerners had an exceedingly high threshold of embarrassment; the authors of conduct tracts routinely implored their readers not to urinate in public or adjust their underclothing when sitting at table.[7]

Yet by mid nineteenth century, middle-class Americans had come to envisage the ideal home as a peaceful, proper island of repose, a "beneficent shield" from the outside world.[8] The domestic ideal was the polar opposite of the hustling, impersonal economic marketplace. "Home, sweet home" was, in fact, its true antithesis, a private refuge where middle-class Victorians sought rest and leisure and learned the virtues of unselfishness.

By the 1840s even the physical shapes of homes altered to reflect the new domestic values. In the eighteenth century most American homes followed a basic design, with the important rooms—the hall and the parlor—in the front and a kitchen and work area in the back. Family members and servants did not sleep in separate rooms but grouped around the parents' bed in the parlor. With rising prosperity and a growing sense of the home as a private enclave, this haphazard arrangement no longer suited. The 1840s saw a movement among housing reformers and architects for a more "moral" domestic architecture, one in which the home became "a refuge from the outside world, a fortress designed to protect, nurture, and strengthen the individuals within it."[9] The new emphasis on domestic intimacy required more private spaces for family members. The rising popularity of "balloon-framed" homes allowed builders to add a second story, designed to allow each individual a room for sleeping, reading, or private contemplation.[10]

Within this enclave women assumed responsibility for the physical care of the family and, even more important, for their moral and spiritual upkeep. Citing the "universal prevalence of the benevolent or disinterested feeling in our sex," Sarah Hale, editor of *Godey's Ladies' Book* and an influential arbiter of antebellum taste, spoke for many when she declared that women simply possessed "a higher degree of moral qualities than man." "Hence it is," Hale concluded, "that she is qualified, even when deficient in what the schools call learning, to be his teacher and model."[11] The values that nineteenth-century Americans found increasingly incompatible with life in the economic marketplace—tact, gentleness, selflessness, and love—were lodged securely in the home, under the watchful gaze of women.[12]

The emphasis on privacy reflected the rising importance of personal intimacy in middle-class family life. Of course, Victorian husbands and wives usually deferred to the formulaic gender roles of their time, even referring to each other as "Mr." and "Mrs.," but, as their personal letters suggest, they viewed marriage with a continuing expectation of romance and affection.[13]

Yet the parent-child bond, especially the one between mothers and children, was the home's true emotional center. Indeed, in many ways nineteenth-century domesticity was really about the importance of children in American culture.[14] Instead of venerating old age, Americans celebrated youth. In the early decades of the nineteenth century younger citizens abandoned the powdered wigs, knee breeches, and long tailored coats of a previous era—fashions designed to accentuate a nicely turned calf or an expansive belly, then considered to be the best features of an elderly gentleman. During the Napoleonic era the nipped waistlines of men's tight pantaloons and the gauzy fabrics of women's empire dresses flattered youthful figures and, in fact, copied the kinds of clothing worn by young children. Even family portraits, especially as they became more afford-able to the middle classes, no longer portrayed boys and girls as stiffly posed min-iature adults. By the end of the eighteenth century, children were beginning to take on a more individual aspect, holding a favorite toy or pet and seated within a loving domestic circle. Instead of formal stares into the middle distance, fam-ily portraits often displayed a ring of fond glances from parent to child, and child to parent, signifying high levels of domestic bliss.[15]

The valuing of children coincided with an important demographic shift. Between 1800 and 1850 the birthrate for urban white women dropped from 7.04 to 5.42; by 1900 it had fallen to 3.56.[16] As the United States was industrializ-ing, large rural households became pragmatically unnecessary and children them-selves less affordable.[17] But fewer children did not mean less responsibility for mothers and fathers; the falling birthrate also reflected the rising importance of individual offspring. Unlike their counterparts among the working and immi-grant poor, the sons and daughters of the middle class had no real economic function; they were, in a sense, the psychological and spiritual projects of their parents.[18]

Of course, few middle-class homes were as private or intimate as many Americans thought they were, at least in comparison to contemporary standards. Urban families routinely took in paying boarders or hired live-in servants; visit-ing friends and relatives settled in for extended stays.[19] Women were not neces-sarily isolated by domesticity either; many created emotionally intense, extensive social networks with other wives and daughters, intimately bonded by "love and ritual."[20] And, of course, for nearly all women home was a place of work, not leisure. The new "cult of domesticity" meant that women devoted far more time and attention to homemaking: baking and cooking elaborate meals, scrubbing and cleaning, doing laundry and supervising domestic servants. Because such tasks were not paid and did not require specialized expertise, Americans found it increasingly difficult to define them as work, even though by mid century the average housewife spent many tiring hours a week completing them.[21]

The new middle-class domestic ideal also stood in sharp contrast to the daily realities many other Americans faced. For the poor and working classes Victo-rian domesticity was an unaffordable luxury; in the case of African American slaves, it was a highly prized but illegal one.[22] Families with limited economic means, especially recent immigrants, depended on extended kin to locate work and housing. And, even though working-class families might aspire to middle-class standards, few could afford to keep their children in school and the mother at home. In an economy in which workingmen could not assume they would receive a "living wage," wives and children necessarily worked to supplement an inadequate, often sporadic family income. Women on their own had even fewer choices. By definition typically female jobs—seamstress, domestic servant, factory worker, even schoolteacher—did not pay enough to support a family. Indeed, the economic privilege of middle-class wives and mothers created sharp disadvantages for women with fewer financial or social resources.[23]

Even those safely within the bonds of middle-class domesticity endured its obvious shortcomings. In the pre–Civil War decades the emerging women's rights movement began its long campaign against the legal inequities of marriage. In particular its proponents attacked the principle of coverture, which gave a husband the right to all of the property owned by his wife and rendered her invisible in the eyes of the law. Some of the movement's early leaders advocated a less patriarchal model of marriage built on "mutual dependence" between men and women. Women's rights leader Lucy Stone scandalized the public by refusing to take Henry Blackwell's last name when she married him; others, even more radical, spoke euphemistically of a woman's right to decide when and how often she would become a mother. Still, most nineteenth-century women's rights advocates sought to reform rather than reject the middle-class family. Only the most radical spoke of liberalizing divorce laws or, even more dangerously, of the possibility of "free love." On the whole the American women's rights movement viewed traditional marriage as a protective institution for women; its proponents assumed that any attempt to weaken its bonds would only increase men's personal freedom at their wives' expense.[24]

Middle-class conventionality and its exaltation of "true womanhood" also hastened the absence of men from the family circle. In the eighteenth century most child-rearing advice was directed at fathers, assumed to be the primary moral teachers of children. But this role diminished as the domestic ideal centered spiritual instruction in the mother-child bond. In a practical sense the reality of a middle-class father's daily commute to and from work also weakened his patriarchal authority. Father remained the head of the household, responsible for financial decisions and discipline of the children—but in many ways the home itself was becoming feminine territory.[25]

Still, the middle-class ideal exerted a powerful pull. Whether or not reality actually measured up to the happy visions of "home, sweet home" described in prescriptive literature, many Americans apparently thought it should. And Protestant theology and practice became a powerful means toward the realization of that ideal.

The Problem of Risk

One important benchmark for the emergence of the redemptive family is the publication of Congregational theologian Horace Bushnell's famous book on *Christian Nurture* in 1847. This eloquent argument for the salvific role of godly parents gave a specifically Christian rationale for middle-class family life—and a middle-class rationale for Christianity. Indeed, Bushnell argued, "religion never thoroughly penetrates life, till it becomes domestic."[26]

On one level Bushnell's views are easy to summarize. The goal of every parent, he contended, was to envelop each child in Christian love from the point of birth. If the atmosphere of the home exuded true religion from every crevice and the parents took daily pains to demonstrate their faith, then it was entirely possible that, as Bushnell famously phrased it, the child might "grow up a Christian, and never know himself being otherwise."[27]

At the time, Bushnell's views elicited heated controversy. After an initially favorable response to a public presentation of several sermons on Christian nurture, the Massachusetts Sabbath School Society agreed to publish them for wider circulation. But a growing barrage of criticism, spearheaded by conservative Congregational theologian Bennett Tyler, frightened the society into suspending publication. In the face of predictions that the Christian nurture theology, especially what appeared to be its weak view of original sin, represented a "great calamity" for Christianity, Bushnell republished his sermons and buttressed them with a mound of historical data on infant baptism. In 1861 the final version of *Christian Nurture* included several additional essays offering further explanations of the Christian nurture process.[28]

Despite the controversy it aroused, Christian nurture theology did not offer guaranteed salvation, and, indeed, as is perhaps already evident, imposed some difficult new burdens onto pious parents. Still, it was a considerable improvement over existing models of Christian child rearing. Bushnell's system was conceived in response to the evangelical understanding of childhood faith, one that emphasized the need for individual conversion and offered parents little ultimate control over the eternal destiny of their children.

Raising children has always been and always will be a risky endeavor, but early-nineteenth-century middle-class parents faced a daunting array of hazards. On the most basic level they confronted the real possibility of losing children to premature death. Rates of infant mortality remained high throughout the nineteenth century: on average children under five accounted for 40 percent of all yearly deaths, and this figure did not drop until the early twentieth century, with the advent of public health movements and more systematic inoculation against fatal childhood diseases such as measles, smallpox, and diphtheria.[29] Parents could well anticipate losing at least one of their children to illness or accident—according to estimates, one in ten children died before the age of one, and in some urban areas the number was one in four.[30]

Nineteenth-century American parents found it increasingly difficult to find comfort in ascribing their loss to a wise and righteous Providence. Personal diaries of mothers document this shift; nineteenth-century accounts tend to be emotionally intimate and given to minute examinations of an individual child's emerging personality—observations rarely found among Puritan fathers or eighteenth-century household record books. They are also deeply tinged with personal anxiety, as children gradually slipped "out of the hands of God and into their mothers' warm, if nervous, embrace." Mothers could neither prevent the death of infants nor depend on an all-powerful God for their survival.[31]

Nor could they ensure their eternal destiny. The traditional Christian understanding of sin, shaped by Augustinian theology, as both inborn and sure ground for divine punishment meant that no one escaped its toils. The logic of this system extended even to the child who died within minutes of birth. Strictly speaking, it did not matter if the child ever had the opportunity to commit a conscious act of rebellion; as one of Adam's descendants, even a newborn infant was fully liable before God. Although, as we shall see, logic did not always dictate practice, a child's untimely death was still a serious matter for parents, both emotionally and theologically.

Evangelicals, Families, and Children

Not surprisingly, the democratic ethos of early-nineteenth-century American society forced Protestant theologians to account for sin in less deterministic ways. It is easy to exaggerate the extent to which Protestant clergy preached infant damnation—even the most rigorous Puritan thinkers certainly differentiated between the rational demands of a theological conviction and the emotional necessity of believing that a dead son or daughter was safe in the arms of a loving

God.[32] But by Bushnell's time Protestant theologians had become reluctant to consign anyone to damnation without some form of explicit consent.

As it developed in the late eighteenth and early nineteenth centuries, evangelical revivalism offered a popular solution to the problem of sin. Without stinting the fact of human evil, it emphasized human agency and free will—any repentant sinner was morally able to stand and walk down the aisle to the foot of the cross. In other words, evangelicalism took away the corporate burden of sin and made its terrors as well as its solution more of an individual responsibility.[33]

But this posed problems for families. Evangelicalism's characteristic language of sin and conversion, as well as its populist ethos, revolutionized the staid, hierarchical rhythms of Puritan New England and the Anglican South. To be sure, it was not uncommon during a religious revival for entire families to undergo conversion experiences within a short span of time—most often when converted wives returned with husbands and children in tow.[34] Yet, as historian Christine Heyrman notes, revivalistic religion could also tear families apart. "For those to whom Canaan's language long remained an unintelligible tongue," she writes, "the conversion of beloved relatives could lead to enduring emotional estrangement. Transformed by their newfound zeal, dutiful sons and daughters, affectionate siblings and spouses . . . [could become] remorseless, relentless, seemingly heartless in dealing with loved ones."[35]

Some evangelicals even hinted that family relationships were an impediment to full religious consecration. Revivalist Phoebe Palmer, for example, interpreted the untimely death of two young children within the space of three years as a form of divine discipline. "After my loved ones were snatched away," she wrote in her journal in 1831, "I saw that I had concentrated my time and attentions far too exclusively, to the neglect of the religious activities demanded. Though painfully learned, yet I trust the lesson has been fully apprehended. From henceforth, Jesus must and shall have the uppermost seat in my heart." Palmer's subsequent career as an evangelist and spiritual guide began when she recognized her first allegiance to God, not family.[36]

Evangelicalism's often demanding piety also posed problems for children. Any child below the "age of accountability," which could be as young as three or as old as seven, was theoretically incapable of full salvation. Indeed, although miraculous cases did appear, religious revivals required emotional and physical rigors sometimes beyond the reach of many mature adults, much more small boys and girls. Since the Reformation, Protestants had entertained lingering doubts about the capacity of children to perceive Christian truth. The emotional volatility of the very young, in fact, suggested that they were not fully human and were dangerously vulnerable to an animal nature that lurked within. Puritan parents, for example, did not allow infants to crawl on all fours, as this was far too reminiscent of a nonsentient beast; tiny infants stood upright in wooden walkers until they learned to stand on their own.[37]

And, in fact, children were more likely to find their way into critics' accounts of backwoods revivals, as evidence for the fundamental irrationality of such conversions. One such story, published in 1810, told of a meeting in which a group of adults, praying in a ring for the conversion of a young man, brought a weeping little girl into the center, telling her "she must pray to the Lord for the power of the Spirit, or she would go to hell." In the course of this revival the emotional temperature continued to rise, affecting young girls most directly. According to their unsympathetic observer, several "tore their turbans from their heads, and behaved more like beasts than human beings." Other examples of "obscene conduct" soon followed: one girl who was struck "insensible" by revivalistic preaching was picked up bodily and carried around by a group of men, even after the women present protested against the impropriety.[38]

Within a revivalistic framework children were at particular risk. Evangelicals encouraged early conversions, but they worried about their authenticity.[39] Parents could rigorously prepare children for salvation down the road, but they could not prevent a tragic outcome. Concerned families had primary recourse to tract literature, most of which was oppressively didactic, replete with instructive examples of upright boys and girls overcoming temptation or dying happy deaths. Although suffused with emotion, evangelical literature for children was largely devoid of empathy for the weak or spiritually vulnerable.[40] And, indeed, the young lives that evangelical children read about seemed to defy all theological logic and experience. One would question how many young readers really aspired to imitate a girl like Elizabeth Waterman Orchard, who, before she died, at age nine, constantly warned her brothers and sisters that, if they persisted in too much play, they would "go to a place of misery, after death." Or, take the example of twelve-year old Peter Melville, who in the throes of death cried out, "Oh what will become of those children who idle about on the Sabbath-day, who swear and steal! Oh, shocking! Shocking! Oh what a blessing to have good parents."[41]

Authors rarely altered their prose to accommodate younger sensibilities. As one popular account explained, "Children are men and women in miniature, and when we place before them memoirs of youth of their own stature, they are

equally interested, entertained and profited."[42] Jacob Abbott, in his popular treatise *The Young Christian* (1832), similarly admitted in his opening paragraphs
that he had "made no effort to simplify the language," assuming that the young
readers would automatically profit by the character-building stories he had
compiled in the volume.[43] Like most early-nineteenth-century Americans, evangelicals did not distinguish early childhood as a distinct psychological stage requiring special attention. Before the advent of graded school systems, adults
gauged a child's maturity on physical size rather than chronological age; hence,
a child, or youth, could be anyone from age seven to the early twenties. Abbott's
book was in fact written for adults to read to their children—defined in the text
as people from the ages of fifteen to twenty-five.[44]

Evangelical tract literature did not, therefore, skimp on awful truths. One
pamphlet, addressed "To a Child," informed the reader that, even though "play
and amusement" were fine to a point, "you did not come into the world merely
to play and be amused." Indeed, "the world in which you now live, is a world of
snares, and sin, and sorrow. You will continue in it, however, but a little while,
and then you must die, and go up to heaven and be happy, or down to hell and
be miserable forever."[45] In one depiction of "A Dialogue between a Father, and
His Son George, about the Cannibals in India" the parent manipulates his child's
curiosity and horror toward a redemptive purpose. "Ferocious as they truly are,"
George's father intones, "you are sprung from the very same, fallen, ruined, corrupted *root* they came from." When the increasingly distressed young George
pops the inevitable question, "what must I do to be saved?" his father urges him
only toward "fervent, fervent, and persevering prayer."[46]

Real-life adults were similarly direct and unsentimental in presenting religion to children. New Englander Lucy Larcom, coming of age in the 1820s, recalled her "first real unhappiness" when "someone told me, one day, that I did
not love God. I insisted, almost tearfully, that I did; but I was told that if I did
truly love Him I should always be good." As she related, a "feeling of sudden
orphanage came over me like a bewildering cloud." Small wonder that her early
musings led her to assume "that only grown-up persons could be Christians, from
which it followed that all children must be heathen."[47]

Since few children fit the exemplary mold of popular tract literature, many
evangelical parents resorted to various means of "breaking the will" to prepare
them for conversion. Although the severity of such measures varied—and certainly not all evangelical parents practiced cruelty to their children—sometimes
Christian formation could veer uncomfortably close to modern definitions of

abuse. In 1831 Baptist minister and former president of Brown University Francis Wayland described a harrowing ordeal with his fifteenth-month-old son that involved depriving the infant of food and human company for nearly two full days, at the end of which, Wayland reported, the child became thoroughly, even slavishly, obedient. Although Wayland's case was extreme, breaking a child's will could demand harsh spiritual discipline, commensurate with the child's inborn bent toward evil. No natural child, many evangelicals believed, could submit to either God or parent without decisive, sometimes psychologically violent, intervention.[48]

Evangelical parenting was not for the faint of heart. The much-reprinted letters of the English cleric Legh Richmond issued stern warnings about "parental neglect" as the root of all evil. Richmond was the model of parental vigilance, with his "never-ceasing anxiety, his constant watchfulness, his daily and hourly prayers" and his "constant inculcation of divine truth." Infusing pious lessons into every waking moment, Richmond forbade "all games of chance" as well as "fishing, field sports, dancing, the theatre, oratorios, and other sources of gratification, which he thought to be inconsistent with the spirit of religion."[49]

Although few parents probably found Richmond's methods attractive enough to emulate, they ignored them at their peril. Protestant authors regularly served up haunting stories of debauched children from upright Christian families, as warnings to neglectful parents. The fate of Aaron Burr, the doomed grandchild of the saintly Jonathan Edwards, was particularly sobering; if this young man from a formidable Christian lineage had gone wrong, then what might lesser folk expect? (Collier pointed to the comforting fact that Burr had been orphaned early in life.)[50] The underlying message of such accounts was truly daunting: although godly parenting required daily vigilance, there was no guaranteed result. In the end, despite the power of an evangelical free will, God still maintained the final say. From the perspective of the godly parent, salvation seemed to be an entirely random gift, beyond the reach of any human agency.

Christian Nurture

Bushnell's answer to such dilemmas was clear and compelling. Citing Lamentations 4:3 ("The daughter of my people is become cruel, like the ostriches in the wilderness"), he excoriated parents who, like the biblical ostriches leaving their eggs in the sand to be warmed only by the sun, let their children fend for themselves spiritually. Yet, he argued, the revivalist emphasis on personal decision making could only result in such "ostrich nurture." The logic of evangelical conversion, he argued, gave parents no compelling reason to look out for the spiritual welfare of their children, except to hammer away at the dangers of sin, the flesh, and the devil. Revivalism, as Bushnell saw it, was intrinsically detrimental to family relationships. It forced parents to "indoctrinate [children] soundly in respect to their need of a new heart; tell them what conversion is, and how it comes to pass with grown people; [and] pray that God will arrest them when they are old enough to be converted according to the manner." In the meantime parents could only "drill them" into the "constraints" of religion, "turning all their little misdoings and bad tempers into evidences of their need for regeneration." Such treatment Bushnell denounced as a nurture of "despair"; after a time "the bread of life itself, held before them as a fruit to be looked upon, but not tasted, . . . finally becomes repulsive, just because they have been so long repelled and fenced away from it."[51]

On one level this portrayal seems unfair. Evangelical child rearing was hardly the callous exercise Bushnell described. When, for example, Methodist evangelist Phoebe Palmer labored for the conversion of her six-year-old daughter, Sarah, the two experienced great spiritual agony and deep intimacy. For many suspenseful hours mother and daughter prayed, sang, and lay silently together on Sarah's bed, waiting for the Spirit to complete its work, Phoebe deeply mindful of the "solemn, unfathomed responsibility" of "God's chosen ones relative to their children."[52] Many evangelical parents recognized some familiar emphases in Bushnell's theology. When Bushnell and the great revivalist Charles Finney met in Hartford, they found that they shared a common emphasis on "Christian experience, sanctification, and holiness." Finney later recommended *Christian Nurture* to his daughters, as an aid to proper child rearing.[53]

Yet Bushnell was not taking issue with particular methods of conversion; in a much larger sense *Christian Nurture* marked the end of a revivalistic era and the beginning of a new effort to normalize the sanctification process. In its entirety Bushnell's theology brought God closer to human reach, an emphasis that places him at the forefront of an emerging liberal strain within Protestant Christianity, emphasizing divine immanence in human reality. Bushnell, however, was much more willing to embrace God's supernatural presence in human affairs than most of the liberal theologians who followed in his path. He would not have disagreed with Phoebe Palmer's desire to see her daughter converted from sin. But he would have wondered why the two spent so much time in such prolonged agony. Little Sarah was closer to salvation than her anxious mother had dared to hope.[54]

Yet Bushnell was no blind innovator. In many ways his theology was an attempt to recover an older Protestant tradition within a nineteenth-century democratic ethos. Christian nurture theology, for example, partially recovered the "federal theory" of Adam's sin, embraced by the Puritan divines. This theory explained the connection between Adam's individual sin in the Garden of Eden and humanity's subsequent fallen state by emphasizing Adam's role as the representative of the human race. Adam's role, in fact, paralleled Christ's role as humanity's representative on the cross. Bushnell did not subscribe to mechanistic notions of original sin, but he emphatically upheld its corporate aspect. Sin was not just an individual experience—perhaps chosen, perhaps not—but a corporate state that required a broad response. Christian nurture theory also stood within a relatively long Protestant understanding of conversion as a gradual, unfolding process. The Puritan divines in particular had emphasized the necessity of "preparation" for conversion and understood the importance of external influences on the development of young souls. Bushnell's antipathy toward revivalism and his emphasis on infant baptism also placed him in sympathy with many nonevangelical Protestants in confessional Lutheran and Reformed churches.[55]

Nor was Bushnell the only one framing alternatives to the evangelical child-rearing model. Since the first decades of the nineteenth century the Sunday school movement had been operating under the assumption that children could respond appropriately to a call to conversion. Although most Sunday school leaders continued to stress the need to warn children about their natural depravity, a growing awareness of the spiritual plasticity of early childhood encouraged teachers to find signs of grace even in the very young.[56] *Christian Nurture* also echoed a much larger conversation about spiritually effective child rearing, much of it authored by women. From the early decades of the nineteenth century maternal associations provided a forum for women to pray jointly for the salvation of their children. Lydia Maria Child's *Mother's Book*, published in 1831, fully anticipated Bushnell's emphasis on domestic atmosphere and parental example. Warning that "the influences of the nursery" could excite a child's "evil propensities," Child, a Unitarian, urged mothers to exercise their moral power in positive ways, reminding them that "every look, every moment, every expression, does something toward forming the character of the little heir to immortal life."[57]

Yet, even without overstating its innovativeness, Bushnell's Christian nurture theology codified a powerful new understanding of the family's religious role, one that has shaped American Protestant thinking ever since. Indeed, Yale president Noah Porter praised Bushnell's theology for initiating "a revolution in the expectations and aims and results of all the families that truly deserve the name of Christian."[58] To begin with, Bushnell elevated mothers and fathers into positive agents of grace in the lives of their children. He urged parents to recognize the "organic bonds" that linked families together spiritually, arguing that their actions had a direct, though perhaps unconscious, influence on an unformed character. Whether parents liked it or not, Bushnell warned, every word or deed shaped their children's developing moral consciousness; from the moment a mother cuddled her newborn baby she began to determine the child's future ability to perceive a loving, ever-present God. "We can never come into the true mode of living that God has appointed for us," Bushnell declared, "until we regard each generation as hovering over the next, acting itself into the next, and casting thus a type of character in the next, before it comes to act for itself."[59]

Bushnell's theology also instituted new regard for the child's spiritual awareness. He argued for the basic integrity of a child's religious faith, even in its most rudimentary form. Proper Christian nurture followed a developmental rubric, beginning "just when the nurture of the body begins." "It is first to be infantile nurture—as such, Christian; then to be a child's nurture; then to be a youth's nurture—advancing by imperceptible gradations, if possible, according to the gradations and stages of the growth, or progress toward maturity."[60]

Thus, Bushnell stressed, any attempt to break a young child's will was nothing short of "dreadful." Childish obstinacy was not an indication of original sin, he argued, but the outgrowth of a natural human desire to explore and challenge boundaries. Overzealous parents who sought to conquer their child's inquisitiveness in the name of religion risked turning out a "coward, or a thief, or a hypocrite, or a mean-spirited and driveling sycophant." Wise mothers and fathers worked on bending, not breaking, their child's will through patient repetition, recognizing that the goal was to impart an internal sense of power and control, "to teach it the way of submitting to wise limitations, and raise it into the great and glorious liberties of a state of loyalty to God."[61]

Despite the fact that, initially at least, Bushnell received his most favorable press from Unitarian periodicals, he did not believe that infants were sinless.[62] Indeed, he held that children born to "depraved and vicious" parents came into the world with a clear moral disability, as if during her pregnancy the mother had denied her fetus adequate physical nutrition. When temptations arose later in life, this child would be hard pressed to fend them off. But Bushnell believed that the child's openness to environmental factors could also work in positive ways. The sons and daughters of Christian parents who had prayed faithfully for them from conception onward possessed a lifelong spiritual advantage. A Christian upbringing sensitized the child to God even before the advent of conscious thought; he or she would remain fundamentally receptive to divine love as intellectual understanding of Christian doctrine developed over the years.[63]

Bushnell was not, of course, issuing anyone a free pass into salvation; if anything, he was raising the stakes for Christian child rearing much higher than before. For, if parents could positively affect their child's spiritual state, they could, even more easily, place obstacles in the path. Bennett Tyler, one of Bushnell's sharpest critics, was one of the few who pointed this out amid the clamor over total depravity. Tyler argued that Bushnell asked far too much of parents as models and shapers of Christian virtue, expecting them "to be more faithful than Abraham, or Isaac, or Jacob, or Aaron, or Samuel, or David; and more faithful than any parents whom he has ever seen, or of whom he has ever heard."[64] All of these famous biblical parents had seen their children go astray; how could nineteenth-century middle-class Protestants expect to do any better?

The Christian Home

There were, of course, ways to lessen the risk. In the 1840s and 1850s a new genre of Protestant literature about the Christian home energetically responded to Tyler's challenge. Advice on Christian child rearing grew quickly in specificity and scope, delineating a domestic environment that might not eradicate all occasions for sin but could certainly limit the possibility of a random encounter.

Bushnell himself, in the final version of his argument, published in 1861, included a range of specific guidelines for proper Christian nurture. He pointed out that parents might aid spiritual growth through godly play as well as thoughtful celebration of birthdays and religious holidays. Although he was consistently mindful of the danger of hypocrisy in childhood religion, Bushnell emphasized the importance of outward, physical practices as a means of grace. Thus, he advocated regular family devotions, recitations of the catechism, and Bible memorization as well as careful attention to a child's dress and diet. In a young child, he warned, the "devils of dyspepsia" could easily "choke the godlike possibilities"; indulgent, "sensual" eating habits—partaking, for example, of coffee, sweets, and other "addictive" foods—all too often led to less innocent forms of excess. Good table manners and high-minded dinner conversation similarly prepared a soul for God, as did personal cleanliness and tasteful clothing. The foppish "little gentleman" or exquisite young daughter strung with expensive jewelry, both ostensibly their parents' darlings, were dangerously far from grace. "Dress your child for Christ," Bushnell pleaded, "if you will have him a Christian; bring every thing, in the training, even of his body, to this one final aim, and it will be strange, if the Christian body you give him does not contain a Christian soul."[65]

Within a Christian domestic setting, advocates promised, the right use of proper means could only result in salvation—suggesting that the rise of family religion at midcentury was an important aspect of a larger routinization of piety that followed in the wake of the antebellum revivals.[66] One author enthused that "God means what he says in the promise, that if you train up your child in the way he should go, he will not depart from it when he is old. The longer we live, and the more we observe the courses of Divine Providence, the more our faith in such promises is confirmed."[67] As Presbyterian James Collier wrote, "It is true that God is sovereign in the bestowments of his grace, and that there is no converting power in even the most faithful religious training, when viewed by itself; yet there is a heaven-ordained connection between the means and the end, and of all the means that are blessed by the Holy Spirit to men's salvation, none are more influential than those lodged in *the Christian family*." Indeed, Collier promised, "With a uniformity resembling the operation of nature's laws, God is seen to hear and answer the prayers of the parents for the children."[68]

The expectation of family togetherness extended beyond life itself. Victorian visions of the afterlife typically featured heavenly mansions and cozy cottages, mirroring the growing spiritual power of family bonds in the earthly realm.[69] Within Bushnell's logic even a relatively brief exposure to the atmosphere of a godly home could have eternally beneficial consequences. A Christian family, even one torn apart by premature death, could look forward to a reunion in eternity. Collier thus imagined a "blissful scene" with a "glorified parent standing in the midst of a happy group," exclaiming, "*we are all here!*"[70]

The emergence of Mormon polygamy and its particular theological interpretation of family life offers a striking example of this desire for eternal certainty. Founder Joseph Smith introduced the practice of multiple wives in the late 1830s; a full rationale came several years later in a series of revelations about "eternal" and "celestial" marriage. According to these revelations, polygamy was allowable, and theologically necessary, because sanctified human relationships continued beyond the grave. Since human beings were themselves both matter and spirit and their heavenly existence merely an exalted form of their earthly lives, a properly sealed marriage—that is, one conducted in a Mormon temple—would literally last for all eternity. Celestial marriage also placed Mormon fatherhood on solid theological ground. In the afterlife Mormon husbands could look forward to special honor as patriarchal heads of families; men who married several wives would further increase their future reward, possibly even achieving fully divine stature in the world to come.

In 1852, after the Mormon trek to Utah, Brigham Young publically declared polygamy a central doctrine of the Latter-day Saints, much to the consternation of the Protestant world they had left back east. Mormons argued, however, that they were not rejecting the Protestant family ideal but, rather, augmenting it. As Lawrence Foster has argued, Mormon defenses of polygamy sounded "more Victorian than the writings of the Victorians." "To an almost unparalleled extent," Foster writes, "the Mormon religion really was *about* the family; earthly and heavenly family ideals were seen as identical."[71]

Few Protestants would have found such arguments persuasive; in their view domesticity was simply not possible without Christianity. As former Mormon John Hyde declared, "The Mormon polygamists have no HOME." Instead of a well-appointed parlor and a cozy fireside, Mormon families lived in "small disconnected houses, like a row of outhouses," or they crowded together into one building, "outraging all decency." Polygamy not only degraded men and women, but it also corrupted children. According to Hyde, visitors to Salt Lake City found Mormon youth undisciplined and immoral, "the most whisky-loving, tobacco-chewing, saucy and precocious children [they] ever saw." The lesson was clear: homes without a recognizably Christian physical form and corresponding sense of spiritual order simply could not produce morally decent children.[72]

Secular Salvation

Of course, in a larger sense middle-class parents' worries about the future were not easily quelled by eschatological promises. Piloting children toward salvation was no mean task, but it was hardly their only challenge. The secular demands of the market economy, emerging in the pre–Civil War decades, required Christian parents to live within a difficult series of paradoxes: their children had to be both loyal and independent, unselfish and shrewd, pious Christians headed aggressively toward worldly success. Godly mothers were at the center of the conundrum: the spiritual traits they embodied were antithetical to the demands of the marketplace, yet they were given primary responsibility for raising sons who would someday succeed there.

Prevailing American attitudes toward children owed much to John Locke's rationalistic model of childhood and Jean-Jacques Rousseau's story of Emile, the boy who personified a secular paradigm of innocent freedom. Rousseau's famous treatise argued against any form of premature indoctrination; a child should be allowed to live fully, to learn in accordance with his own developing needs, not with a parent's arbitrary demand. Thus, Rousseau kept his Emile a functional pagan until he reached young adulthood, assuming that abstract religious ideas were simply nonsense to his innocent, simple mind.[73] When another French-man, Alexis de Tocqueville, visited the United States in the 1830s, he found the spirit of Emile firmly within the American system. "In America," he ob-served, "the family, in the Roman and aristocratic signification of the word, does not exist." A young man in the new democracy did not have to depend on his father for land or inheritance; born as the "master of his thoughts," he "is soon master of his conduct."[74]

In a free economic and religious economy, middle-class parents could not pass along financial or spiritual security to their children. They could not man-date a professional or romantic choice any more than they could ensure a child's religious conversion. The central dilemma of nineteenth-century middle-class parents—in many ways still true—was to "do justice to American ideals of in-dividualism while, at the same time, saving that freed and expanded will from indulging in the corruptions plaguing American society."[75]

This need to balance freedom and order was not unique to nineteenth-century parents, but it was particularly acute for them, especially for parents of young boys. Victorians identified the mature man as one who had achieved "self-mastery." Thus, the opposite of manliness was not femininity but childishness—it was no accident that both infant boys and girls wore long skirts, the dress of women, to symbolize their dependency. The essence of the child's immaturity was an inability to inspire the respect and trust of others. The competitive mar-ketplace of American society rewarded entrepreneurs but, even more so, those who demonstrated the middle-class virtues of moderation and restraint, the signs of a good credit risk. Astute parents, therefore, worked to create what David Riesman would describe as an "inner-directed" personality in their children. In-ternal restraints, not fear of punishment, would ultimately separate the thought-less child from the mature man.[76]

Figure 1. Victorian mother and children at prayer (S. S. Pugh, Christian Home Life: A Book of Examples and Principles. *New York: American Tract Society, 1864, frontispiece).*

Bushnell's model of Christian parenting provided the answer. Stressing the virtues of obedience and submission, it allowed feminine piety a meaningful role in the rearing of both sons and daughters. In contrast to the earlier evangelical model, it counseled love as the primary means and freedom as the intended result. "The too frequent use of the rod, or the resorting to those methods of ingenious *torture* which form with some the chief staple of family government," Collier wrote, "tend rather to harden than soften the young and tender heart. . . . We need not resort to the rod when a word or a look may suffice."[77] A similar account counseled that a "wise liberty must be allowed to children, in combination with the requirement of perfect submission and the exercise of self-restraint. Children are being trained to think and act for themselves in after-life; and in order to this, the golden mean must be found between a rule so strict as to destroy all independent action, and unchecked license."[78]

Christian parents who did not rely on traditional means of breaking the will had to assert control over their children with more subtle techniques. Indeed, Bushnell counseled, conscientious parents needed to be more vigilant about their own behavior than about their children's. "Every hour," he wrote, "is to be an hour of duty, every look and smile, every reproof and care, an effusion of Christian love."[79] Parents could not afford a single lapse of attentiveness but, as one guidebook counseled them, were to be always "solemn, tender, prayerful. Let the look of your countenance indicate the unutterable anxiety of your soul for their salvation."[80]

The emotional climate of a Christian home was a critical factor in its success. "For the honour of Christianity," Collier wrote, "then, no spot where it is claimed should be cheerless and joyless."[81] Many pious authors assured their readers that domestic religion was itself a recipe for personal happiness. Truly Christian families were "the most contented and happy" and their relationships "an unfailing source of pleasure."[82] They urged all family members to "take a cheerful view of every thing, and encourage hope"; to "keep a strict watch over yourself" when feeling irritable from "sickness, pain, or disappointment"; and, "when pained by some unkind word or act, ask yourself, 'Have I not often done the same and been forgiven?' "[83]

Clearly, such advice impacted mothers far more than fathers and daughters more than sons. Prescriptive literature from the 1840s onward offered very different advice about anger to women and men. Open displays of temper were simply "unfeminine" and to be avoided at all costs; masculine aggression, however, served a purpose in the wider world. Mother's job, then, was to watch the emotional thermostat at home, to train her sons to channel their anger and their daughters to deny it.[84]

The "praying mother," so central to nineteenth-century autobiographical accounts, exerted a powerful and costly control over her children. G. Stanley Hall, for example, remembered his mother as a "saintly woman" who never showed "a single symptom of anger or even impatience with three children at a trying age about her." But her private journals, written during the 1850s, reveal deep spiritual struggles. "The power and extent of individual influence has been a theme of frequent meditation of life," she wrote in the summer of 1857, "and how fearful the thought that I may have already set in motion influences for evil which are to have a widening range through all time." She recorded her resolve to "order my speech, my every tone of voice, all the particulars of manner which go to make up the general deportment. . . . I am a mother, and what is my influence on my children on whose young hearts are made ineffaceable impressions which have a bearing on their character through time, and also their future destiny? It is a solemn inquiry and awakens sad reflections." Mrs. Hall determined to maintain "greater watchfulness" over her behavior, "that in all things my mite of influence may tell for good on my children to the remotest generation." Hall, the psychologist and the son, found her efforts at self-control both admirable and oppressive. "I think she had an almost morbid dread of conflict of any kind," he recalled. "She could not endure antagonism or criticism, and seems to have had nothing less than a passion for getting and keeping in amicable relations with every acquaintance." Family quarrels caused her particular anxiety. "Perhaps," Hall wondered, "she felt that she should have prevented all our bickerings if her heart was full enough of love and reproached herself that harmony did not always reign."[85]

Hall's account reveals how closely Christian child rearing dovetailed with the developing canons of middle-class behavior. At midcentury a multitude of conduct manuals and etiquette books—the secular counterpart of the Christian home literature—offered rules for life in an open, increasingly anonymous urbanizing society. By the middle decades of the nineteenth century city dwellers in particular could no longer identify an individual as middle-class simply by dress or deportment. As the advice literature warned, social counterfeits of various types easily mimicked the outward signs of conventionality. It was not difficult for these types to ingratiate themselves into proper society and then make off with everything from the family silverware to a daughter's virtue. The solution, at least in part, was to internalize middle-class virtues and to uplift the importance of sincerity and "character," qualities presumably beyond the reach of a confidence man or a vulgar parvenu.[86]

Yet the only final assurance of middle-class virtue was a Christianity instilled from birth. Indeed, conduct that issued only from a social desire to impress was by definition selfish and insincere. True courtesy "rises out of the well-spring of grace in the renewed soul," one etiquette authority reminded his readers. "The Scriptures teach a courtesy of which the politeness of the world is only the cold and lifeless image."[87] Sarah Hale agreed that the Bible was the most fundamental guide to social etiquette. She organized her own conduct manual around seven commands of Christ, arguing that "the gentleman or lady who will conform their conduct to the perfect pattern of 'good will' needs few other rules for the 'etiquette of good society.'"[88]

Bushnell's promise that parents could begin molding their children's character from birth gave Christian families a unique advantage: a child raised in a godly home was the epitome of sincerity, having never even acquired evil habits in the first place. Indeed, Bushnell believed that by three years old the child's character was virtually determined; half of the parents' opportunity was fulfilled or forever lost.[89] In other words, godly and conscientious parents had the power to set even a young infant on a virtuous life course and to all but ensure the future flowering of the habits required for economic and spiritual success.

Homes and Churches

Bushnell did not, however, intend Christian homes to become islands of forced cheerfulness. Christian nurture required a supportive Christian environment, which Bushnell envisioned as a series of concentric rings "with the family and mother in the center."[90] He reserved some of his strongest criticism for the individualism that isolated families beyond the realm of human need or assumed no common interests between the home and its larger social world. "A national life, a church life, a family life, is no longer conceived, or perhaps conceivable, by many," he complained. "We only seem to lie as seeds piled together, without any terms of connection, save for the accident of proximity, or the fact that we all belong to the heap."[91]

Bushnell insisted that the organic connections unifying family relationships also united home and church. He lamented the decline of infant baptism among American Protestants, arguing that it was a necessary signifier of the intrinsic ties between the parents' and the child's faith, based on a holy presumption that the child's seed faith would one day mature. On the strength of this argument Bushnell urged churches to grant baptized infants and children a special form of catechumenate membership. As soon as they were physically able, he declared, children should join in Sunday morning worship, prayer, and singing.[92] Together, church and home would provide a moral shelter for vulnerable children, where they might be "kept in purity, saved from the world, and led forth under all tender examples of obedience and godly living; and it will be strange if that nurture of the Lord does not show them growing up in the faith, to be sons and daughters, indeed, of the Lord Almighty."[93]

A few of Bushnell's more perceptive critics, however, recognized the claustrophobic implications of his theology—that is, the inevitable narrowing of Christian experience when the middle-class home becomes the primary site of religious nurture. Princeton Presbyterian Charles Hodge, for example, found much he liked in *Christian Nurture* yet objected to Bushnell's fundamentally "naturalistic" assumptions. In Hodge's view Bushnell failed to distinguish between ordinary and supernatural saving grace; he placed Christian conversion on the same plane as a "cultivated intellect." ("He has not advanced an inch beyond Pelagius.") "The whole tenor of this book is in favour of the idea that all true religion is gradual, habitual, acquired as habits are formed," Hodge complained. "Every thing must be like a natural process, nothing out of the regular sequence of cause and effect." In other words, parents need not—should not—expect their children to receive any divine visitations or wrenching encounters with a Righteous Judge. Bushnell's God, Hodge argued, was a thoroughly safe, domesticated deity.[94]

John Williamson Nevin, from Mercersburg Seminary, also found much to like in Bushnell, particularly his critique of "the reigning individualism of the age."[95] Yet, to Nevin, a confessional theologian with a firm appreciation of the church's liturgical role, Bushnell did not go far enough. His emphasis on the salvific power of a godly home meant that, in the final analysis, no other social institutions were really necessary. A home can never play the role of the church, Nevin argued, and parents should not even try to play the part of religious intermediaries. Nevin was similarly unimpressed by Bushnell's endorsement of infant baptism. Since in the end, Nevin argued, Bushnell's Christian nurture depended on natural human processes rather than supernatural means, Bushnellian parents might as well put a ring on the infant's finger as sprinkle baptismal water on its head.[96] "Faith must have a basis . . . beyond itself, on which to rest," Nevin declared. But in Bushnell's scheme, he argued, the wider historical importance of ecclesiastical ritual and tradition really meant nothing at all. Each parent was, in the end, a lone priest and each child a single congregant in an isolated domestic church.

Hodge and Nevin were in the minority, although a century later others would resume their critique. The majority of Protestants found the prospect of domestic self-sufficiency oddly comforting. As the Presbyterian *New York Observer* declared in 1855, if Christianity were "compelled to flee from the mansions of the great, the academies of philosophers, the halls of legislators, or the throngs of busy men, we should find her last retreat with women at the fireside. Her last audience would be the children gathering round the knee of a mother; the last sacrifice, the secret prayer, escaping in silence from her lips, and heard, perhaps, only at the throne of God."[97]

Of course, American Protestants were also working busily to ensure that such a scene would never come to pass. In the late nineteenth century the Christian home became an important tool of Protestant empire building, facilitating the emergence of a diverse denominational infrastructure of missions, education, and reform. The Christian home ideology survived and flourished through an energetic renovation, largely engineered by women, of drawing room piety into a grand strategy for the conversion of the world.

Chapter 2   Protestant Homes and Christian Civilization

Although the Christian home ideal originated in the sentimental confines of the antebellum middle class, the post–Civil War generation gave it a vigorous public agenda. Protestant missionaries, reformers, and teachers—most of them women—extolled the Christian home as key to the moral transformation of American society and the world beyond. As a Baptist author enthused, making a "happy home," one in which "love reigns supreme, and amiability, affection, cheerfulness, joy and peace are the natural conditions of family life," was "preeminently millennial work."[1]

Modern readers may find this a curious construction. Over the past century home has become—symbolically, if not actually—a place for personal escape from social pressures at the end of the working day, hardly the location for much "millennial work." But a century or more ago American Protestants did not assume such a radical differentiation of public and private space. They saw the home, and to a similar extent the church, as mediating institutions within a larger social whole, simultaneously occupying both sacred and secular space, the private as well as the public sphere.[2] As such, it was pivotally important in cultivating both personal piety and the moral renewal of society, for as Methodist bishop Isaac Wiley declared, the "sacred institution" of the home fulfilled God's purposes for "the welfare of human beings in their social relations" and "with regard to his Church and Kingdom on the earth." As one Protestant educator put it, "public morality is the sum of private morals . . . as is the individual, so is the nation."[3]

This chapter outlines the role of domestic Christianity in forging and maintaining that link. During the late nineteenth century the home increasingly defined the essence of American Protestantism and as such played a crucial part
in its civilizing mission to the world. "Only in the sphere of Christianity does
the true idea of home become fully developed," Presbyterian Samuel Phillips
wrote in 1860. "Home with the savage is but a herding, a servitude."[4] Methodist H. A. Boardman agreed that "wherever the Bible is, there the family will be
found." The Christian family was the bedrock of Western morality, far superior
to "the brute-like commerce of Socialism," the "hydra-headed monster of Polygamy," and "the no less hideous gorgon of Divorce."[5] The language of domestic
Christianity brimmed with the same righteous certitude that informed American political rhetoric. Boardman, for example, cheerily borrowed a line from
manifest destiny, referring to the home as a "domestic empire" with "a code which
is binding upon all alike."[6]

Indeed, Protestants were certain that Christian homes were central to the
task of nation building. The family altar, one minister argued, was "the chief
factor in hastening the universal sway of the kingdom of God." Godly homes,
he declared, ensured a peaceful social order. "To lose family prayer out of our
homes is to lose the rudder of the ship of state."[7] The view of Christian families
as miniature state institutions was, by the late nineteenth century, a common
insight. In a popular series of articles published in 1840 Amherst College president Heman Humphrey described the family as "a little state, or empire within
itself, bound together by its patriarchal head." Although several decades later
Humphrey's patriarchal emphasis was a bit out of date, the hopes and fears he
projected onto Protestant family life were as fresh as ever. With the reuniting
of North and South after the Civil War, the civilizing functions of the Christian home became integral to the new national order.[8]

This chapter offers two extended examples of this process, in the outer and
inner lives of American Protestants. First, the post–Civil War home missionary
movement offers a particularly good example of the growing importance of domesticity in Protestant evangelistic and civic agendas. A following section describes ways in which Christian domesticity gave churches deeper access into
the private worlds of individual members, exemplified by the successful institutionalization of the family altar within Protestant households. Such methods
served the churches well, especially as a way of enlisting wide and enthusiastic
lay participation on behalf of denominational objectives. Indeed, the Protestant

domestic strategy allowed churches to harness the cultural power of the Christian home as "the strongest human institution on the face of the earth," situated at the very heart of late-nineteenth-century Western civilization.[9]

The civic agenda of domestic Christianity was, to a large degree, engineered by middle-class Protestant women, whose lives increasingly transected both the public and the private realm.[10] Domesticity, even in its most restrictive forms, always held open the possibility that women's responsibility for the home might require more direct efforts to ensure public morality; allegiance to one could logically intensify commitment to the other.[11] By the latter decades of the nineteenth century possibility was becoming reality. As Chautauqua lecturer Emily Huntington Miller declared in 1882, "No woman can do the best work for her own home whose work *ends* there; the more blessed her own garden, . . . the readier should be her sacrifice for that labor by which the deserts of sin may be changed into the garden of the Lord." Miller readily accepted the sentimental notion that home was "woman's kingdom," but, she declared with millennial enthusiasm, "surely the golden age of that kingdom is but now dawning upon it."[12]

In the postwar period women's organizational ambitions closely matched denominational aspirations. While antebellum Protestants had assumed that Christian homes would reproduce by the power of love and moral influence, the next generation took a more pragmatic approach. Northern postbellum Protestants were quick to realize that the Union victory in the Civil War was the result of bold plans and organizational efficiency. The work of the United States Sanitary Commission and its evangelical counterpart, the United States Christian Commission, mobilized thousands of volunteers on behalf of northern troops. The Sanitary Commission eventually numbered over ten thousand local auxiliaries; huge "Sanitary Fairs" in Chicago and Boston raised hundreds of thousands of dollars and provided invaluable administrative experience for the women who organized them. After the war ended women's groups voiced a determination to continue working together on behalf of the unfortunate. When the Woman's Central Association of Relief disbanded, in July 1865, its officers declared that they would not allow the "common bond" that had formed among the nation's women to "weaken or dissolve."[13]

The Civil War cemented among American Protestants the conviction that society would never be Christianized unless the religion of "home, sweet home" moved beyond mere sentiment into a broad, synchronized campaign. Thus, the postwar period saw a decidedly unsentimental effort to expand the reach of domestic Christianity through a variety of mass-produced material means, including coordinated efforts of denominational agencies for missionary and educational work and the creation of standardized resources for spiritual nurture.

Domestic Christianity was an infinitely pliable religious concept. The theological ideas undergirding it were a mile wide and only inches deep, their relative shallowness an advantage in a time of mounting religious controversy. In contrast to the multitude of divisive issues that loomed by the turn of the century—the truth and uniqueness of Christianity, the ordination of women, the veracity of the Bible—the Christian home ideal was not unduly weighted with complicated theological baggage. Advocates could appeal to a fairly benign set of biblical texts and leave the rest of the argument to a prevailing middle-class consensus within their churches. But this made middle-class Protestantism an easy target for its growing array of critics. Religious conservatives, many of them leaders in what would become the fundamentalist movement, took easy aim at the rickety theological underpinnings of domestic religion. Protest against Gilded Age religiosity, in fact, required them to reject the notion of human progress, of God's immanence in American society, and the redemptive power of family life—in short, the entire edifice of late-nineteenth-century Protestantism.

More liberal Protestants, however, remained heavily invested in a domestic strategy of nurture and outreach. More than simply a sacred space for Christian child rearing, home became a means of bringing order and cultural unity to a society in which both seemed to be in increasingly short supply. By the turn of the century Protestants had invested the home with such a daunting array of responsibilities that churches almost seemed redundant to the success of Christianity. Protestants evangelized, worshiped, and nurtured within the domestic context; what then, they might well have asked, were churches for?

Home Missionaries

After the Civil War, under the leadership of Protestant women, Christian domesticity took on an aggressively evangelistic cast. By the turn of the century an array of denominational mission organizations, flanked by a powerful women's temperance movement, had mobilized the sentimental idealism of the antebellum generation into an aggressive arm of Protestant outreach. Women's home and foreign missions, moral reform societies, and national humanitarian and educational efforts formed the largest mass movement of women in American history to that point, overlapping but greatly outnumbering membership in the much more visible women's suffrage movement.

The rise of independent women's missionary movements was in many ways a logical outcome of the domestic ideal, but certainly not envisioned in the 1840s. The original ideal of the Christian home presupposed the constant presence of a submissive, godly mother. In fact, because he believed so firmly in maternal influence, Bushnell had opposed woman suffrage as "a reform against nature." In his view the prospect of women in the voting booth boded only ill for Protestant families. Bushnell predicted an increase in divorce, especially in wives who voted differently than their husbands, and painful levels of domestic conflict. Indeed, Bushnell prophesied an erosion of femininity if female suffrage ever became the rule and, in its place, a new race of "shrill" and aggressively masculine women.[14]

And, to be sure, many of the early leaders in the institutionalization of the Christian home were women who saw such work as an alternative to the egalitarian rhetoric of the women's rights movement. In 1869 antisuffragist Catherine Beecher and her sister Harriet Beecher Stowe codified Christian domesticity in a popular treatise on *The American Woman's Home*. The book provided architectural models literally combining a home, church, and a school as well as pages of detailed instruction on the minutiae of the Christian house, from the proper arrangement of a room to the right ordering of kitchen work (see fig. 2). Religion pervaded the domestic realm not merely in the creation of a proper moral atmosphere but in the installation of clothing hooks, the economical preparation of soups and stews, and well-ventilated sleeping quarters. The manual includes an object lesson about little Jim, a good child who goes to sleep "in a most Christian frame," having said his prayers dutifully. Yet, when morning comes, Jim "sits up in bed with his hair bristling with crossness, strikes at his nurse, and declares he won't say his prayers—that he doesn't want to be good." The problem, the Beecher sisters explained, was not the child's innate sinfulness but the fact that the child, "having slept in a close box of a room, his brain all night fed by poison, is in a mild state of moral insanity." The development of a Christian character, they argued, required far more than just moral instruction—environment could in many ways determine the daily state of one's soul.[15]

To the Beecher sisters the distinguishing features of a Christian house were order, efficiency, and industry, practiced by parents, children, and servants alike. In a similar vein Mary Mann, the wife of journalist Horace Mann, published a

Figure 2. The Beecher sisters' Christian home (*Catherine Beecher and Harriet Beecher Stowe*, American Woman's Home *[1869; rpt., Hartford, Conn.: Harriet Beecher Stowe Center, 1975], 23).*

book entitled *Christianity in the Kitchen,* explaining the elements of a Christian diet. "Compounds like wedding cake, suet plum-puddings, and rich turtle soup, are masses of indigestible material," she warned, which "should never find their way to any Christian table."[16]

Such attention to detail had a clear moral purpose. Although Catherine Beecher sharply opposed woman suffrage, she argued that a woman who knew how to run a proper home had far more clout than she could ever achieve through the ballot. "There is a moral power given to woman in the family state," she declared, "much more controlling and abiding than the inferior, physical power conferred on man." If a woman brought a truly Christian family to a destitute settlement, Beecher argued, "soon its gardens and fields would cause 'the desert to blossom as the rose,' and around would soon gather a 'Christian neighborhood.'" Before long a church would appear, offering opportunities for literary and social gatherings and "safe and healthful amusements." Soon after, "colonies from these prosperous and Christian communities would go forth to shine as 'lights of the world' in all the now darkened nations." Thus, Beecher concluded, "the 'Christian family' and 'Christian neighborhood' would become the grand ministry, as they were designed to be, in training our whole race for heaven."[17]

Although Beecher's conclusions about women's roles set her apart from many of her contemporaries, few would have questioned her fundamental assumptions. Indeed, Bushnell's original vision of Christian nurture discussed the role of the home in the "out-populating power of the Christian stock." He argued, "if the children were identified with religion from the first, and grew up in a Christian love of man, the missionary spirit would not throw itself up in irregular jets, but would flow as a river."[18] Whether or not they agreed on the extent to which women's place was in the home, late-nineteenth-century Protestants willingly supported a myriad of efforts to bring the home's influence to bear on the wider world, including the realm of politics. "Home is our place," suffrage orator May Wright Sewall declared in 1881. "To stay in it and perfect it, to rear in it noble sons and noble daughters, we must open and legitimate political power." Indeed, she concluded with a flourish, "a domestic necessity compels it."[19]

The Women's Christian Temperance Union (WCTU) represented one of the most successful efforts to link domestic Christianity with a political agenda. When the organization first formed in 1874, it followed a more overtly religious program of "moral suasion." Annie Wittenmyer, the WCTU's first president, emphasized the importance of "gospel temperance," arguing that it was God alone who had called women into the work. Members promised to resist the temptation to form alliances with other like-minded groups, since they had been "in a peculiar manner called of God" to lead the nation toward moral renewal.[20]

Frances Willard, who became president of the WCTU five years after it was founded, was an ardent advocate of political involvement in prohibition and women's suffrage—both in the name of "home-protection." "It is not enough that women should be home-makers," she declared, "but they must make the world itself, a larger home."[21] Decrying the artificial barriers between the home and the political world, she urged on her followers a sanctified campaign of "gospel politics" to extend domestic virtue to American society more generally. Thousands of Protestant women fervently believed in her cause; by 1885 the WCTU boasted 200,000 members, and over the next five years that number grew by 70 percent. Willard herself became one of the most beloved, even revered, figures in American Protestant culture by the end of the century, an intriguing blend of "true womanliness" and organizational genius.[22]

The women's home mission movement, organized in the 1870s and 1880s, offers a less known but equally striking example of domestic Christianity's aggressive social program. Before the Civil War, Protestant home missions consisted mainly of sending churches, pastors, and Sunday schools to the advancing frontier, a movement spearheaded by the formation of the American Home Missionary Society in 1826. After the war, however, focus shifted toward evangelizing the country's newly accessible populations of "elbow heathen"—unassimilated immigrants, newly freed slaves, and Indian tribes in the West. To critics who decried the formation of yet another set of voluntary organizations, home missions advocates promised that evangelism at home would actually streamline larger global efforts. As Methodist bishop Isaac Wiley told a Chautauqua audience in 1884, "If we can take care of Christian America, American Christianity will take care of the world." Although foreign missions would continue to attract the most money and volunteers, home missionaries could experience the romance of cross-cultural encounter, without the arduous and often fatal necessity of overseas travel required for foreign missions.[23]

Since Protestant women were denied access to preaching as a means of evangelism, home missions emphasized education as a primary means of uplift. In 1888, for example, a Baptist missionary noted that "preaching to congregations" was no longer part of successful evangelistic work; far more effective were efforts at establishing schools, doing "house to house teaching," and making personal calls to mothers and children at home. Implementing Catherine Beecher's vision, women's groups concentrated their efforts on establishing Christian homes among the poor and culturally unassimilated, aiming to produce "clean homes, clean hearts, and clean lives."[24]

These aims coincided with government policy toward freedmen in the years after the Civil War. The great indictment of slavery had been its "degradation" of family life; abolitionists had fervently argued that the essential immorality of the peculiar institution was the denial of legal marriage to slaves—not to mention the immoral conduct of slave owners toward female bond servants. In such a system slave parents could not guide their children's moral development, much less protect them from sexual license. After the war the Freedmen's Bureau, given the task of reconstructing slaves into citizens, immediately began encouraging couples to contract legal marriages and to establish stable nuclear households. The Fourteenth and Fifteenth Amendments furthered this goal, establishing the civil and political rights of black males and thus emphasizing the husband and father's civilizing role as the representative head of his individual family.[25]

Denominational leaders were quick to recognize their potential contribution to this task. After the Civil War northern Protestant denominations and freedmen's aid societies sponsored a flood of teachers into the southern states. Male-run mission boards initially emphasized the necessity of rudimentary education as a means of training a new generation of black pastors who would in turn Christianize their race by establishing local congregations. Missionary officials soon discovered, however, that it was not only cheaper but more efficient to employ female teachers instead of men, because these women were able to expand their work beyond the classroom and into the "cabins of the people," where they would presumably have a more permanent impact. The domestic setting, in other words, began to prove far more strategic to Presbyterian home missions than the training of local pastors. Other denominations soon came to the same realization. Three women's groups—the Women's Home Missionary Society of the Methodist Episcopal Church and the Woman's American Baptist and the Woman's Baptist Home Missionary Societies (two cooperating wings based in Chicago and Boston)—arose directly in response to changing perceptions of missionary work in the postwar South.[26]

The changing character of Christian domesticity spurred a multitude of efforts. After the Civil War northern Baptist women raised hundreds of thousands of dollars toward the education of black clergymen; others had gone south to work as teachers under the auspices of the American Baptist Home Missionary Society (ABHMS). In 1873 a young Baptist woman, Joanna Moore, moved to New Orleans to work among black churches, having held an unsalaried commission from the ABHMS to work with freedmen in refugee camps during the war. As knowledge of her efforts, and her need for financial support, spread northward, Baptist women formed the Woman's Baptist Home Missionary Society in 1877. In short order they supplied Moore with a salary and four female assistants.

By the early 1880s, Moore was concentrating on building Christian homes across the South. In 1883 she established the Training School for Mothers in Thibodeaux, Louisiana, offering a ten-day course in housekeeping, hygiene, temperance, and childcare, as well as family prayer and Bible study. In 1885 she began disseminating the principles of Christian domesticity in a small magazine, called *Hope*. The contents included a serialized version of the Training School curriculum and practical articles for African American mothers on such subjects

as "Chewing Gum" and "How to Wash Dishes." In 1893 Moore expanded her
study program into a four-year "Fireside School," modeled on the Chautauqua
movement and designed for use by all members of the family. She instituted a
"Parents' Pledge" in which both mothers and fathers promised to make their
homes "as comfortable and attractive as possible."[27]

In similar fashion Methodist and Baptist women's training schools in the
South aimed to teach the principles of Christian family life as well as "theory
and practice of housekeeping" by placing students in "tastefully and economically" appointed model "industrial homes." Students did not receive a traditional
literary education but daily classes in home economics, physiology, hygiene, and
care for the sick. Missionaries insisted that such subjects, though deemed by some
to be merely "secular," were "too intimately associated with the Christian training of girls" to be excluded.[28]

The gospel of Christian domesticity also spread to the American West. The
Dawes Severalty Act, passed by Congress in 1887, announced the government's
intention to save Native Americans from extinction through a concerted campaign to civilize them. Instead of forcing the tribes onto reservations, government officials held out the offer of land and eventual citizenship to any individual
who agreed to relinquish old tribal ways. No longer nomadic, polygamous enemies of the United States government, Indians were one day to become model
American citizens by settling down into stable nuclear families.

Missionaries soon became central in implementing this vision. In 1888, in
response to protests by Hicksite and Orthodox Quakers, the United States government reversed a decision to transfer the Indian Bureau from the Department
of the Interior to the War Department. The new so-called Quaker Policy also
gave Protestant denominations much greater access to Indian tribes and more
control over the selection of government agents. The policy also reflected the
widespread Protestant conviction that only acceptance of Christianity would save
the tribes from extinction.

Protestant missionary efforts in the West expanded greatly during the post–
Civil War period, shaped by an urgent awareness that rapid Christianization
would require far more than Bible distribution or evangelistic preaching. By 1898
the Presbyterian Women's Executive Committee had established sixteen Indian
schools and by 1904 had expanded its work across thirty-three tribes in fifteen
states. The Women's National Indian Association, an interdenominational organization formed in 1884, similarly worked to establish schools where Native
American women were taught "to *make homes*, and keep them in civilized and

Christian fashion."[29] With little sense of irony the missionaries gave indigenous women lessons in food preparation, clothes making, care for the sick, and the need to "respect work and be self-supporting." Such instruction, the missionaries believed, formed an essential part of their conversion to "genuine and practical Christianity."[30]

Methodist and Baptist women also introduced the Christian home to European immigrant women. They stationed missionaries in Castle Garden, New York, to intercept new arrivals, and in Boston they established temporary homes ("moral lighthouses") for young women who arrived without friends or family. Baptist and Methodist women's missionary training schools offered courses of study in German and Scandinavian. Between 1881 and 1903 close to a third of the 586 graduates of the Baptist Missionary Training School were from the foreign language contingent—which included, for the Baptists, a two-year course of study consisting of 640 hours of theology and Bible, 480 hours in Sunday school work, 600 hours in the domestic arts, and 912 hours doing fieldwork. The goal of the program, supporters explained, was to provide instruction in "intelligent *Christian Home making*" and to instill in immigrant women "a sense of the obligations resting upon them as *wives* and *mothers*."[31]

But, surely, home missionaries must have recognized that the women they taught knew a fair amount about food preparation and childcare. One can imagine a certain disparity between the reports they sent home and their actual encounters with women living in sharecropper's cabins or reservation lean-tos.[32] But the logic behind their efforts demanded strict attention to the most mundane and trivial detail. If the redemptive essence of a Christian home lay in its atmosphere, itself the cumulative effect of a home's design, ornamentation, and interpersonal behavior, then a class in proper table setting had an undeniable godly purpose. Right behavior and right feeling, more than right belief, were the true marks of an American Protestant conversion.

More than that, the gospel of Protestant domesticity was part of the post–Civil War national agenda. It is not surprising, as historian Nancy Cott points out, that the late nineteenth century saw increasing government efforts to codify and enforce the Protestant ideal, through social purity laws against vice and by direct federal intervention in religious practice. In 1882 the Edmunds Act outlawed Mormon polygamy, denying the right to vote to any man or woman in unlawful cohabitation or plural marriage. Five years later the Edmunds-Tucker Act repealed the Church of the Latter-day Saints' articles of incorporation, and it was followed by government efforts to seize church property. Ultimately, the

Mormon church backed down, rescinding polygamy in 1890 and accepting state-
hood for Utah in 1896. Protestant domesticity, as this episode suggests, was both
a means of raising Christian children and the law of the land, a powerful statement of post–Civil War national unity. The Christian home symbolized the highest fruits of American civilization: its moral purity, its democratic values, and
its spiritual superiority to all other ways of life.[33]

The Family Altar

The Christian home also helped Protestant denominations bring much-needed
inner order to late-nineteenth-century religious life. The rapid proliferation of
national denominational structures after the Civil War was an obvious indication of religious success but also a cause for worry. Between 1861 and 1909 Protestant women established 44 missionary organizations and supported 4,710
missionaries, to a tune of nearly four million dollars. Methodists did not open
their first training school for clergy until 1847; but by 1880 the denomination
had established 11 theological seminaries, 44 colleges and universities, and 130
schools for women. Protestant institutions grew in every direction: Sunday
schools proliferated in individual congregations, fed by a steady stream of literature from denominational presses and trained volunteers emanating from denominational headquarters.[34] Yet, as many Protestants recognized, rapid growth
imposed heavy spiritual costs. In the competitive rush to build new institutions,
the rapidly expanding "salvation machine" might end up compromising both
personal piety and denominational unity.[35]

One place that seemed inherently immune to the deadening effects of
routinization was the spiritual relationship between parents and children. Trust-
ing in Bushnell's promise of the fundamental purity of this bond, late-nineteenth-
century Protestants began to look to the home to compensate for the sins of
the institutional church. Here above all, as Bushnell himself argued, religion
had to be utterly sincere to be effective.[36]

In the late-nineteenth century the family altar thus became central to the
growing ritualization of middle-class Protestant home life. An informal survey,
published by a Boston Congregational pastor in 1891, found wide agreement
among both clergy and lay people about the absolute necessity of a family altar—though, of course, not all followed the practice to his satisfaction.[37] Prayer
books and manuals proliferated, each one framed as an aid to deeper and more

regularized personal sincerity. Ideally characterized by "simplicity of language and directness of supplication," the family altar included morning and evening prayers and Bible reading and, often as not, a hymn or a meditation led by one of the parents.[38] Families often read the Bible through, chapter by chapter and, depending on their ecclesiastical background, offered extemporaneous prayers or read from a common text.[39] Although many prayer books offered a yearly round of daily prayers, supplemented by others for special occasions, some devotionals were more topical. "In this way," one author explained, "may be avoided a feeling of insincerity arising from using a prayer merely because it is marked for the day, while it may have no adaptation to our present feelings."[40]

Sunday churchgoing, another centerpiece of family religion, gradually became one part of a longer observance that began with the Saturday evening bath and ended twenty-four hours later after a regimen that included special Sunday morning prayers, morning worship, Sabbath school for the children, and a second afternoon or evening service.[41] In between, parents catechized their children, allowed them to read morally uplifting literature, and, if they were less strict, took them on a long Sunday afternoon carriage ride. Sunday observance fell within a weekly pattern of religious practices. "We did not merely go to church," social reformer Ida Tarbell recalled of growing up in rural Pennsylvania; "we stayed to class meeting; we went to Sunday school, where both father and mother had classes; we went to Wednesday night—or was it Thursday night—prayer meeting. And when there was a revival we went every night."[42]

The family altar allowed American Protestants to feel a powerful connection with a simpler, more religious past. Nearly every plea for home devotions included a reference to "The Cotter's Saturday Night," a poem about a rural Scottish household. In this idealized, pastoral setting "the priest-like father" read "the sacred page," while the rest of the family gathered around him in deferential silence.[43]

This quaintly patriarchal image suggests that much of the appeal of domestic religion was the quiet orderliness of its routines. Some advocates of the family altar emphasized its utility as an "aid to family government." They assumed that the ritual was the father's responsibility, his public piety an important source of his authority over children and servants. The head of the household "does well to call around him everything which can strengthen his authority over the household," one author reminded. "Can we imagine anything better calculated to effect this than his daily appearance in their midst as . . . their *priest*, leading them with the sacrifices of a broken spirit and a contrite heart, to the mercy-seat of God? Will they not rise from their knees with a more reverent regard for him who has been interceding in their behalf with the Father of their spirits?"[44]

Many advice books assumed that servants as well as family members would attend nightly prayers, for pious as well as practical reasons. "Prayerless brothers," Charles Deems exhorted, "do you know why your servants are so faithless to you? Why they work so slowly, and neglect their work in your absence, and give you so much trouble in a thousand ways? Is it not because you have never, by reading the Scripture to them, by prayer, by personal instruction, shown them that *you* recognized such a thing as duty and such a thing as moral responsibility?"[45]

But the traditional, patriarchal approach was becoming a bit old-fashioned by the post–Civil War period. By this time religious observance had become primarily women's responsibility, as had the popular practice of reading aloud in the family circle.[46] Busy middle-class fathers were increasingly hard-pressed to oversee the spiritual lives of family members and servants; in many homes father's occasional delegation of religious responsibility to mother gradually became a regular habit.

In the late-nineteenth century the family altar also began to follow a more Bushnellian logic, in which the entire family, not just the father, acted as instruments of grace to one another. "Each one should have something to do," one manual declared, "and especially the children."[47] By the late nineteenth century many families practiced "reading around" a text and allowed children to recite verses or pray in turn. In 1883 Lyman Abbott edited a collection of Bible passages and prayers for families, in response to frequent inquiries for "a brief, comprehensive, and adequate manual." Abbott's volume, like many others of this period, was designed to include both parents and children and featured human interest Bible stories of famous men and women.[48]

Protestant parents could perhaps afford to be less didactic, since most could rely on the rapidly proliferating Sunday school movement to provide organized instruction. Once geared toward converting unsaved children, American Sunday schools adopted a motto of "growth, not conquest" in the post–Civil War era. By the 1880s families could assume that their children were receiving systematic training in Bible content, often in a regular, sequential format, though not necessarily an age-appropriate one. Because religious educators could more often assume that children from Christian homes would be long-term attenders of Sunday schools, they presented truth in small, easily digestible bits of knowledge.[49]

Once they were assured that churches would provide the basics of instruction, Protestant parents could afford to be less moralistic and more affective in

home devotions. Indeed, late-nineteenth-century domesticity employed a growing variety of nonverbal inducements to piety, including stitched mottos, portraits of Christ, and large, ornate family Bibles. The very "act of looking" at such
objects, the boundary markers of a carefully constructed Christian environment,
was central to the development of a child's religious imagination and a family's
"collective memory." As Methodist author Isaac Wiley explained, "Our children
are mirrors, living mirrors, which not only catch up the image of every object
and event that comes before them, but by virtue of their vitality they retain
them all."[50]

The Sunday school model also helped direct the focus of Protestant domesticity toward families with young or preliterate children. By the 1890s the
most enterprising religious educators specialized in early childhood education,
drawing on the growing popularity of the European-inspired kindergarten movement. Besides family devotionals, religious educators produced a growing array
of books written especially for "very little people" and their parents, including
simple prayers and stories to be read together.[51]

Few family devotionals, therefore, attempted to address the spiritual needs
of adolescents and young adults. The oversight in part reflected social reality:
awareness of adolescence as a separate life stage was only just emerging by the
turn of the century. Before age-graded schools and curriculum materials became
widespread, categories such as child, youth, and adult could easily overlap. Moreover, before most middle-class couples had access to birth control, babies were
spread across a lengthy period of time; parents might be raising infants and toddlers for twenty years or more. Thus, by the turn of the century young people
looked not to their families but to special organizations such as the Christian
Endeavor movement for spiritual nurture; only a few observers noticed the several-
year gap between parental supervision and participation in young adult organizations, a period that later educators would recognize as particularly problematic.[52]

To many children family rituals could be both a burden and a source of comfort. "Indeed," social reformer Alice Hamilton wrote of her Indiana childhood,
"our 'puritanical' Sunday was distinctly pleasant, probably because it was so different from all other days and followed so strict a tradition. Breakfast, dinner,
supper, on Sunday were unvarying but different from the meals on other days,
and the books we read were 'Sunday' books, and church and Sunday school were
interesting partly because they constituted our rare excursions into the outside
world."[53] New England Episcopalian Ella Gilbert Ives recalled feelings of genuine
rage on the dreary Sunday afternoons when her grandmother set her to reading

aloud from the Bible. "Chapter after chapter I read until my voice stuck in my throat," she wrote in 1915. "But I believe that I owe this practice and one another, the staying quality of my conviction and conversion. After the reading, grandmother made me kneel beside her while she prayed aloud. This was habitual with her whenever we were along together; and the reality of the unseen world so grew upon me as she talked with God, that the wholesome fear instilled became a powerful factor in my training."[54]

Advocates of the family altar issued dire warnings that parents who neglected the rituals of the hearth were not just missing an opportunity for good but were unnecessarily exposing their young to terrible dangers. "All history and all experience," Presbyterian James Russell Miller warned, "proves that nothing but the religion of Christ can be a shelter for our loved ones from this world's dangers and temptations."[55] Thoughtless parents, another writer agreed, would surely find themselves a "melancholy spectacle" when their children had "gone to ruin" and they were left alone "enfeebled, humiliated, mourning over the wreck which their indolence or their errors made possible."[56]

But few Protestant authors seemed to worry about the growing competition from public amusements and the intensifying demands of the white-collar work world. Most of them assumed that, if parents exercised proper responsibility, children would easily succumb to the superior attractions of the "charmed circle" of the Christian home and its clear "talismanic power" over its inhabitants.[57] "If parents would save their boys," Miller advised, "they must make a home-life for the evenings so pleasant, so attractive, so charming that they will not want to leave it for any course of glaring fascinations outside." Miller suggested a range of activities, including "romping," games, music, or "the reading aloud of some racy and interesting book."[58]

Yet for most Protestants such warnings were probably unnecessary. By the end of the nineteenth century family religious observances were, as one self-proclaimed "old-fashioned New Englander" put it, "the natural and proper thing to do."[59] Ray Stannard Baker remembered from his Presbyterian boyhood the enormous family Bible in the parlor as "a kind of household god to be worshiped, a magic talisman that protected the family, and, as much as anything, a warrant of respectability." During his "Bible-ridden" youth, Baker wrote, "even in families of intelligence, the very act of reading [the Bible] was considered a virtue, a kind of magical process for securing divine approval."[60]

For some children the ritual perhaps worked too well. Although a Protestant childhood usually meant absorption of large amounts of religious belief and behavior, such childhood experiences did not always create a need for formal religion in later life. Even William Jennings Bryan, the great defender of orthodoxy, found the experience of growing up in a loving, observant home so satisfying that conversion did not mean a change in his habits of life or habits of thought: "I do not know of a virtue that came into his life as a result of my joining the Church, because all the virtues had been taught me by my parents."[61] For others a pervasive sense of parental love and nurture seemed to undercut the possibility, or the need, of a religious crisis in later life. Journalist Lincoln Steffens explained that because he had been "born in an atmosphere of love," so pure and constant, his own love "had no chance. It began, but it never caught up."[62] Edgar Lee Masters wrote, "I never confessed my sins and took conversion and the church," in part because his parents did not pressure him to and also because of his sense that "my grandfather's piety may have seemed sufficient to cover my Adam inheritance. I revered his religion, and found protection and sustenance in it."[63]

These idiosyncratic accounts point to broader changes in American religious life. As historian William Hutchison has argued, the Christian homes of the late nineteenth century produced a generation of liberal Protestant theologians, clergymen, and social reformers who, in good Bushnellian fashion, never underwent the emotional rigors of conversion. Few, if any, remembered their religious upbringing with animosity or confusion. These men, whose thought would shape the direction of mainstream Protestant culture in the twentieth century, felt the ethical imperatives of their Bushnellian upbringing but without any looming sense of alienation. They grew up knowing themselves both to be Christian and deeply loved by their parents, "sensing that, within broad limits, deviation would not mean rejection either of or by the parental generation."[64]

Dissent

American fundamentalists were clearly different in this respect. It is perhaps counterintuitive to find that these important predecessors of the modern evangelical movement and its profamily emphasis did not share in the sacralizing of domestic space in the late nineteenth century. Yet for theological and cultural reasons fundamentalists maintained an ambivalent, if not openly suspicious, stance toward the Protestant vision of redemptive family life.

The movement emerged in the mid–1870s and 1880s as a vehicle of dissent against Gilded Age religiosity. Although opposition to the German "higher criti-

cism" of the Bible and to the atheistic implications of Darwinian science figured high on the fundamentalist agenda, theological issues alone did not form
the basis for the movement's growing popularity. Early fundamentalism's brac-
ing piety and evangelistic zeal, codified in the revivalistic crusades of Dwight L.
Moody, J. Wilbur Chapman, and Billy Sunday, formed in conscious critique of
the perceived "worldliness" of well-heeled church members in elegant sanctuaries.

One of the movement's primary emphases, especially in its early years, was
the teaching that Christ's return was to come suddenly and very soon. Dispensational premillenial theology, disseminated in Bible institutes and summer Bible
conferences, offered a system of biblical interpretation that unlocked the intri-
cacies of Old and New Testament prophecy, and warned the faithful against fool-
ish capitulation to the "spirit of the age." Dispensational premillennialist
believers did not pretend to know the exact time and place of Christ's return,
but they lived with the daily awareness that it might come at any moment.[65]

One result of this expectant view toward the future was open contempt for
the mainstream Protestant trust in human institutions as agents of progress. Fundamentalists had little faith, for example, in women's suffrage as a means of social uplift and found few good reasons to support any politically based efforts,
no matter how righteous the cause. Although they did not publically oppose
Protestant efforts in education, temperance, and social reform, fundamentalists
often considered them dangerously superfluous, especially in view of Christ's imminent return. "Missions and holiness, rather than ecclesiastical organization
and moral reform, are the spheres in which we must chiefly exert ourselves,"
Boston Bible teacher F. L. Chappell wrote in 1896. "Perfected Christian character is what God now wants, more than any external arrangement of church,
or state, or social order." The "Eleventh Hour Laborers" in the early days of
Chappell's Boston Missionary Training School had no textbook except the Bible
and very little institutional infrastructure—no buildings, no endowment, no standards for enrollment. As A. J. Gordon, the school's founder, declared, "If the
Church had faith to lean less on human wisdom, to trust less in prudential methods, to administer less by mechanical rules" and to look to the "supernatural
power" at its disposal, "who can doubt that the grinding and groaning of our
cumbrous missionary machinery would be vastly lessened, and the demonstrations of the Spirit be far more apparent?"[66]

As heirs to the revivalistic tradition that Bushnell had challenged decades
earlier, dispensational premillennialists were skeptical about the Christian family, reminding their followers that the world was emphatically not their home.[67]

Although a Christian "may attend to business as it becomes necessary for him to transact in his travels," leading premillennialist spokesman James Brookes wrote in 1876, "he takes no part in the strifes and contentions that are going on around him; and he refuses to be enlisted in the advocacy and promotion of any local interests, because he is not at home." Indeed, Brookes exhorted, "the believer . . . will never be at home until he is with the Lord."[68] Similarly, biblical scholar Cyrus A. Scofield rejected the "crude and fleshly" vision of heavenly mansions popular among Victorian Protestants, reminding the faithful that they would experience heaven only as a state of absolute perfection and should not expect anything remotely similar to human life on earth.[69] This standard of rectitude was not necessarily typical of fundamentalism later in the twentieth century—and indeed, most revivalists had at least one standard sermon on the glories of the "old-fashioned home." In its early stages, however, the movement drew a clear contrast between its own rigorously individualistic piety and the softer spiritual tones of the Christian home ideal.[70]

Late-nineteenth-century fundamentalism was peculiarly immune to sentimentalism, especially the upwardly mobile pietism of middle-class Protestant households. The "higher life" spirituality that fast became characteristic of the movement centered on the "emptying of self" in preparation for divine in-filling. As Gordon explained, "the wind always blows toward a vacuum. Let your heart be empty of self-confidence, and of self-will, and the Spirit can come in and bear you whither God would have you to go." Similarly, in a convention address on "Dying to Self," a young Christian and Missionary Alliance woman urged her listeners not to "seek for religious pleasure, for emotional feeling, and the gratification of our sensibilities, even of our highest, but let us seek Him, glorify Him, and live for Him."[71] As these statements suggest, both the rhetoric and practice of fundamentalist piety was starkly different from the emerging ethic of self-discovery and development that followed in the wake of Bushnell's Christian nurture theology.

Full-time evangelists were especially clear that their peripatetic calling required a life apart from domestic comforts. In 1890 New Englander A. B. Earle recalled the time when, in the course of a fainting spell, he thought he was near death and relayed a good-bye to his wife, instructing his friends to "tell her that I died in the harness." To the young evangelists in training in his audience he emphasized "the necessity of being away from your homes. If you are going to be working evangelists," he declared, "you are going to be sojourners." Over the course of his own fifty-four years of marriage Earle figured he had been away for nearly thirty.[72] Frank Gaebelein, son of the well-known Bible teacher Arno C. Gaebelein, admitted to an interviewer that in his early life he rarely saw his father. "Many people feel that because he was my father and a great Bible student that he gave me all sorts of biblical instruction," the younger Gaebelein explained. "Actually he never did, simply because he travelled so frequently. I can't remember a half hour of Bible instruction from him."[73]

When evangelists went on tour, they often knowingly subjected their families to considerable hardship. Early in his career, as Harry Ironside later confessed, "I, personally, felt that I should rely upon the Lord alone for my temporal support and that of my family, without making our needs known in any way to other people whether saved or not." Ironside's "random reminiscences" included several harrowing instances when financial aid came through only at the last minute, allowing him to continue on his evangelistic travels. Almost as an aside, Ironside recalled packing his wife and young son into trains with only a few dollars to live on. In later life he revealed some guilt over these absences in a letter to a friend, written shortly after his wife had suffered what was to be a fatal heart attack. "I do wish I did not have to be away so much while she is ill," he confessed, "but that is one of the trials of the path which one must enter while seeking to minister Christ to others. I often feel like saying with the bride in the Song of Solomon, 'They have made me the keeper of the vineyards, but my own vineyard I have not kept.'"[74]

In a sense the erratic domesticity of the fundamentalist father had a theological warrant, reflecting the reserved but watchful role of God the Father in much dispensational teaching. In this system of biblical interpretation God ruled by imposing moral guidelines for each period of sacred time, or dispensation. In times of trouble or confusion the fundamentalist believer could rest assured that God's "plan" for humanity was still in place; in spite of difficult earthly circumstances, the divine master remained serenely in control. As prominent dispensational theologian Lewis Sperry Chafer warned, "the creature's most God-dishonoring sin is that of departing from the position and estate in which by creation and divine arrangement he has been placed." Like a wise though distant father, God always knew best.[75]

Enthusiasm for Christian domesticity required a sense of God's presence in human institutions, a this-worldly orientation that most early fundamentalists rejected and Protestant liberals affirmed. The Protestant rationale for the redemptive family reflected the late-nineteenth-century quest to humanize Jesus as a historic, ethical figure and to emphasize his lived experience in first-century Palestine rather than his supernatural, miraculous powers. As Methodist author J. S. Mill explained, home-based religion required a God who was thoroughly incarnated within every realm of human experience. Mill was particularly fond of one "helpful motto" reminding family members that Christ was not only the "head of this house" but also the "unseen guest at every meal, the silent listener to every conversation."[76] In other words, God was continually present in Protestant kitchens, dining rooms, bedrooms, and parlors, pleased to view a family enjoying a meal or doing chores together, without ever once raising their voices in pain or anger.

Conclusion

By the end of the nineteenth century the majority of Protestants accepted the need for home religion without dispute. The Christian home had proven immensely important in mobilizing Protestant women for evangelism and social reform. It offered Protestants a unifying symbol in a time of growing social conflict, and it promised to keep rising generations of American children safe from worldly snares and temptation.

Christian homes, in short, duplicated nearly every function of the institutional church. Ideal Christian families met together for worship and gave children and servants a rudimentary religious education there. They collected religious iconography for their walls and maintained small libraries of morally appropriate literature. The home was also the place from which missionaries and social reformers drew inspiration to evangelize the heathen, raise the fallen, and transform the social order.

Yet in many ways domestic Christianity was far weaker than it seemed. Indeed, the readiness of late-nineteenth-century Protestants to collapse home and church into one institution was based on a mix of anxiety and pragmatism. Post–Civil War Protestants deputized the home as an arm of the church without any clear historical, biblical, or theological warrant—an oversight that would prove fateful decades later, when the essentially Victorian middle-class nature of the Christian home ideal could no longer be taken for granted. But that realization was slow in coming. In the early twentieth century Protestants would use all the cultural tools in their repertoire to rework the old-fashioned Christian home into a more modern version. And its appeal, a few decades late, would far exceed its immediate usefulness or its intellectual depth.

Chapter 3

From Christian Home to Christian Family

SOMETIME AFTER THE turn of the century middle-class Protestants began to talk less about the Christian home and more about the Christian family. The difference in meaning between the two terms says volumes about the shifting role of mainline Protestant religion in domestic life during the early twentieth century. *Home* connoted an older Victorian ideal of an enduring, divinely ordained moral institution, emphasizing order, privacy, and piety. *Family* was a more twentieth-century term, not an abstract ideal or a physical place but a set of fluid, roughly egalitarian human relationships.[1]

The Christian family, as popularly described by Methodist educator George Walter Fiske in 1929, was relatively easy to identify. It was, first of all, child centered, avoiding the old-fashioned authoritarianism as well as the "new-fashioned home anarchy" he saw as distressingly characteristic of far too many families. It was also democratic, built on "mutual respect for personality." In truly Christian families, according to Fiske, husband and wife were equals, and they treated their children with "constructive discipline based on a reasoning obedience to reasonable requests." Parents and children shared an equal voice in the "family council."[2] Christian family life also included regular times for prayer, worship, and instruction (for this Fiske suggested a variety of texts from Methodist publishers). Carefully selected religious artwork graced the walls of children's rooms, and the family gathered regularly at the phonograph to listen to the "noblest music."[3] Home was, in short, a "laboratory," a place where children could daily observe religion being lived by godly parents. Fiske even endorsed Christianity as good "divorce insurance," for it "teaches reverence for personality and the rights of others. . . . It makes people more considerate and more patient, more thoughtful of others." "The religion of Jesus," he declared, "is the surest stabilizer of the family also because it teaches the finest kind of friendly teamwork and develops stable character in the process."[4]

Fiske's Christian family was not specifically Christian, at least in terms of belief or experience, but a loosely religious version of the early-twentieth-century middle-class companionate family. In contrast to the role-oriented, patriarchal Victorian family, the new middle-class ideal was generally egalitarian, flexible, and attentive to the developmental needs of children. Home was a place to relax and have fun—the early twentieth century saw a proliferation of board games, children's literature, and opportunities for parents and children to enjoy together.[5]

Of course, Fiske's genial description belied the pressures on both family life and organized religion in the early twentieth century. By the 1920s moralists were decrying the negative consequences of the new ease and freedom. Critics took aim at the emancipation of youth and the decline of marriage, citing the dwindling birthrate and the rising number of divorces. A new sexual ethic also appeared to undermine the future of the family. Birth control, as a means of delaying and spacing conception, became a middle-class norm by the 1920s; for many couples recreational sex could, at least theoretically, continue past the wedding ceremony.[6] By the 1920s old-fashioned patterns of courting on front porches and family parlors, always within the watchful gaze of adults, had all but disappeared. With the advent of the automobile and the movie theater, dating promised couples new levels of personal and sexual intimacy within the anonymity of large urban public spaces.[7]

By the 1920s, not just traditional Victorian morality but religion itself stood open to question. Doubt was already losing its social stigma by the turn of the century, especially among the well-educated. New scientific thinking promised better, more certain paths to knowledge, transforming the religious skeptic from the pathetic, marginal figure typified by the old "village atheist" into a heroic individualist. The "tough-minded" refused to accept the easy blandishments of organized religion; they demanded scientific standards of truthfulness, steadfastly avoiding what Charles Norton termed the "great sin" of "insincere profession."[8] By the 1920s heroic individualism had given way to a more relaxed cynicism about religion, typified in H. L. Mencken's description of "Christendom" as "that part of the world in which, if any man stands up in public and solemnly swears that he is a Christian, all his auditors will laugh." While religious institutions remained strong in terms of membership and financial support, they were fast losing their capacity to command attention or shape public opinion.[9]

But liberal Protestant theologians avoided a moralistic response to these social trends, preferring to construct a positive engagement with modern culture. The heart of the New Theology, a movement that dominated Protestant seminaries from the 1870s through the 1930s, was the conviction that religion must adapt to new forms of pragmatic, scientific thought. Advocates of the New Theology rejected older ideas of divine transcendence and wrath and argued that God was immanent within human institutions and, indeed, implicitly revealed through them. They were convinced that the Kingdom of God lay in religious ideals working within human activities and, indeed, that the modern world was itself a unique incarnation of Christian principles. The New Theology took a decidedly optimistic view of human sinfulness and emphasized the potential for growth and development in each individual. Ethical concerns, rooted in a view of Christ as a great exemplar of moral behavior, also defined the theological agenda of the late nineteenth and early twentieth centuries. The New Theology promised a less metaphysical, more pragmatic form of religion; the truth of a doctrine lay in its practical results, not in its propositional clarity.[10]

The Christian family ideal neatly intersected liberal Protestant theology and the shifting norms of American middle-class society. Like its secular counterpart, the Christian family was democratic, egalitarian, flexible, and fun-loving. Religion was, of course, central but never in an intrusive or didactic way; in the Christian family Christianity blended imperceptibly with the twentieth-century canons of middle-class behavior.

But, as the Protestant family ideal continued its slow merging with middle-class behavior, it was sometimes difficult to tell which preceded which. In 1929 one Christian educator warned parents that "any practice or situation in the home which makes life hectic, uncertain, disorderly, or unfriendly is a direct inhibition to sound spiritual growth."[11] A Yale professor similarly admonished, "Our understanding of [Christ's] teachings depends upon the quality of our own family life."[12] According to the emerging logic of twentieth-century Christian domesticity, failure to achieve harmony at home could put one's spiritual life in jeopardy—a truism that would have surprised most of the authors of the New Testament. But by the early twentieth century American Protestants saw religion as both a primary cause and a direct effect of domestic tranquillity.

This chapter, which covers a fairly long period, from the turn of the century to the early 1930s, charts the uncertain passage of Bushnell's Christian nurture theology into modernity. Throughout this time Protestant educators never stopped insisting on the primacy of the home as a teacher of religion. Yet few recognized how complicated the project had become. Not only had the middle-class family changed significantly from Bushnell's day, so had Protestant ideas about the method and content of religious training. Although the new approach, fundamentally shaped by the Progressive education movement, promised a more trouble-free experience of Christian parenting, by the eve of World War II, it was clearly faltering. In the moral tumult of the 1920s and the economic chaos of the Great Depression, both religion and family relationships proved to be far more complicated than anyone had been prepared to guess at the turn of the century.

The Progressive Vision

Family and *home* were not the only words in transition in the early twentieth century: in a similar fashion *personality* began to replace *character* as a means of describing the essential person.[13] Increasingly, professional educators and social scientists—and lay people as well—employed the language of relationships to describe the domestic ideal. Just as homes once nurtured character, families would shape personalities.

Psychological categories, not abstract moral principles, gradually dominated descriptions of twentieth-century domesticity. Terms such as *motherhood* and *fatherhood* began to sound quaintly Victorian; modern people increasingly preferred to talk about themselves relationally, as parents and children, wives and husbands. During the first two decades of the twentieth century, an era dominated by the social optimism of the Progressive movement, this new emphasis promised much.[14] Sociologists, pioneers in a new discipline of social research, were generally sanguine about the future of the family, viewing it as a flexible, resilient institution in transition toward a more open, democratic form.[15] Their optimism stood in marked contrast to the pessimism of social workers and moral reformers, who pointed to rising divorce rates—one in every seven marriages by the 1920s—as evidence of widespread family dissolution.[16] But, during the opening decades of the twentieth century, moral alarm among professional elites diminished as a social science language of progress and possibility increasingly dominated talk about the family.

During the Progressive Era women, for example, heard much about the importance of "scientific housekeeping," the application of the latest management and social science principles to work in the home. Some enthusiasts even sought to incorporate George W. Taylor's studies in worker efficiency, in which he employed a stopwatch to study the various movements involved in completing industrial tasks. "The housekeeper," wrote one such advocate, "must learn to perform each task with the smallest possible number of motions and without any that are awkward and unnecessary." Eliminating waste and inefficiency would bring women true liberation: "more liberty, more rest, more intelligence service to her loved ones, . . . [and] the coming of peace and happiness to numberless anxious and overburdened souls."[17]

Even the design of homes reflected the new emphasis on health and individual freedom. Reformers and architects argued that the old Victorian homes were simply too big and sprawling to keep clean. The new bungalow styles were much smaller, with well-engineered kitchens and more efficient architectural planning. The formal Victorian parlor, packed with curios and overstuffed furniture, was replaced by a combination living and dining room space, "less a place for display and more a staging ground for family activities."[18] Enthusiasts, as always, promised that more efficient home design and the faithful use of "labor-saving devices" would result in more leisure for women; though the promise did not come true, the expectation certainly survived.[19]

Although architectural reformers rejected the Victorian language of moral influence, they continued to insist on the importance of a healthy environment. Indeed, growing awareness of developmental psychology made the design of a house, and especially the placement of rooms, more important than ever. The nursery, for example, needed to be adjacent to the parents' bedroom to reinforce the child's sense of well-being. Architectural reformers also believed that a good home included a separate space just for the children, a room for messy projects or physical play.[20]

Children also became the object of empirical research. The child study movement of the 1890s, presided over by psychologist G. Stanley Hall, promised to "revolutionize" the work of parents and teachers. Armed with piles of new data about the "contents of children's minds," medical doctors, psychologists, and social scientists offered mothers advice on an ever-growing array of topics.[21] Maternal intuition would no longer suffice: "scientific mothering" required empirically tested, standardized methodologies. Some of the advice no doubt tested the resolve of even the most self-consciously modern parents. John B. Watson's 1928 text, *Psychological Care of Infant and Child*, advocated an unyielding regimen of meals, naps, and rigid positive and negative reinforcement of behavior. Watson, in particular, warned against too much coddling and play with infants, as this would foster dependent, self-centered attitudes.[22]

But, more often, early-twentieth-century American culture valued children for their natural, even primitive qualities. Hall, in fact, viewed childhood as a metaphoric recapitulation of human evolution, from a state of semisavagery toward a more "civilized" level of awareness.[23] Thus, the mischievous antics of a Tom Sawyer, Peter Pan, or Penrod offered a winning antidote to the overcivilized and stultifying quality of modern life. Parents began to dress their infants and toddlers in rompers instead of the long restrictive gowns of Victorian childhood, to allow them more freedom to explore the surrounding world. Toys designed for individual tastes or gendered preferences became a staple of playrooms and nurseries.[24]

The educational philosophy of John Dewey provided the intellectual foundation for the modern family. His emphasis on the intuitive, spontaneous development of the child encouraged parents to facilitate but not to force the growth of intellectual or emotional capacities. To Dewey children were not the moral or psychological blank slates John Locke once envisioned, nor were they the empty vessels that nineteenth-century parents hoped to fill. Rather, Dewey believed that education began "unconsciously almost at birth" as the child commenced an encounter with the world, and it continued in more formal settings as "the art of . . . giving shape to human powers and adapting them to social service."[25] Following Dewey, progressive educators saw children as, in effect, tiny seedlings, born more or less complete, with enormous potential for growth and development.[26]

Religious educators of the early twentieth century, encouraged by the work of anthropologists and empirical psychologists, did not worry unduly about inborn traits or failings; human nature, they believed, was infinitely pliable and profoundly susceptible to the power of external example.[27] Indeed, William James saw the act of imitation as an inherent psychological necessity, arguing that thought does not exist in isolation but that every psychological impulse includes a drive to complete a specific action. In a reciprocal sense early-twentieth-century psychology opened the possibility of molding the personality by disciplining the brain through regular repetition of a desired behavior. In effect "action formed character."[28] Not surprisingly perhaps, the early twentieth century saw the rise of popular interest in self-improvement psychologies as well as metaphysical movements such as New Thought and the many "positive thinking" methodologies that drew from it. New Thought advocates argued that any person could effect self-improvement by the systematic formation of desirable mental and physical habits. Thus, the repetition of simple phrases ("Be happy, be happy, be happy") might eventually result in a mental readjustment and a positive change in behavior.[29]

This understanding gave parents a new advantage in molding their children toward adulthood, but it also introduced new risks. Parents no longer needed to fill their children's minds with religious content, since the real key to creating Christian thinking was following Christian behavior. But, of course, they had to watch what they said and did more closely than ever; Christian behavior now amounted to far more than certain religious activities, such as prayer or Bible reading. But, in effect, enlarging the sphere of Christian training really reduced the level of urgency about any one particular set of tasks. Personal piety, in other words, was no longer a prerequisite for godly parents; what mattered was creating the right environment to maximize the growth of an individual child's personality.

In sum early-twentieth-century family life put a new premium on individual comfort and personal growth, whether through scientific technique or carefully tended natural development. In many ways, of course, this emphasis was hardly new; the ethic of self-development was already deeply embedded in Victorian middle-class culture. Nor was the emphasis on individual personality as central as it would become in the years after World War II.[30] But it does represent a clear shift in middle-class values. The older Victorian ethic of economic and emotional restraint, theoretically enabling a parent to manipulate a child's conscience with an expertly raised eyebrow, was giving way to a new ethic of desire.[31] The modern era, with its consumer economy and ready access to transportation and entertainment, opened doors to individual pleasures and duties, especially for women and young people, as never before. Even the shape of modern family rituals—the observance of Christmas and Easter or the marking of special events such as births, deaths, and marriages—emanated more from the commercial marketplace than communal norms set by traditional ethnic or religious practice. Families could appropriate them at will—or perhaps improvise their own, but they could not require similar observances from future generations. The decision to perpetuate or abandon the family altar, the Easter egg hunt, or the Christmas goose was, increasingly, entirely up to the children.[32]

Alert readers may have already guessed that the narrative of the Christian home and family is very much a story about women. Just as emerging ideas about "woman's sphere" were central to nineteenth-century domesticity, the early-twentieth-century changes in middle-class women's work and aspirations helped drive the companionate family model. The burgeoning white-collar sector of the economy at the turn of the century brought increasing numbers of young, middle-class women into the work world for the first time. Whereas previously most women had worked as teachers or domestics, many members of the new female work force ended up in offices, libraries, schools, and hospitals, many of them in jobs that had not existed before the invention of the typewriter and the telephone.[33]

Fewer and fewer women opted for missionary or church parish work. By the early 1900s women's missionary organizations were already beginning to worry about a shortage of volunteers, as the rising generation was not filling their mothers' places either at home or abroad. Women's religious work no longer seemed to be engaging the "best" women, and observers began to note that gray hair increasingly predominated at missionary meetings. Some missionary supporters pointed to a general decline in female altruism, especially in the alarming proliferation of cigarette-smoking flappers, "saturated in luxury" and "trained only in the art of pleasure and amusement." Others quietly stopped advertising themselves as "women's" missionary groups, in vain hopes that interested laymen would boost attendance figures.[34]

By the 1920s women's groups were having difficulty even defending their independent existence, as, in the name of administrative streamlining, denominational executives pressed them to consolidate with larger male-dominated church agencies. Women protested, worrying that consolidation would mean the practical end of any meaningful involvement by the masses of laywomen in the missionary cause. As Baptist laywoman Lucy Peabody wrote in 1927, "Our place and contribution seem to be at this moment in question. . . . No great plan of men which weakens or lessens this work of women or removes from them responsibility and initiative really marks a gain."[35]

In other words, the intrinsic ties between religion, domesticity, and womanhood, so central to the Victorian ethos, did not survive very far into the twentieth century. The language of loss or gain is not necessarily appropriate here: in the nineteenth century religion had been women's means of access into the public sphere, but the twentieth century allowed other choices. Women not only achieved the right to vote in 1920 but also a growing array of professional opportunities in social work and related fields. Still, the changing configuration of gender and religion at the turn of the century had a clear impact on mainline Protestant family life. In the late nineteenth century Protestant women had created and pursued a civic agenda on behalf of the home and by virtue of their role as domestic and social homemakers. As Frances Willard declared, women's moral influence drew not "from what woman *does*" but from "what she *is*." As the source of women's moral authority, family life had an intrinsic social dimension.[36]

But when these presumptions failed, the contours of home life—and Christian home life as well—began to narrow and to become less public. The home was still a primary place of women's work, but it was less and less a source of social influence. In the early twentieth century the slow disappearance of the word *home* in favor of more relational terms such as *family* symbolized not only changing social patterns but also a permanently altered relationship between middle-class Protestant women and the social order.

Religion and the Family

In 1903 Auburn Theological Seminary president George Stewart warned a gathering of Protestant educators about the "sore lack of moral and religious instruction in the homes of our land, even in the religious homes." Few households still maintained a traditional family altar, Stewart guessed, and he concluded soberly that "we cannot count on it for the advancement of home religion, unless we can rebuild it. It is not now an appreciable religious force."[37]

Although his pessimism was perhaps exaggerated, Stewart's sense of rapidly changing times was not entirely inaccurate. Turn-of-the-century religious faith did, in fact, lapse into "spiritual crisis," as supernatural assumptions encountered scientific rationalism in the form of evolutionary theory, biblical criticism, and empirical psychological analysis of human spirituality. While the Protestant denominations generally maintained healthy growth rates and institutional budgets, their cultural presence, especially in American cities, was rapidly outstripped by rival institutions. The unquestioned dominance of Protestants in the Victorian age did not last long into the twentieth century.[38]

But the men and women in Stewart's audience were not worried. Indeed, the first gathering of the Religious Education Association (REA) at which he spoke marked a new shift in Christian nurture strategy, designed to maintain Bushnell's carefully orchestrated balance of home, church, and Sunday school but within the nondogmatic world of the modern family. The new generation of religious educators wanted church schools to keep step with the latest pedagogical improvements—more child-centered instructional techniques and developmentally graded curricula—and they wanted to bring "right assistance" to the home, explicitly recognizing its subsidiary role in shaping the spiritual lives of children. John Dewey, speaking before the same gathering in 1903, envisioned religious education as "bringing the child to appreciate the truly religious aspect of his own growing life, not . . . inoculating him externally with beliefs and emotions which adults happen to have found serviceable to themselves."[39] Religion was not an external force applied to a child's nature by parents or teachers but an intrinsic capacity waiting to be developed under their wise example.

The Religious Education Association played a formative role in shaping early-twentieth-century domestic religion. Guided by leading educators, theologians, psychologists, and philosophers, the REA rejected the old didactic Sunday school model in favor of a multidimensional, child-centered approach. The new education would address the needs and questions of developing children in every area of life—home, church, school, and play. Religious education, explained George A. Coe, "is simply education that completes itself by taking account of the whole child, the whole educator, and the whole goal or destiny of man."[40]

The new goal of religious education was self-realization. If human beings were by nature religious, as William James suggested, then, their happiness required unleashing that capacity in early childhood. Although progressive educators talked frequently about the overriding imperative of "personality development," they were not necessarily concerned with cultivating a child's native charm; in the religious sense *personality* connoted one's ability to achieve spiritual power and social connection, the emergence of a fully "radiant" self. Moral backbone still figured in this process: one could not free a child's personality without some shaping of external behavior. Even within the Progressive educators' more fluid conception of religious formation, personality development still required a certain amount of character formation.[41]

Most religious educators understood these goals as thoroughly in line with Bushnell's idea of Christian nurture. Writing in 1924, Yale professor Luther Weigle declared that "the modern movement for the better religious education of children owes more to Horace Bushnell, doubtless, than to any other one man." In Weigle's view Bushnell not only anticipated the modern aversion to religious "indoctrination," he also facilitated the "emancipation of the child" into a freer atmosphere of religious questioning and doubt. A. J. William Myers, another leader of the progressive education movement, found in Bushnell an endorsement of the modern companionate family style, particularly the "camaraderie between parents and children" found in "the more intelligent homes." "The desirability of such an atmosphere is so recognized," he concluded, "that it needs no argument." Myers also interpreted Bushnell's theology as an attack on "the whole intrenched doctrine of total depravity," an ideal "no longer a question among liberal educators."[42]

But, of course, the similarity between twentieth-century Christian nurture and Bushnell was largely superficial, even when Bushnell's heirs interpreted his views correctly. The two systems operated on vastly different premises about God, children, and parents, differences that were becoming more obvious as the twentieth century progressed.

Parents Meet the Experts

Since children did most of their early learning in the home with their parents, religious educators began to pay keen attention to these interactions. In good Bushnellian fashion Coe described parents as "instruments in the divine hand for playing upon the divinely constructed strings of human nature," by the power of their example "promoting or holding back the triumph of God's kingdom on earth."[43] But, unlike Bushnell, Coe and his peers believed that good parenting—even good mothering—required careful training. "One can scarcely believe how many incompetent homes there are, even in prosperous America," one REA official declared in 1911. It was indeed fortunate that "the wealth of experience, knowledge and skill in the training of the young" among educational professionals "is available to parents for solving the problems of home care, training, and instruction."[44] "One often thinks longingly of 'instincts,'" Lewis Sherrill agreed several decades later, "but there is no instinct to guide us to successful parenthood; indeed, we soon discover that we are completely ignorant of many important details." Even "natural impulses which we do have," he warned, "often lead to hurtful acts."[45]

By the 1920s the advance guard of religious educators was becoming more and more convinced that, left to themselves, most parents were just not up to the task of teaching religion to their children. Their growing awareness of Freudian psychology, which by the post–World War I era had filtered into the popular consciousness as well, further accelerated concerns about problem homes.[46] Articles in *Religious Education*, the REA's flagship periodical, for example, warned that parents who talked to their children about God in crude anthropomorphic terms could unwittingly introduce lifelong religious aversions. One boy, in a study by Sophia Lyon Fahs of Union Seminary, had been taught to think of God as a "white-bearded, stern old man," and turned to "stealing and sex play with little girls" as a coping device. Other children were reported terrified of vivid sunsets, windy weather, or being alone in the dark—all the unfortunate result of their parents' pedagogical ineptitude.[47]

Even mothers, once unquestioned religious experts, now required manuals on spiritual nurture, preferably those "reviewed by competent educational authorities" employing the latest "approved educational methods" and "worked out in the laboratory of a Christian home."[48] Many of these manuals included a series of daily lesson plans, each with a short object lesson, a picture, and a song or activity for the mother and child to do together. To ensure that mothers used these lessons properly, some authors even wrote their lesson texts in actual "baby talk." One story for three-year-olds, in the popular manual by Methodist Anna Freelove Betts, included a reproduction of a painting by Millet, *Bringing Home the New Born Calf*, a printed story about "Baby Moo Moo," and a poem about "The Cow" by Robert Louis Stevenson. Betts provided a short commentary for mothers to read: "See the maid milking the cow. What do you see in the pail? It is brimming full of white, warm milk." Although the story had no specifically religious content, Betts also included a one-line prayer for mothers to read at the conclusion of the lesson: "Dear God, I thank you for the nice fresh milk from the bossy cow. Amen."[49] Betts also placed a "Mother's Creed and Prayer" at the opening of her manual with an acknowledgment that "mother-love is sent of God," followed by a prayer in which a mother asked that "I may better understand the needs of my child and lead him in the natural unfolding of the life thou has given him." The prayer's thinly veiled didactic rather than devotional purpose was evident in the mother's petition to "realize that religion and morality are closely related to good health and sound physical vigor."[50]

The prevailing air of unreality evident in Protestant advice literature for parents probably reached a pinnacle of sorts in such manuals. It is, of course, impossible to know even roughly how many mothers read these books to their children or, more important, what they or their children thought about them. Although children's Bible story books remained the most popular items of religious instruction in most Protestant homes, Anna Betts and her husband, George, were influential and well-known in Methodist publishing circles, she as an author of frequently reprinted object lessons for children and he as editor of the Abingdon Religious Education Text series.

Most Protestant educators, however, were not seeking the opinions of individual parents and children. In the late 1920s and 1930s many more took inspiration for church-based programs from secular sources, especially the parent education movement.[51] Although the REA maintained a "department of the home" from 1906 to 1920 and gave special attention to home issues at the 1911 and 1918 annual conventions, the formation of the secular National Council of Parent Education in 1924 sparked more general interest among mainline Protestants.[52] In 1927 the Federal Council of Churches created a Committee on Marriage and the Home headed by Leland Foster Wood, in connection with the Commission on the Church and Social Service. The committee's chief work, it appears, was creating numerous pamphlets and bibliographies on subjects related to marriage, parenthood, dating and courtship, and "family life." With only one full-time staff member other forms of outreach were slow to materialize.

Most of the actual programming issued from the International Council of Religious Education (ICRE), an organization oriented toward church workers instead of academics.[53] In 1931 the ICRE set up a Joint Committee on Family and Parent Education, composed of representatives from the Federal Council of Churches, National Congress of Parents and Teachers, the National Council of Parent Education, and the Child Study Association of America. The committee established contact with some sixty individual congregations carrying out family-related educational programs. In 1931 the ICRE also declared a year of special emphasis on the Christian home, offering local congregations a year's worth of programming, including a monthly schedule of activities. Thus, for example, in November and December families could discuss "religious values in holidays" and, in May and June, "religious values and dangers for children (or young people) in the vacation time."[54] In 1936 the ICRE issued a bulletin on *Home and Church Sharing in Christian Education* and held a summer conference at Lake Geneva, Wisconsin, which resulted in further initiatives for adult education. ICRE "Schools in Christian Living" emphasized family life through a special conference in 1938 and an experimental "family camp" first held at Lake Geneva in 1939 for fifteen families.[55]

In tight economic times denominational support followed more slowly. But in the mid–1930s a number of church bodies began developing their own programs, in some cases taking on additional staff workers. Most of the denominational effort resulted in informational bulletins, parent magazines such as the *Christian Home* (a joint venture by Congregationalists and Southern Methodists), adult education textbooks, and occasional conferences.[56] In the 1930s Southern Presbyterians issued certificates for "Accredited Christian Homes," whose members signed an agreement to maintain the family altar, to go to church regularly as a family, and to send the children to Sunday school.[57] "On the whole," one observer concluded in 1937, "the statement that the Protestant churches have become family-conscious seems justified." She noted that, though "only a small proportion as yet have instituted specifically planned programs for their work with the family, . . . the leadership is very much awake and at work."[58]

Modern Family Altars

The open question behind all of these efforts, however, was about content. In what sense were parents still teachers, and what exactly were they to be telling their children about Christianity? Throughout the early decades of the twentieth century the language of moral absolutes played an increasingly limited role in mainline Protestant discourse about the family. The bloodshed of World War I delivered a body blow to liberal optimism, but did not sever its dependence on the social sciences. Mainline Protestant educators and family experts—academics such as George Coe, Henry F. Cope, Hugh Hartshorne, and A. J. William Myers—viewed their field as a subspecialty within the secular social sciences and rarely attempted to reintroduce specifically religious concepts into the conversation. "Strikingly," Presbyterian Lewis Sherrill concluded in 1937, "the goal suggested by religion and that suggested by psychology and sociology are essentially the same, in respect of marriage and family life. Both religion and these sciences have in view the stabilization and enrichment of personality in marriage partners and children."[59]

The new partnership between home and church, in fact, militated against the inclusion of factual content. In 1903 George Stewart felt obligated to reveal that he was still "old-fashioned enough to believe that the teaching of objective truth is a function of the home." "I confess I do not have that fear of explicit forms of truth," he said, "which is sometimes thought—mistakenly, I believe—to be inconsistent with wise pedagogical methods." Stewart was still prepared to insist that Christian home training include basic doctrine as found in "Scripture, in hymns, in liturgies, and in creeds and catechisms."[60]

Stewart, however, was in a minority. Family experts increasingly emphasized personality formation as the primary task of home religion. "In vain do we torture children with adult religious penances, long prayers, and homilies," declared Henry F. Cope, author of a popular book on *Religion and the Family* (1915). Presbyterian authors Constance Hallock and Emma Speer described the home as a "powerful educational agency." "Here life is lived, not talked about," they enthused. "It is [the child's] laboratory, and he learns to do by doing; his experience is unified."[61] As Leland Foster Wood, head of the Committee on the American Home of the Northern Baptist Convention, explained, family religion was also the perfect antidote to dry dogma. "Religion in the home . . . is to be thought of as the atmosphere and climate in which the members of the domestic circle live in fellowship with one another and with God. In . . . the mingling of life with life, and in hearts knit together, religion dwells, and God is manifest in the midst."[62]

The question, of course, was whether such nurture would still be definably Christian. Certainly, as George Stewart conceded, many Protestant parents gave their children a solid moral education in "truthfulness, sobriety, cleanness in speech, unselfishness, service [and] good manners." But, he declared in 1903, "the besetting sin of today is . . . leaving God out of the account."[63] It would be another forty years, however, before anyone took Stewart up on his objections.

Up through the 1930s the most forward-looking religious educators counseled against introducing outmoded rituals, including the family altar, into modern homes. Part of their aversion had to do with the Victorian formality and sentimental piety they rightly associated with it. Most tended to see the family altar as a relic of the days before the automobile, the movie theater, and the department store blurred the parameters of middle-class life. But, informed by the insights of popular Freudianism, they also emphasized the importance of creative "adjustment" rather than resistance to modern-day circumstances. By the mid–1930s a Baptist author thus concluded, "Not every family in this complicated age of living can arrange for the daily worship around the family altar, but the deeper meanings of prayer and a sincere prayer-life may be cultivated in any family."[64] Regina Westcott Weiman similarly advised that "it is better that the child remain absent from family prayers until he has a fair understanding of what God is and how He works in this world of ours." Weiman suggested "nonreligious rituals" geared toward the child's spiritual awareness, such as "the setting aside of fifteen minutes once a week when every member would do something for the betterment of the family life, . . . [such as] keeping fresh flowers on the table or welcoming father home. There is no end to the possible list."[65]

These educators were not, of course, the first Protestant leaders to recognize the futility of pushing for a standard most of their membership had long since abandoned. Still, mainline churches provided relatively little guidance on such matters, at least partly because religious educators and pastors were not interested in enforcing moralistic standards. Their goal was to create a whole-some set of relationships within a Christian family, not to police certain behaviors. The Christian child was not a Scripture-quoting, rule-abiding model of comportment but a growing individual psychologically well adjusted and internally well equipped to face the challenges of modern life.

Social Isolation

Christian Family Brown was a play, published in 1936, dramatizing the godly home. The cast included "Father John," "Mother Anne," and four children, Nancy, Jerry, David, little Merry, as well as the obligatory "Grandma" and Carl, the boy next door. All are uniformly cheery and unselfish, despite their moderate circumstances and the fact that Grandma must stay with them while her other son, Henry, is off on an expensive vacation. The children enjoy simple hobbies, mostly rock collecting and music, as well as poetry, good literature, and the small but tasteful etching selected by the family. They maintain a meager Family Fund, chiefly by doing outside errands, and convene the Family Brown Executive Council, in which every member has an equal vote, before spending anything. (In episode 2, "The Sharing of Labor," they vote to buy new glasses for Grandma instead of buying a radio or a new dress for Mother.)

God does not make an appearance until the last scene, when the Brown family holds a "Thank You Party" to celebrate Grandma's decision not to move back in with the well-heeled Henry. Non-Christian Carl is mystified when Father quietly refers to the eight members of Family Brown. After taking a quick tally, Carl protests: "But—there are only seven of you, aren't there?" "No," Father smilingly replies. "Eight. There's another one of us that you can't see, but He's our partner just the same. Even though we don't talk about Him a great deal, we all know He's here." Carl is clearly flummoxed until little Merry explains: "Daddy means God. He's always been a part of our family, ever since it started." That said, the family, and Carl as well, gather to list their blessings and sing a few of their favorite hymns, including, perhaps not surprisingly, "Blest Be the Tie That Binds."[66]

Except for God's invisible presence, this Christian family has little contact with the outside world. Packages arrive, Carl appears for brief visits, and members frequently exit and enter stage right. But nothing of importance occurs off-stage. Our attention is focused always on the Brown's living room, described as "pleasant" and "comfortable, though its furnishings give evidence of a careful choice rather than of an indiscriminate luxury." The set includes "a few good paintings" on the walls and "a well-filled bookcase" as well as a piano, a few musical instruments, and flowers, "arranged artistically." "It is obviously a room much loved and lived in."[67]

The rather obvious dramatic weaknesses of this simple play illustrate a significant intellectual limitation in mainline Protestant assumptions about religious families. Worldly business rarely intruded into all of the many books and pamphlets about Christian family life, though during this time Americans endured a world war, a revolution in manners and morals, and a cataclysmic economic depression. The play shows Father John and Mother Anne capably maintaining the proper atmosphere for godly growth in their children. But the cast in this Christian family drama includes no outsiders, not even a friendly minister or Sunday school teacher. The neighbor Carl, who drops hints that his own family life is less than satisfactory, cannot influence any of the Brown children toward the wrong; indeed, the end of the play finds him happily singing hymns along with the rest.

In many ways the Brown family's social isolation reflects the social science of its time. Before World War I sociologists had viewed the family as "a strong, if troubled, institution, whose difficulties were tied to the larger problems of social reform." By the 1920s, an age preoccupied with the self and its proper adjustment to society, sociologists were more interested in human interactions within the family than with its external role in society. According to sociologist Ernest Burgess, the family was "a unity of interacting personalities"; it was "less a thing or a structure," as historian Robert Griswold explains, "than a process that changed over time as the individuals within it changed."[68] Family sociology of the 1920s and 1930s thus represented "a total eclipse of the broader community and neighborhood perspective characteristic of social work and sociology before World War I." Families were simply "islands of adjustment, floating on an impersonal social sea."[69]

This inward turn reflected the debt of family sociologists to the rising importance of psychology during the 1920s and 1930s. They traced a wide variety of social problems to faulty family relationships, arguing that individuals who were well adjusted to the needs and demands of others were the least susceptible to antisocial behavior. Environmental circumstances, like poverty or urban disorder, were less important to a child's outcome than the quality of interpersonal relationships. Indeed, during the Great Depression family sociologists discovered that people from flexible, open, democratic homes weathered hard times much better than more tightknit, role-oriented ones. Good parenting, in other words, helped people survive the economic woes of the 1930s.[70]

Mainline Protestant faith in the essential power of the Christian family mirrored the assumptions behind this model. Thus, among moderate and liberal Protestants discussions of the family and religion gave only passing notice to secular amusements, consumerism, even adultery or divorce. A few authors made veiled references to adolescent sexuality, but, for the most part, they seemed to assume that the family was a safe enclave set apart from larger social problems. Even when religious educators recognized the growing complexity of modern family life, they did not do so with much alarm. "Parents now share with the school teacher, church school teachers, club leaders, favorite actors of the screen and radio, the employer, and many others, the building of the character of their children," Speer and Hallock wrote. Yet they counseled parents not to worry or to try and shield their children from nefarious influences: "The constructive and honest religious attitudes of the parents, their method of evaluating life, form a spiritual climate in which the children grow naturally to a sense of kinship with the rest of the world, and of a responsibility to it."[71] A Methodist educator similarly affirmed that the primary responsibility of Christian parents was to "accept" modern life "without emotional upset." "We cannot prevent change," he counseled, but, with a "proper consecration of talents," an "intelligent understanding" of the needs of young people, and a "friendly attitude" toward them, "we can make change a stepping-stone to the achievement of a higher Christian experience."[72]

Similarly, Wood warned against "pagan influences" in modern society—specifically, cynicism, materialism, self-indulgence (which for this Baptist author centered on the use of alcohol), nationalism, and "unwholesome amusements." But he insisted that the power of a Christian home was far greater than any of these. In the case of modern entertainment culture wise parents need only provide "more simple, more creative and more wholesome forms of recreations, . . . to satisfy the needs of those who hunger for fellowship."[73]

Since the nineteenth century Protestant parents had relied on public schools to reinforce moral instruction at home and church. Children of all denominational backgrounds sat through Protestant prayers and Bible readings, in symbolic recognition of that faith's central role in shaping American civilization. Even by the turn of the century, as religious diversity became an inescapable fact, the "common schools" played a special moral role. The American public school, as one enthusiast put it, was "a miniature Christian republic" and "the people's university for training young America in . . . Christian civilization."[74]

But the old tripartite alliance of home, school, and church fell increasingly out of balance in the early twentieth century, in favor of the most secular of the three. Parents and religious educators both recognized that, in terms of educational standards, social power, and even the weekly allotment of time, home and church would be hard-pressed to compete with public schools. As a distraught Pennsylvania mother explained in 1930, "I have to compete for time not only against regular school hours, but against all sorts of extracurricular activities, such as football, basketball, innumerable plays and school and class benefits, Latin and other clubs, etc. These have an undoubted value for the child, but when the sum total is so great that my child *never* has time to consider the welfare of anyone but himself, *never* has a chance to learn to serve others, it makes systematic home training almost impossible."[75]

Caught in a spiraling competition with the outside world, many parents struggled to find a moral center. The great popularity of movies among small children was a particularly difficult point of conflict. In the early twentieth century children most often attended in groups, rarely in the company of a parent, and many watched shows almost daily. Although these films were hardly racy by current standards, they did attract the worried attention of parents and social reformers who objected to their often violent appeal to impressionable youth.[76]

In 1930 the *Christian Century* published a running debate about the "menace of the movies" on American youth, blaming parents as the chief culprits behind the moral demise of the nation's children. "If the boy turns out to be a thrill-hunting hooligan, or if the girl a sex-saturated sophisticate," the editor declared, "the parent is directly to blame."[77] In the absence of any nuanced consideration of environmental factors, mainline Protestants could not really look anywhere else. What moralism remained in liberal Protestant discourse was directed primarily at modern parents.

But the challenges to Christian formation in the early twentieth century went far deeper than "sex-saturated" movies or the access of adolescents to cars. Broad social changes in the nature and purpose of family life weakened the pull of tradition and the possibility of didactic instruction. For many middle-class people home was becoming a "way station," or a "branch office," not an object of sentiment or a means of moral coercion. But the social sciences, on which

Protestants had decided to rely, offered few intellectual models for understanding the integral relationship of families and other social institutions—neighborhoods, cities, schools, or churches. Declining faith in Victorian womanhood also, in a way, contributed to the family's social isolation. Once the link between the home and society, twentieth-century women occupied an increasingly ambiguous position in both, not really speaking on behalf of the home nor fully eligible to enter the public sphere. Domestic religion entered the twentieth century with a relatively impoverished sense of social connectedness and an inflated belief in the home's intrinsic moral power.

The story of religion and the family in the early twentieth century is paradoxical. Progressive educators had rejected Victorian didacticism in order to make Christianity a more natural and pervasive aspect of Protestant home life. In a sense formalistic observances such as the old family altar were simply not religious enough to meet the spiritual needs of the twentieth century. But attempting to expand the realm of religion attenuated its power to shape behavior in meaningful ways. As Winthrop Hudson observed, "the long-term tendency of the progressive religious education movement was to persuade the individual that there was no fundamental contradiction between his own desires and the demands of God, and the net effect was to leave the individual conscience undisturbed and untroubled by any deep-seated conviction of sin."[78] Stretched to include all manner of domestic practices, family religion ultimately became not the sole source but, rather, one option among many for achieving domestic happiness.

Chapter 4

Protestant Families in Wartime

THE VAST INFRASTRUCTURE of family religion in the 1950s rested on a host of contradictory impulses buried deep within the waning culture of 1930s liberal Protestantism. By all rights the economic catastrophe of the 1930s and the looming shadow of yet another world war should have chastened confidence in any social institution, including the family, as the sure solution to every social problem. But, in fact, the tumultuous events of the late 1930s and 1940s reaffirmed Protestant faith in the importance of domestic and spiritual ties; the war years inspired an even greater commitment to domestic Christianity and a new outpouring of public optimism about the redemptive power of the home. "In a time of world crisis," a National Council of Churches pamphlet declared, "the Christian home offers the best hope for building a better future." "For if Christian homes really succeed, little else matters," another report sturdily declared in 1940. "They will carry all else with them." The widely reprinted "creed of a religious educator" similarly lauded the home as "the one complete and effective democracy" with "security for tossed and confused spirits" and the means by which "society itself becomes more and more fashioned into the Kingdom of our God and of his Christ."[1]

FROM THE CREED OF A RELIGIOUS EDUCATOR
I BELIEVE IN THE HOME
I looked into the past and saw the crude beginnings of the Home.
I saw it being nurtured in struggle, surviving through social change,
    maintaining its inner spirit and its essential ministry to mankind
    even through transformations in its outward forms.

I looked into the world about me and saw the Home stricken hard by
    changing standards, threatened by the collapse of its economic
    system, and fighting for its life against machines and false cultures;
But still I found it going on its way, changed and yet unchanging.
It remains the one complete and effective democracy;
It provides security for tossed and confused spirits;
It affords in its own life, practice in putting its ideals into action.
It takes the strange mixture of experiences that an aimless society tosses
    into every growing life and gives them meaning, weeds out their
    dross, and centers them around some single purpose set attractively
    in the soul.
When this purpose becomes Christian the Home becomes Christian and
    through it society itself becomes more and more fashioned into the
    Kingdom of our God and of his Christ.
I believe in the Home.

I BELIEVE IN THE CHURCH

The Church has been my spiritual home.
I have memorized its scriptures.
Its hymns have nourished me in defeat and fortified me in temptation.
Its history has thrilled me as I have followed its fortunes down the
    centuries.
Its persistence and its power, in spite of so much folly and wrong in its
    human leadership, make me believe that God believes in it too, and
    has yet some great work for it in the world.
I know well the mistakes and weaknesses of the Church. I am saddened
    by its pursuit of foolish whims; distressed by its fatal divisions;
    discouraged by its absorption into materialistic ideals that it is set to
    oppose.
But also I know well the latent idealism of its members.
I am aware of the vision and courage of its wisest leadership.
I am conscious of the unused powers of costly plants, and working
    membership and growing persons.
I see what it can become in transforming the world if it ceases to serve
    itself and once more becomes enamored of its power as a servant of
    human good.
I believe in the Church.

In less guarded moments, of course, church leaders began to voice worries
about the future viability of family religion. They placed little faith in parents
as disciplinarians or as religious teachers, even as they publicly insisted that Christian homes could singlehandedly bring about a better world. Perhaps if World
War II had not intervened, the entire system might have collapsed on its own.

Certainly, in the neoorthodox movement, liberal Protestant pedagogy had a host of powerful and articulate critics. But the edifice remained standing. World War II brought a new sense of moral emergency to Protestant churches and a deepening commitment to American civil religion. This complex mixture of patriotism and piety rested on some deeply shared assumptions about the importance of religious faith and the necessity of strong homes and families, assumptions that closely matched ideals already embedded in mainline Protestant culture. The war years, then, created a powerful new rationale for domestic Christianity, forestalling for decades the serious reassessment that was, by this time, long past due.

Religious Illiteracy

By the late 1930s, when the "lost generation" of the post–World War I years began to settle down to raise their children, Protestant church leaders began to fear that these young parents had nothing meaningful to say about religion. "We are trying to hand on a religion which we ourselves do not wholly believe," one commentator despaired.[2] The disturbing possibility arose that the parents, who had themselves been raised in an antidogmatic, antiritualistic age, might raise their own generation of religious "illiterates."

In 1935 Willard Sperry, dean of the Harvard Divinity School, reported that the average young man he encountered was mostly indifferent toward religion— "a decent, attractive, instinctively healthy fellow" but "simply without the slightest idea about what it means to be troubled in conscience. He is not in revolt against his own past because there has been nothing at home to revolt against." Sperry used a Depression era metaphor to describe this exhaustion of "what we might call private religious capital." The current store of moral money in the bank, carefully invested by sober Victorian forebears, had provided enough for the World War I generation to live on but was not sufficient for their children.[3] Edward Scribner Ames found similar "evidence of pathetic confusion" even among "the most enlightened communities of American life." Religiously indifferent parents, he complained, had no chance of passing on a spiritual heritage to their bored and rebellious children. "No wonder," he concluded with a sigh, "there is confusion and uncertainty."[4] Sperry was content to allow his Ivy League parents a genteel agnosticism in the face of their children's spiritual questions; if necessary, qualified professionals could be called in to provide doctrinal specifics. "I think we shall do well," he advised, "to make our peace with the fact that our children will probably get most of their detailed religious instruction from persons other than ourselves."[5]

But Sperry's urbane counsel was lost on most other Protestant church leaders. By the mid–1930s they had settled in the rather daunting conviction that parents—even the functional agnostics at Harvard—were key to the church's future. Scattered evidence from the 1920s and 1930s suggests a general decline in family-based religious practices. A 1930 study of white American-born seventh-, eighth-, and ninth-graders found, for example, that only one in eight participated in family prayers.[6] A Louisville pastor's study of his Presbyterian congregation in 1929 unearthed the dismaying fact that not one of his members reported holding regular Bible reading or prayer in the home. "My own family being the only in the Church with a family altar," the crestfallen minister concluded, "was a significant revelation."[7]

Robert and Helen Lynd's 1929 study of "Middletown" offered a similarly bleak, almost anarchic, view of middle-class religious and family life. As a Middletown businessman explained, "The home was once a sacred institution where the family spent most of its time. Now it is a physical service station except for the old and infirm."[8] The Lynds queried pastors of six leading churches about the family altar, and found that at the very most only 10 percent of the homes in any given congregation observed the practice. The same ministers were willing to guess that anywhere between 10 and 30 percent of their parishioners read the Bible at home at least once a week—but this was mostly speculation. As one pastor confessed, "I've no way of knowing how many read their Bibles."[9] Speaking before the Federated Club of Clubs, a Middletown pastor concluded that "the home is failing to instruct the children religiously as it should. The family altar, set times for devotional reading and discussion, are not as common as they were formerly. People do not seem to be ready to acknowledge that they value such things any less, but excuse themselves on the ground that they are too busy. It has been crowded out of the family program."[10]

Middletown parents seemed incapable of formulating, much less enforcing, consistent moral or religious practices. Sundays were a difficult case in point. One set of parents, the Lynds reported, let their children swim on Sunday but drew the line with playing golf. Another allowed their children to make popcorn on Sunday but not make candy. "All along the line," the Lynds concluded, "parents may be seen fighting a rear-guard fight, each father and mother trying to decide 'what's right.'"[11]

A study of family ritual, covering a lengthy period from 1880 to 1946, documented many of these concerns. The students of the Depression and World War II generation, surveyed by researchers from the University of Pennsylvania, practiced far fewer formal religious observances in the home than had their late-Victorian forebears. Of 138 interviews with Philadelphia area residents the authors found a high incidence of agnosticism among middle-class families, alongside scattered remnants of nineteenth-century ritual. "Grace is frequently said at meals, and in many different forms," they reported. "Bedtime prayers are as common. Children were taught them by a parent as soon as they were old enough to talk, and they were 'heard' each night, often kneeling, for many years, after which time a good proportion of the children continued them individually even on to college age." But in most of these families ritual had become increasingly child centered, fluid, and negotiable. "There is," the sociologists observed, "less of the ritualistic gathering of the youngsters around the feet of the family patriarch for a period of instruction, and more of the ceremony which entails joint enterprise and display of individual talent." The authors summed up the generational change by observing that in the World War II generation "the exclusive sectarian tone dropped out to give way to a broader interpretation of religion and family responsibility toward it," resulting in "present-day rituals which express a religious attitude that is serious, but not narrow; an attitude of responsibility that is educating and interesting even to small children, rather than tiresome and deadening to them." Thus, "sherry before dinner may become as much a ritual as family prayers before going to bed; and listening to a Sunday night radio program may be the center of a ritual complex as much as the reading of the Bible."[12]

Religion was certainly a part of home life in the pre–World War II years, but its exact purpose was often uncertain. In a recent study a mainline Presbyterian who had grown up in the Philadelphia suburbs before World War II offered an apparently typical description of religion as identical with "proper, respectable living." In his words, "Religious principles and social principles sort of blend together; I was taught to be honest, to be responsible, and to love my family." His parents never broached specifically religious subjects. This Presbyterian child "merely observed their behavior and inferred from it that they believed in God." Although his parents certainly did pray, often kneeling together at night, he never knew "what they prayed about, because they prayed in the privacy of their bedroom."[13]

Walter Lippmann's famous description of the "acids of modernity" certainly seems to fit these accounts of middle-class religious life. Although the modern person attempts to live according to the dictates of individual conscience, Lippmann wrote, "when he searches his conscience, he finds no fixed point outside of it by which he can take his bearings." Indeed, he concluded, for most people religion is only "one phase in a varied experience; it no longer regulates their civic duties, their economic activities, their family life, and their opinions. It has ceased to have universal dominion, and is now held to be supreme only within its own domain." Modern life, with its often jarring and unconnected processions of experience, demanded a complex series of loyalties that were at one time ordered by traditional institutions. But in the twentieth century, Lippmann concluded, "the religious synthesis has dissolved." The modern person "no longer believes genuinely in any idea which organizes his interests within the framework of a cosmic order."[14]

Institutionalizing Christian Parenthood

In the late 1930s hard pragmatic reasons also drove the renewed emphasis on the Christian home, despite all the evidence of decline. The onset of the Depression severely limited church finances and programs. Religious education professionals found themselves the first to be let go as budgets tightened, and many congregations reported that they could no longer afford to buy Sunday school curriculum materials. In some cases families stopped attending public worship because they could no longer purchase Sunday clothes or afford to drive a car.[15] In situations like these, the cost-saving potential of home-based religious instruction clearly increased its attractiveness. At the very least such efforts removed the risk of duplicating services: families would take up more responsibility for religious training, and the church would become more of an extended family.[16]

The drive for economic efficiency sometimes made the institutional church look a bit superfluous. In 1939 Nevin Harner, an inventive Methodist educator, suggested—only partly in jest—a franchise scheme to farm out religious work through Christian homes, which would operate as "branch offices wherein much of the real business of the Kingdom is transacted." "Let the church, therefore, become a mere office building—a place where a number of home-consultants would have their headquarters." Thus, Harner continued, "there might be a person specially trained in religion; another in psychology; another in medicine; yet another in homecraft; and so on. These advisers would ply back and forth between the central church and the homes of the congregation, bearing help and guidance of the sort required at the time when it was needed most." Harner quickly noted that such an extreme innovation was not really necessary, but other religious educators were dead serious in their belief that "the church would make more progress if it would take its message and its help into the home, . . . rather than spending so much effort and money in maintaining an elaborate building to which it generally insists that the people come if they are to be served."[17]

The new emphasis on family religion in the late 1930s also reflected the New Dealers' enthusiasm for programmatic solutions to moral problems. "A religion that does not function or that does not square with the facts at hand about life is not respected," one church educator declared in 1937. Church-sponsored parent education programs, she argued, had the advantage of incorporating an empirical approach, based on parents' needs and a "scientific method of thinking," in order to "increase parental satisfactions and skills."[18] Ideals for family religion, in short, reflected an odd and contradictory mixture of pragmatism, worry, and unbridled optimism.

Yet, despite their uniformly upbeat tone, parent education programs were undertaken in a spirit of growing pessimism. "The influence of the home is so much greater than the church, in most cases," an ICRE bulletin noted despairingly in 1935, "that the efforts of the church sometimes seem almost futile."[19] As one particularly candid Presbyterian leader explained in 1934, "A generation ago when religious leaders were concerned over the state of the church, they coined a slogan which read, 'Family religion cures sick churches.'" "The argument looked good on paper," he noted dryly, "but it failed to work in practice." Faced with the conclusion that churches could no longer "exploit" the family for their own spiritual benefit, Presbyterian leaders were beginning to realize "that the home must be saved not for the sake of the church but for its own sake."[20]

By the 1930s mainline Protestant leaders had already begun to worry that the family was not a spiritual resource but a liability requiring careful supervision. While many continued to invoke Bushnell's Christian nurture theology, few perhaps really believed that domestic life was in any way salvific, at least apart from extensive, well-planned church programming.

The Neoorthodox Critique

Not surprisingly perhaps, by the 1940s family religion and the theological ethos that had framed it were the subject of increasingly abrasive public critique. In his groundbreaking 1937 book, *Moral Man and Immoral Society*, Reinhold

Niebuhr took direct issue with the liberal theology of "adjustment." Against the darkening backdrop of European totalitarianism, he passionately decried the moral compromises inherent in all human social institutions, taking particular aim at the pieties of liberal Protestant social theory. Can the victims of social injustice be asked to adjust to their oppression? "Our contemporary culture," Niebuhr declared, "fails to realise the power, extent and persistence of group egoism in human relations."[21]

Niebuhr's trenchant critique of liberal humanism helped launch a neo-orthodox movement in American theological circles. Neoorthodoxy held no sympathy for either liberalism or fundamentalism; it sought to recover foundational Christian doctrines of sin, salvation, and divine revelation yet without reverting to antimodern formulas. Neoorthodox theologians emphatically rejected the liberal view of divine immanence, arguing for a transcendent, mysterious God who stood in radical judgment of human pride and selfishness.

Neoorthodoxy held significant implications for religious educators, particularly their hope that families would somehow rescue flailing Protestant churches. If, as Niebuhr argued, all human institutions were fundamentally flawed, then even the hallowed Christian family might—in fact, must—fall under careful scrutiny. "All human groups tend to be more predatory than the individuals which compose them. The most tender emotions may characterize the relations of members of a family to each other," Niebuhr wrote, "but the family as such is easily tempted to gain its advantage at the expense of other families." Echoing Marx's critique, Niebuhr noted "the tendency of family loyalty to accentuate covetousness" and "the family instinct as the very basis for private property."[22]

Niebuhr also had very little practical patience for liberal pedagogy. As a pastor in inner-city Detroit, he found the dominant philosophy of religious education simply "absurd." "We are told by a delightful 'expert,'" he wrote in 1928, "that we ought not really teach our children about God lest we rob them of the opportunity of making their own discovery of God, and lest we corrupt their young minds by our own superstitions. If we continue along these lines," Niebuhr declared, "the day will come when some expert will advise us not to teach our children the English language, since we rob them thereby of the possibility of choosing the German, French or Japanese languages as possible alternatives." Children needed to learn their own tradition thoroughly before they attempted to decide on an adult faith, because, as Niebuhr wrote, "appreciation must come before criticism." "I have a dark suspicion," he continued, "that some of these modern religious educators do not really know what religion is about. They want a completely rational faith and do not realize that they are killing religion by a complete rationalization. With all their pious phraseology and supposedly modern pedagogy they really are decadent forces."[23]

In 1942 Union Seminary professor H. Shelton Smith took specific aim at George Coe and the Religious Education Association and the entire enterprise of family-based religion as it had developed into the 1930s.[24] Smith, a former Religious Education Association board member, opened his book on *Faith and Nurture* by deriding the liberal emphasis on personality development—"almost an obsession with the modern religious educator."[25] The assumption that personality only emerges from a process of social interaction, Smith argued, means that "persons lose their transcendent meaning and value." Indeed, the near idolatrous worship of human personality was, in Smith's view, ultimately antihuman, devaluing individual persons as the mere end products of the socialization process. With an eye to totalitarian Europe, Smith found it "no surprise" that the "complete socialization of human value should be followed by some sort of dictatorship, whether of the Left or of the Right."[26]

Smith would not have been surprised to find God a shadow member of the Brown family. Liberal theology, he argued, put human and divine within the same narrow box: the emphasis on persons as an interactive community implied that "contact with God may be made only indirectly through social relations."[27] God only became real within the loving interactions of a human community, or, in Smith's caustic phrase, "where self-realizing persons creatively adjust themselves to their natural and social world."[28]

Neoorthodox critics of liberalism hoped to restore God to a transcendent realm and bring a prophetic edge to Protestant religion. They called on their fellow believers to resume without apology conversation about sin, forgiveness, and divine transcendence. Neoorthodox theology proclaimed a transcendent God, no longer the genial but mute "unseen guest" at the dinner table but One who has tried all human institutions and found them wanting.[29] Smith openly scoffed at the middle-class pieties of religious socialization, pointing out that "great religious prophets have always transcended the experiences and insights of the social culture in which they grew up."[30]

The neoorthodox critique of religious education included a rejection of a child-centered church. Although certainly a necessary means to perpetuate the church as an institution, "the religion of the child," Smith observed, was usually "a relatively pale edition of the faith of the older generation."[31] "The Church should remember," he declared, "that great periods of religious rebirth have not emerged as the results of child-nurture. Religion has always come alive in the adult consciousness, and has usually involved a break with the religion inherited in childhood."[32] Smith, in fact, doubted whether children really benefited by progressive education techniques. An emphasis on inquiry and experimentation certainly made sense if, as educators assumed, the child came into the world spiritually intact and needing only growth and development. But Smith found the interrogative approach to teaching religion "a form of vacillation, cowardice, or superficiality."[33] Such overconfidence in the child's predisposition to faith served them no better than the old revivalist view of infants burning in a lake of fire.

In *Faith and Nurture* Smith argued that neoorthodoxy was a truer heir to Bushnell's Christian nurture theology than the pallid humanism of the liberals who claimed his mantle. He believed that twentieth-century religious education had overplayed Bushnell's critique of revivalism into a fundamentally nonempirical assumption that children are "by nature already in possession of a life-principle which requires, not repentance, but spiritual development. . . . Thus in effect it obscures the radical nature of repentance as a condition of participation in the Kingdom."[34] Neoorthodoxy, Smith argued, restored Bushnell's original intent to take the family seriously as a means of grace—not just an empty backdrop for the child's spiritual unfolding.

Smith stopped short, however, of an all-out critique of domestic Christianity. In fact, his book ends with a strong hint that, as a "nonsectarian" religious institution, the family might still be more important to the future of ecumenical Christianity than the divided Protestant church. The real root of the problem, Smith concluded, was the weak ecclesiology of American church life, especially when it came to the process of Christian nurture. "Religious educators seem to have been less concerned with the nature of the Church than any other professional group in religion," Smith observed. The church seemed a purely instrumental means to an end, an institution to be "tolerated" as long as it did not get in the way of "real religion." Without a clear sense of what churches were for, Smith argued, liberal pedagogy placed an enormous and insupportable burden on families for Christianizing children in an increasingly pagan society.[35]

Not surprisingly, some liberal religious educators reacted to the neoorthodox challenge with anger and distress. William Clayton Bower described it as a "totalitarian" reaction and warned that the neoorthodox pedagogy of "indoctrination, coercion and propaganda" was based on a "pre-scientific and primitive concept of the nature and structure of reality." Liberals took particular umbrage at neoorthodoxy's attempt to reintroduce doctrinal content into religious formation. To George Coe, for whom doctrine was at most a "resource" for curriculum planners, neoorthodoxy presaged a dangerous tilt toward authoritarianism. "To put the matter abruptly, the church is represented as the authoritative teacher of the thoughts of God," imposing a set of "intellectualistic presuppositions" on impressionable children.[36]

For the most part, however, the liberal establishment ignored Smith's challenge. Just a year before the publication of *Faith and Nurture*, in 1941, Harrison Elliott, Coe's successor at Union Seminary, published a ringing defense of liberal pedagogy, affirmatively answering the question "Can Religious Education Be Christian?" The volume is a relatively standard statement of divine immanence, human development, and the power of love, with little indication that Elliott had taken the neoorthodox challenge to radical faith seriously. Indeed, the Religious Education Association virtually ignored Smith's book and published only one brief and scathing review in *Religious Education*.[37]

The late 1930s and 1940s hardly seemed a time for religious controversy. The postwar years brought even more concerted attempts to institutionalize family-based religion, articulated through the crisis language of neoorthodox theology and built on a renewed conviction that a child-centered church family was the key to spiritual renewal. The Presbyterian General Assembly in 1946 reported a dangerous inattention to the spiritual needs of the nation's children. "It is ironical enough," the Board of Christian Education report declared, "that in Christian America where there was least excuse the children were all but completely ignored," but in war-torn communist Russia "children were regarded as important and their needs given priorities comparable to the armed forces." "The Fascist and Communist states have nothing at all to teach us about freedom and democracy," the Christian Education board admonished, "but they have everything to teach us about the importance of children." That year Presbyterians began gearing up for a major new Christian education campaign incorporating parents as the first teachers of religion and adopting a decidedly neoorthodox theological tone. As the following chapter will discuss in more detail, Cold War rhetoric and neoorthodox crisis theology were, for a time, a potent combination.[38]

More religious education programming was probably not what Smith and the other neoorthodox critics had in mind. But perhaps it was simply not possible for any post-Bushnellian mainline Protestant to envision religious life with the Christian family somewhere in the equation. Whether it deserved to be or not, the Christian family would remain at the center of twentieth-century mainline Protestant religious imagination.

Family Religion in Wartime

In a larger sense, however, the effort to institutionalize family religion was not a matter of choice. During the war years the federal government issued clear directives about the strategic importance of the Christian family. In 1939 President Roosevelt, addressing a White House Conference on Children in a Democracy, voiced direct concern about "the children who are outside the reach of religious influences, and are denied help in attaining faith in an ordered universe and in the fatherhood of God." The final report of the conference denounced "the menace of totalitarianism" that threatened American freedom as well as the "neglect of spiritual values" that threatened to widen the "disorganization of our world." Citing an earlier government study on *Recent Social Trends* (1933), the author of this report decried the declining role of churches and parents in providing the necessary moral education to the rising generation and issued a firm call for renewed efforts. Recognizing the potential legal difficulties in mandating any particular forms of religious instruction, the government report noted with approval the beginnings of nonsectarian, community-based efforts—many more fully realized after the war in the "release time" program for children. But "the difficulty of the solution of the problem which our generation has inherited," the report continued, "does not in any sense relieve the churches of responsibility for the religious nurture of the children and the youth of the Nation. . . . Pending the working out of a more adequate program for the total education of the child, they should make the utmost use of the educational opportunities that they now possess."[39]

Such statements reflected the successful effort to mobilize the home front during World War II. In 1940 the United States military was only the eighteenth strongest in the world, behind the major powers as well as the Netherlands, Portugal, Sweden, and Switzerland. In the months following Pearl Harbor, as in Roosevelt's words, "Dr. New Deal" gave way to "Dr. Win the War," the military buildup enlisted the wholehearted participation of every American man, woman, and child. Citizens did more than just collect aluminum scraps and carry rationing cards; winning the war against Germany and Japan also required sacrifice of social service funding. During the 1940s federal support for relief programs declined drastically, offset by a rising standard of living within the war-based economy.

Although few Americans on the home front questioned this change of priorities, they did begin to worry about the war economy's effect on children. In the shift toward military production some hard-won regulations about child labor fell by the wayside. Between 1940 and 1944 the teenage workforce grew from one to nearly three million, and more than one million students dropped out of high school. Fears of "juvenile delinquency" sharpened during the war, accelerated by perceptions that mothers in war production were neglecting their children. Harrowing stories of abuse and neglect as well as the antisocial exploits of "eight hour orphans"—teenage prostitution rings, gang warfare, climbing rates of venereal disease and premarital pregnancy—soon became grist for child psychologists and anxious media exposés.[40]

Yet few Americans on the home front questioned their enlistment in the war effort. Indeed, American parents looked to government leaders with unique trust during the Depression and war years. Eleanor Roosevelt, for example, fielded thousands of questions from anxious mothers and fathers and wrote on family-related topics regularly in popular magazines. She generally counseled tolerance and avoidance of authoritarian methods, "emphasizing the importance of creating a democratic atmosphere in the home in which parents served as group leaders and children as occasional participants in the family's decision-making process." Eleanor's advice was hardly original, and she had no special expertise in the study of early childhood, yet, just as destitute Americans wrote to the Roosevelts asking for second-hand clothes or help with paying bills, parents trusted the First Lady's wisdom on matters pertaining to family life.[41]

During the war Protestant educators received a constant stream of governmental admonition from politicians such as Minnesota governor Harold Stassen, president of the ICRE in 1942. In an address entitled "Christian Education Faces Wartime Needs" Stassen proposed a vigorous quasi-military campaign of outreach that included maps and surveys to locate children beyond the reach of a religious education program, widespread radio programming, and a popular campaign based on the publication of "appealing, picturesque" little booklets, designed by a team of child psychologists and church educators. "Of course," Stassen continued, "I do not propose that we violate the fundamental principle of separation of church and state. But, if religion is to be vital, the decisions of state, the decisions of the community, the decisions of the commercial world must not be made entirely shut off from the fundamental precepts of our religious belief." "It is not enough," Stassen declared, "that we interpret our religion as to what it means in terms of personal morals and personal conduct. We must also interpret it in terms of national morals and national conduct."[42]

Law enforcement officials echoed his concern. During the 1940s J. Edgar Hoover's paean to the Sunday school as a "crime prevention laboratory" was reprinted in a variety of religious periodicals and won him a loyal following among church leaders. In 1948 Edward Elson, Hoover's pastor, published a thoroughly admiring account of the Presbyterian convictions behind the FBI director's war against communism and vice. "Reared on the Shorter Catechism, the Bible, and disciplined worship, it is perfectly natural," Elson enthused, "that his zeal for righteousness would make him a relentless antagonist of gangsters and lawbreakers."[43]

Such ties were not new, of course; in the late nineteenth century the Christian home had served as a similar point of connection between nationalistic and religious ideals and as an index of national superiority. A half-century later the difference was that the church and state were hardly equal partners; government was far more explicit in articulating its own role in the old partnership, and in charting its direction, than were mainline Protestant institutions.[44]

In March 1943 government and religious leaders inaugurated Christian Family Week, calling on Protestant, Catholic, and even Jewish leaders to join with the U.S. Office of Civilian Defense in "focussing general public attention upon the importance of the family in our democracy," and its spiritual needs in particular. (The following year, apparently in deference to Jewish participants, the event was renamed National Family Week.) In their joint response secular and religious authorities stressed the "place of religion in establishing and maintaining the home and in fulfilling family life" and "the basic place of the family in a democratic society." Together they recognized the practical value of religious institutions in providing childcare for working mothers and emotional support to bereaved and separated families.[45]

Government initiatives thus provided the basic structure for expanding church-related efforts. In April 1943, a month after the inauguration of National Family Week, the ICRE began a program entitled "United Christian Education Advance," designed to increase "home cooperation." In a manner reminiscent of the New Deal's "blue eagle" campaign, participating churches issued window stickers to families that enrolled by working through a brief checklist printed on the back ("We Cooperate in the Ways Checked," i.e., grace at meals, regular Bible reading, maintaining a "quiet place" for individual meditation, a family council, as well as subscribing to church periodicals and regularly attending church and Sunday school) (see fig. 3). Families then placed the sticker on their front window, the blue outer side proclaiming to the community that "This Church Home Is Cooperating in the United Christian Education Advance" and the red inner side reminding them of the checklist.[46]

THIS **CHURCH HOME** IS COOPERATING IN THE

Above is a reproduction of the Church Home Window Sticker, exact size. The stickers are printed in blue on the front side and in red on the back. The following lines are printed on the back:

WE COOPERATE
IN THE WAYS CHECKED
(Check any desired number)

_____ 1. Having grace or blessing at meal time.
_____ 2. Regular Bible Reading and Prayer.
_____ 3. Having a "quiet place" as an altar for individual use.
_____ 4. Subscribing for and using a church paper.
_____ 5. Subscribing for and using a periodical on home life.
_____ 6. Planning together in "family council."
_____ 7. All sharing in home work and play.
_____ 8. Regular attendance at Sunday school and church.
_____ 9. Support of Christian work at home and abroad.
_____ 10. Enlisting and helping other families in similar activities.

Figure 3. The Christian home and American patriotism (*"Advance in Home Cooperation,"* International Journal of Religious Education *[April 1943]: 15). Permission from Ministries in Christian Education, National Council of Churches of Christ.*

In many ways a renewed focus on parents made good sense, psychologically and spiritually. As many children of those times remembered years later, a parent's reactions to war-related news often made a permanent impression. Some children never forgot the sight of a parent's tears at the news of Pearl Harbor or a mother's daily fortitude in the face of her husband's absence. Moreover, by the time the United States entered World War II educators and many parents were familiar with the problems British children encountered when their parents sent them from war-torn London to homes in the countryside. Studies by Anna Freud and Dorothy Burlingham, and John Bowlby's "attachment theory," argued that children who stayed with their parents fared far better emotionally, even during the London blitz, than those sent away to the countryside.[47]

Wartime itself opened up an important religious conversation among parents worried about their children's emotional health. The long-established connection between religion and emotional security took on an entirely new dimension for families facing painful separation and bereavement. In 1943 Selective Service included fathers in the draft for the first time. By April 1944 they numbered over half of new inductees, nearly 115,000 men. By late 1943 through December 1945 men with children made up nearly a third of all those drafted into the armed services. The effect on American families was widespread: by mid–1945 the army reported over 2.8 women and over 1.8 children receiving family allowance benefits, each, no doubt, with their own story of anxiety and loneliness.[48]

Family religion during wartime offered the security found in order and enumeration, often echoing the awkward cadences of military jargon. The ICRE, for example, included a program of family life education with a list of eight "comprehensive objectives": getting each member of the family to "participate willingly and helpfully in the responsibilities and work of the home," to "accept his or her share of responsibility for maintaining the happy and harmonious fellowship of the home," and "to enable the parents of young children to appreciate their grave responsibility for the early religious and moral training of their children." The manual also offered a lengthy set of "criteria for determining whether a home is Christian." This list made only a passing reference to doctrinal issues—"the viewpoint or philosophy of life that prevails in the experience of its members"—and focused on "basic assumptions with reference to the meaning of existence" ("Are its thinking and its purposing based on Jesus' attitude and teaching regarding the supremacy of personal values?" "Are the rearing of children and the comradeship of the home regarded as fellowship with God in his creative activities?"). A second set of criteria dealt with the quality of relationships within the family ("Is the life of the family conducted on a democratic basis?" "Do all members of the family participate to the limit of their ability in the decisions of the family affecting the rights and welfare of all; in determining major policies, in planning projects, and in accepting responsibility?"). A third and fourth set of questions surrounded steps parents were taking to create "a home that is increasingly religious" ("Does its daily life exhibit reverence, awe, wonder, joy in the realization of the presence of God?" "Are the relationships between the parents and particularly their emotional adjustment to each other such as to give the children a sense of security, stability, poise, and confidence?") and, finally, "to educate their children as Christians" ("Is the family life so ordered that it leads to a sense of at-home-ness in the universe, a feeling of security and confidence?").[49]

In a similar fashion Congregational author Florence Taylor provided parents with a checklist for assessing whether or not their children were "normal." The list of traits—"incessant activity," "ceaseless questioning," "refreshing sincerity"—no doubt worried some parents of introverted children.[50] But this idealized portrait did make clear that the American Christian family stood firmly in line with the aims of democracy and freedom and in presumed contrast with the regimented younger citizens of Nazi Germany or Stalinist Russia. Indeed, Frank Capra's famous series of training films for American soldiers, "Why We Fight," powerfully juxtaposed footage of carefree, laughing, sunburnt American children with the sad, desperate faces of their counterparts in enemy lands.

World War II strengthened the identification of Christian families with democratic values, imposing a heavy burden on them as the primary location for the preservation of American civic life. Like the church, they were "menaced by towering economic and political institutions which are self-seeking, competitive, coercive, [and] secular." But, also like churches, homes were to be places where kinder cooperative virtues might prevail and grow to transform American society. This faith seemed to have no foreseeable limits. Indeed, as one postwar periodical concluded, "Not the battleships in the harbor but the homes on the hills guarantee the future of America. Not the marble columns of the banks on Main Street but the children kneeling for the bedside prayer gives us assurance of a strong future nation."[51]

Conclusion

American mainline Protestants entered the postwar years with their faith in the Christian home at an all-time high. The war had offered vivid proof of the importance of home life—soldiers yearned for it in letters home, their longings amplified in mass-produced popular music and their triumphant return to wives and children fast becoming a central element of national iconography. But, more than that, World War II elevated the superiority of the Christian home as the true foundation not only of church life but of national moral and civic virtue. The virtues of personality development and adjustment touted by progressive educators took on a new urgency in the battle against European totalitarianism and a new practicality with the advent of parent education training and character education.

The need, of course, was for more extensive programming linking the home and church together. In 1946 planning officials in the ICRE concluded that they had "no alternative than to proceed upon a course which will lift its philosophy out of the pages of a booklet and put it at the heart of all its endeavors." And, certainly, no Protestant educator argued with the need for "adequate printed resources"; the looming problem, as the ICRE document put it, was that "the average parent lacks initiative and imagination and experience in teaching religion." Indeed, "to aid fathers and mothers to become intelligent and skillful parents is a task of startling but thrilling magnitude."[52]

Yet, beneath the growing enthusiasm for family-based educational programming, old problems persisted. The parents of the postwar era were in many cases the children of the religiously illiterate generation of the 1930s—in other words, a thin reed on which to build an ambitious educational program. The other old problem concerned the content and methodology of family religion. Didactic, Bible-oriented training was long obsolete. And, although character education in such virtues as generosity and courage had a clear purpose while the nation was at war with Germany and Japan, the cold war, with its invisible enemies and fears of subversion, created a more ambiguous climate. Were American virtues the same as Christian virtues? Where might one draw the lines separating a definably Christian body of teaching and tradition with suburban middle-class socialization? Not surprisingly, the heyday of Christian family life in the 1950s also brought into sharp focus all of the ideology's inherent flaws. The postwar era, for all its idealization of the suburban middle-class family, marked the end of a long and increasingly unrealistic Protestant discourse about the family and the beginning of a new and even more difficult one.

Chapter 5

Praying to Stay Together in the 1950s

THE FAMILIAR ICONOGRAPHY of the 1950s Protestant family usually depicts two well-dressed, incredibly happy parents with their relentlessly well-adjusted youngsters in tow, all headed down the sidewalk toward the church of their choice. A vaguely colonial church spire in the middle distance suggests that their destination is not a Pentecostal meeting house, a Jewish synagogue, or even a Roman Catholic cathedral but, instead, a solidly respectable mainline Protestant congregation.

The postwar decades did, in fact, mark a huge groundswell of middle-class Protestant family piety, much of it centered in mushrooming suburban neighborhoods, another familiar hallmark of that time. During the 1950s some sixteen million Americans moved to the growing rims of cities, their migration facilitated by low-cost government loans and mass-produced housing. Church statistics for the postwar years are the stuff of legend. During the 1950s church membership grew faster than the population; by the end of the decade some 65 percent of Americans claimed affiliation with a religious institution, marking an all-time high, even for a heavily churched country such as the United States. Upwards of 90 percent of the American public professed faith in God and in the power of prayer. The new religiosity quickly poured into religious institutions. Following two decades of decline in church giving, postwar Protestant churches found themselves suddenly full of new members and their yearly budgets growing. Thousands of brand-new sanctuaries soon dotted the suburban landscape, most of them abandoning the traditionally vertical lines of Protestant church buildings in favor of a strong horizontal profile. New church designs

contained many of the comforts of home: well-appointed parlors, coffee and conversation rooms, and cheerful, well-equipped Sunday school wings for their burgeoning numbers of young children.[1]

The religion of family togetherness in the 1950s has been much reviled,
lampooned, and critiqued, and it is probably unnecessary—and impossible—to
add much new to the story here. This chapter considers the domestic piety of
the 1950s within a longer historical perspective, as in one sense the culmina-
tion of a Protestant tradition and in another a major point of transition into a
new religious and social era. It is, of course, hard to separate the story of 1950s
mainline piety from its swift demise in the following decades. Within an amaz-
ingly brief span of time mainline Protestants dropped all hope of redemption
through family religion, in the face of massive defections by the very children
raised in those close-knit, presumably pious homes. But to tell that story in all
its complexity, as the next chapter will attempt to do, we must first consider
the "golden age" of cold war domesticity.

Continuities and Discontinuities

Most historians agree that the fabled 1950s family was a demographic aberra-
tion, shaped by the booming economy and drive for togetherness in the postwar years. Divorce rates, for example, were extraordinarily low during this time,
at least compared to long-term trends. Since the Civil War the figure had been
rising about 3 percent a decade and increased sharply in the years right after
World War II with the breakup of many overly hasty war marriages. But the
1950s saw the smallest increase in the divorce rate for any decade during the
twentieth century and, in fact, a return to pre–World War II levels. Postwar
Americans also married younger and in greater numbers than their parents or
grandparents. The average age of marriage for men fell from 26.7 years in 1900
to 22 years in the 1950s; for young women it dropped from 24 to 20. And, of
course, these couples began producing children early and often; the long-term
decline in the U.S. birthrate, which sharpened during the Depression and war
years, rebounded during the 1950s to produce a baby boom of unprecedented
proportions. By the end of the decade American parents produced nearly as many
new babies as their counterparts in India.[2]

Not surprisingly, these family demographics created an unusual time for
mainline Protestant churches. The typical new joiners, according to numerous
studies, were that well-scrubbed family of four, although some of the data sug-

gested that it was the children, not the parents, who were leading the way into church. A distressingly high proportion of parents appeared content to drop their children off for church and Sunday school and then, like writer Annie Dillard's father, "drive by at noon . . . , saying, 'Hop in quick!' so no one would see his weekend khaki pants and loafers."[3]

Still, during the 1950s family and church stood at the center of a broad national consensus. The three authors (Protestant, Catholic, and Jewish) of a piece on religion for the 1960 White House conference on "The Nation's Children" declared that "there is no doubt but that the United States is essentially a nation which grew out of convictions as to man's individual honor, freedom, and dignity, and these convictions were based on religion." The authors encouraged American parents to "take a page from the practice of pioneer families" and maintain home prayer and Bible reading. Such habits, they declared, would enable "children to withstand those forces which are contrary to family standards because of the godly strength which accrues to family standards through family worship."[4]

In many ways, however, the culture of the 1950s was not necessarily a sharp departure from social changes taking place during the war years and before. The rising birthrate of the 1950s, for example, began with the departing soldiers and their war brides in the 1940s, a time when family ties certainly carried at least as much mythic power as they would during the cold war. In contrast to the extremely low birthrates of the Depression years, the early 1940s saw an unprecedented jump in babies born. Some demographers, in fact, date the baby boom phenomenon from 1940 to 1960, covering a period of constant population growth, fueled by postwar immigration but most of it coming from native births.[5] Nor was the emphasis on family piety anything new for Protestant churches. Although the exigencies of the cold war added an element of urgency, many of the beliefs and practices about domestic religion were thoroughly grounded in assumptions carried since the 1930s, a fact that explains both their success and their eventual failure.

The Religion of Togetherness

Togetherness was the touchstone of cold war domesticity, reflecting both the fears and aspirations of middle-class Americans. The vaguely defined dangers of communist subversion and the more imminent threat of nuclear annihilation put a premium on the kind of security family life seemed to promise. Indeed, home bomb shelters and the compact design of the typical suburban ranch house literally drew middle-class family members into close proximity, warmed by the cathode rays emanating from their electronic hearths.[6]

Children seemed particularly vulnerable to danger. Experts warned parents to be alert not only about communist subversion but also about the possibility that their son or daughter might encounter unsavory influences in their own homes. Even as innocent a pastime as comic book reading could plant sadistic fantasies in a young boy's mind; in 1954 a Senate Subcommittee to Investigate Juvenile Delinquency met to plumb the connections between comic books and teenage crime. Television, even in its infancy, prompted fears of "zombification" in the nation's children. Doctors warned parents about "TV squint," "TV tummy," "frogitis," and a host of other physical maladies directly attributable to television viewing. More urgent worries about violence and the commercialization of the nation's "vast wasteland" would soon follow.[7]

But the other side of fear was the doggedly optimistic conviction that the American family was the only hope for the future of the free world. The famous showdown between Nikita Khrushchev and Richard Nixon at their 1959 "kitchen debate" pitted the time-saving wonders of a suburban tract home against the ponderous might of Soviet weaponry. The core of U.S. superiority, Nixon repeatedly reminded the truculent Russian premier, rested in the safety and abundance enjoyed by millions of middle-class families. As historian Thomas Hine remarks, "Nixon seemed to be making a stand for American values right in the setting that was most meaningful to Americans, in the heart of the suburban house—the modern push-button kitchen."[8]

Even so, togetherness was far more than a grim cold war necessity. Parenting was also supposed to be fun. In his best-selling *Baby and Child Care* Dr. Benjamin Spock encouraged young parents of the 1950s not to worry unduly about following correct procedures. Most babies, he wrote, are "friendly and reasonable" people who want nothing more than to "fit into the family's way of doing things." Parents, in his view, possessed a similar bent toward goodwill and cooperation; their main challenge was not to damage their children by forcing them into unnatural directions.[9]

Mainline Protestants were by now thoroughly familiar with this child-centered, positive thinking family ethos—and they had played no small role in creating it. They had long held the conviction that the family was the key to all forms of social progress; it was but a small leap from that conviction to the general theme of the 1954 Methodist National Conference on Family Life, "The

Christian Family—The Hope of the World." "The Methodist Church is not going to miss the timetable of social emergence of concern for family life," church officials confidently declared. "At a time . . . when the general public and Social Agencies of the land are turning to the family as the one hope for the growth of sound persons to make a safe world, . . . the Methodist Church is pressing toward the restoration of the religious life of the home, summoning the family to its divine vocation."[10] Clearly, family religion continued to evoke millennial passions even among the this-worldly Protestants of the 1950s. "When the church is once more in the home," George Buttrick promised his Madison Avenue (New York City) Presbyterian congregation, "public worship will have a new glow, preaching a new grip on all life, the church school will have its rebirth, and our bloodshot world a Christian hope and health."[11]

For perhaps one final moment mainline Protestants found themselves at the center of white, middle-class American culture. The theme of Christian Family Week in 1951, "Children Deserve Christian Homes," offered a ringing affirmation of the child-centeredness fast becoming endemic to suburbia. "Nothing less is good enough for them!" a Methodist author declared. "The capacity to love and serve children comes near being man's highest capacity," another Methodist agreed. When we say that nothing is too good for my child, he declared, "we are approximating genuine nobility" and taking on a genuinely godlike character.[12]

Although the domestic ideal decisively excluded some groups, the nonwhite and non–middle class in particular, it did extend the Protestant consensus beyond its previous boundaries. After a century of persecution and ridicule, Latter-day Saints, for example, found themselves for the first time in general agreement with American values. Already deeply invested in family, after World War II Mormons enthusiastically surged toward the cultural mainstream on the crest of postwar domestic piety, declaring wholehearted support for the American family altar. Although "Home Night," the practice of spending Monday nights in family-related activities and Scripture study, had begun in the 1930s, this program became increasingly central to Latter-day Saint identity in the 1950s, as "the family became the focus of public relations." Indeed, by the 1950s Home Night had become "Family Home Evening," buttressed by church programs in Family Prayer, Family Scripture Study, and Family Worship—echoing the shift toward relational language among mainline Protestants.[13]

The same is generally true of Protestant fundamentalists. As the following chapter will discuss more fully, the family-oriented culture of the 1950s facilitated a reversal in the movement's separatist stance toward American culture.

The shift may well have been prompted in part by a growing casualty list of disaffected children from solidly orthodox Christian homes. Yet the popular appeal of family religion offered a morally impeachable justification for (at least partly) casting off their old outsider status and charting a cautious course toward the cultural mainstream.

During the postwar years a growing multitude of Christian family magazines, pamphlets, and programs updated Horace Bushnell for the mid-twentieth century.[14] Not one of them doubted that, as Bushnell once argued, domesticity was a fulfillment of Christianity and that "the very vocabulary of the Christian faith is furnished with its richest meaning in Christian family life." Indeed, delegates to a national conference in 1950 on "Christian parenting" agreed that under the aegis of Christianity the family "becomes a redemptive fellowship, a kingdom of God in miniature."[15] The religious nurture of children, a National Council of Churches (NCC) publication declared, was still the "divine mission" of the Christian family.[16]

Of course, one difference between the nineteenth- and twentieth-century versions of Christian domesticity was the role of women. The "godly mother" of the 1950s was far different than her 1850s counterpart, though not necessarily better off in every way. Mother still remained the primary teacher of religion but hardly within an ordered, patriarchal setting. Postwar mothers negotiated a complicated network of competing responsibilities; many testified that they fulfilled most of their religious duties on the road, driving children to and from church-related activities.[17]

The nature of Christian motherhood proved elusive. During the 1950s advocates of family religion promoted Christian domesticity as an antidote to the growing restlessness of the middle-class wife and mother. "Jesus teaches the housewife the dignity of her calling," a Baptist wrote in 1951. "For, when he sanctifies the home by showing that it possesses the Kingdom of Heaven in miniature, the work of the mistress of the home assumes a regal distinction."[18] Such language clearly drew on nineteenth-century views of womanhood but with a twist. Postwar domesticity did not afford women moral authority because of their gender; if anything, motherhood had become fraught with dangerous liabilities. Psychologists warned that a cold and thoughtless mother could work as much harm on her children as a cloying, smothering one. Philip Wylie's overwrought diatribe, *Generation of Vipers* (1942), launched a furious attack against overprotective mothers blamed for producing the millions of young men who were psychologically unfit for service in World War II. In contrast to the earlier era of

Protestant domesticity, Christian family periodicals of the 1950s were notice-ably silent about women's parenting role, suggesting by their silence how mor-ally complicated—or morally vacant—they understood the task to be.[19]

Religious educators continued to stress the "unconscious" nature of religious growth and the absolute power of parental example, adopting a consistently up-beat tone to emphasize the importance of a positive emotional framework. Two Baptist authors used a combination of biological metaphors to describe the de-velopment of a "contagious" religious conviction. "Your children may inherit your blue eyes, big feet, or fortune," they explained, but "they cannot inherit your Christian faith. They can only catch it as you expose them to it." The au-thors continued with a comparison between the fictional Smith and Brown fami-lies, both holding generally orthodox beliefs but only the former backing them up with "consistent Christian living." The Smiths met regularly for prayer, "with-out complaining," and volunteered for church projects in a similarly positive frame of mind. In contrast, the Browns spent little time in church, told "white lies," and "complain[ed] freely" about life's adversities. "Each of these families is communicating religious belief," the authors explained. "The real faith taught is that which is lived rather than that which is spoken."[20]

The essence of Christian family life emerged in personal interaction, guided by the rules of middle-class togetherness. At the top of a list enumerating the ten "marks of a Christian home" a Baptist author placed affectionate concern for each member, respect for individual differences, "clean and wholesome tastes in entertainment," and a "general atmosphere of cleanliness and neatness." The bottom half of the list included family devotions, participation in church pro-grams, and, at the end, recognition of the "perfect secret" of the Christian home, that "Christ is the head of this house, the unseen guest at every meal, the silent listener to every conversation."[21] Similarly, family life expert Donald More Maynard emphasized the importance of "wholesome" traits and cooperative, democratic forms of interaction. "A Christian home," he declared, "will be run on democratic principles. There will be no one person to whom the other mem-bers of the family are subservient." In contrast, a devout but authoritarian house-hold failed the test, for it did not "reflect the fine spirit of understanding and comradeship that should be evident in a Christian home." "By no stretch of the imagination," Maynard declared, "can this home be called Christian."[22] Simi-larly, and even less ambiguously, the author of a 1951 book on the Christian home included a multiple-choice questionnaire for parents entitled "Is Our Home as Christian as It Might Be?" The first question, "Is the general atmosphere of the home pleasant?" was the determinative one for the nineteen that followed, only one of which addressed a behavior specific to Christianity, maintaining the family altar. (With a possible 5 points for each answer, a score of 85 or higher meant an "excellent home," 75–84 a "good" one, 65–74 an "average" one, and 50–64 "poor.")[23]

Christian families were distinguished by their capacity for fun. Following the popular format of women's magazines, denominational publications demonstrated this point by profiling exemplary, possibly fictional, families as models for the less well-adjusted to emulate. The Websters, for example, were not only a loving, churchgoing group, but their home was "a preferred place on the list of the neighborhood fun-spots."[24] In a similar fashion the Slifer family lived "abundantly." "If you're searching for a martyr's religion, a religion that gives you a long face, that makes you feel glum, that prompts you to search and search through dusty books to find out what's wrong with the world, then don't visit the Slifers," a visitor enthusiastically reported. "They're optimists." "Although the reading of the Bible has an important place in the Slifer family life," he explained, "they are not too concerned about formal religion. More important to them is love, good will, courtesy, concern for others."[25]

Happiness and security counted for much more than theological rigor. "How can children be helped to feel the religious meaning of doing what is right," the author of a series of leaflets on *Home Guidance in Religion* queried, "without the use of the slightest suggestion of a threat? To say 'God is angry when you act like that' does violence to the child's growing conception of the perfect love of God . . . [and] may lead to the feeling that God is not fair, for in childish conflicts each child feels that he is right." Indeed, the author concluded, "a child should not be made to have a sense of guilt, rather of temporary failure that he can overcome."[26] Far better for parents to cultivate a positive spirit of happiness in their children, if possible, through their own example. "If they would have happy, well-adjusted children," one author counseled, "they need to be happy, well-adjusted persons themselves. Happiness is catching."[27] Christian family magazines also exhorted parents not to moralize but to "leave the preaching of repentance and of God's stern ways with sin to the pastor in the pulpit. . . . We parents are not perfect," a Baptist expert chided. "And we cannot drive our children into the church by repetitious and self-righteous sermonettes. The occasions of our Christian witness to our children must be happy occasions."[28]

Even mild forms of didacticism were suspect during the cold war. The blind faith of a "true believer," in Eric Hoffer's biting description, was a clear sign of psychological pathology, especially as chilling stories of "brainwashed" prisoners of war filtered back from the Korean front. As historian Daniel Beckman writes, "The absolute authority of parents over children . . . became suspect in the face of the Nazi example of authoritarianism."[29] Thus, Harry C. Monro, author of an influential textbook on Christian education, warned of "authoritarian parents, teachers, and ministers" within both the neoorthodox and fundamentalist camps. In a democratic home, he admonished, "the parents conceive their function to be that of freeing their child into his own self-direction and responsibility as rapidly as he can take it, and in all the ways he can take it."[30]

Another important influence on child-rearing advice and Christian education programs of the 1950s was the rising importance of pastoral psychology. In the flush economic times of the postwar years, seminary programs retooled quickly, adding courses and even graduate programs in pastoral counseling and theology. To a large degree the growth of such programs reflected a rising demand by parish ministers, who found themselves devoting an inordinate amount of time to the "cure of souls."

The new pastoral psychologists were highly critical of what they saw as the latent moralism of the Freudian adjustment models characteristic of the 1920s and 1930s. Instead of berating the downtrodden for not being sufficiently wholesome, they argued, Christian counselors should aid in the task of self-realization, as articulated in the writings of Carl Rogers, Eric Fromm, and Karen Horney. Cold war psychology, even in its pastoral application, was profoundly suspicious of social institutions. "It was, after all," as Brooks Holifield writes, "an era of bureaucrats, dictators, and demagogues." The new model, in fact, set personal fulfillment in opposition to social structures; it taught that individual growth required a radical rejection of conformity to the icons of mass culture—including, by implication, church and family. Not surprisingly perhaps, the juxtaposition of this radical individualism with the public-spirited emphasis on "cooperation" in the World War II years was the source of many confusing messages to parents and children. By the late 1950s the dissonance would become nearly impossible to maintain.[31]

Confirming this growing sense of indecision, Presbyterian educator James Smart noted a deep reluctance among educated, middle-class American parents to "indoctrinate" their children with religious beliefs. "The impression . . . has gone abroad that the intelligent thing to do is to let children and young people work things out for themselves, without interference of any kind."[32] In keeping with this spirit, a Baptist mother explained, "We have always tried to give [our children] the reasons and backgrounds for our beliefs, but have said, 'This is what *we* believe. Think it through, and then decide what *you* believe.'" And, she added, "We are not afraid for their ultimate decision."[33]

The goal of Christian parenting closely matched the middle-class suburban definition of happiness and success. A study of the "Crestwood Heights" suburb in 1956 described the goal of family life as "a blend of material well-being, success, social status, good physical and mental health." Most Crestwood Heights described themselves as happy and, the researchers explained, "ascribe their happiness largely to the family."[34] A Ford Foundation study of sixty thousand "successful families" profiled homes in which all the children finished high school, an achievement attributed to a strong family ethic.[35] The Christian families profiled in Protestant magazines hardly appeared any different than their neighbors down the block—if anything, their happiness was more complete because of their religious faith.

The obvious shallowness of this ideal quickly drew a host of critics. Sociologist Peter Berger angrily dismissed the Christian domesticity of the 1950s as "a surrealistic blend of Horace Bushnell, John Dewey, and an emasculated Freud." Dan Wakefield, who reviewed a popular Methodist family magazine for the *Nation*, found its "desperate attempt to be up-to-date" both appalling and amusing. From breathless feature stories about Methodist "All-American" football greats to an awed portrayal of the "Miss Methodist Student Nurse" competition, Wakefield had nothing but scorn for the bubbly, conformist spirit of mid-twentieth-century Protestant Christianity—as he described it, "purely Sinclair Lewis." In a desperate attempt to please "they have dressed Jesus Christ in a grey flannel suit and smothered his spirit in the folds of conformity. The new slick-page Christianity cheerily rises in the midst of a world seeking answers to survival, and offers an All-Methodist football team." But, despite such easy criticisms, domestic Christianity proved durably popular. In the era of Norman Vincent Peale, the relentless congeniality of Protestant family literature matched the spirit of the age.[36]

This mood is most evident, perhaps, in the curiously offhand treatment of nuclear war in Protestant family periodicals. Children of the 1950s learned to "duck and cover" in school drills, played war games during recess, and no doubt went to sleep at night wondering about the possibility of nuclear annihilation; parents worried about creating a "secure" home certainly had a challenge on their hands. In 1959 a National Council of Churches report on children and religion stated that fears of death and dying were the primary concern. The NCC's Department on Children found that it could not keep enough copies of its pamphlet on "Interpreting Death to Children" in stock.[37] Yet, although containment metaphors abounded in Protestant family magazines, the cold war itself rarely appeared. Even in the wake of the Cuban missile crisis in 1962, parents received little guidance for comforting frightened children. One author, for example, advised showing them pictures of cold war "statesmen" to remind them that these "sane, sensible people" are "untiring in their efforts" on their behalf. "Assure him that at this stage in the world's developments," she continued, "we adults are grateful to be dealing with nuclear weapons. Otherwise, we might have a so-called 'conventional' war on our hands at this very moment."[38]

Clearly, one purpose of family religion was to shelter children during a dangerous decade, and in some ways it appeared to have been successful. Many adults who grew up during this time remember their experiences in Sunday school and family devotions with genuine nostalgia. Home became a comforting spiritual metaphor, reflecting what Robert Wuthnow describes as a "spirituality of dwelling." It seems likely that such associations played a role in the resurgence of interest in religion several decades later. As some recent studies have shown, children of the postwar era, who became adults within the anarchic spirituality of the 1960s and 1970s, returned to churches with their children, perhaps drawn by their early memories.[39]

Protestant domesticity also attempted to cultivate a rudimentary social consciousness in parents and children. Its genial, nonjudgmental spirit laid the basis for the ethic of tolerance and "brotherhood" that would animate the civil rights movement in northern white churches during the early 1960s.[40] Of course, the idea that parents could bequeath progressive social attitudes to their children placed powerful new strictures on the details of their interactions within the home. During and after World War II psychological research began to posit a link between child-rearing methods and the rise of fascist and racist ideologies, suggesting that the roots of childhood prejudice lay in the home. The work of Theodor W. Adorno, Gunnar Myrdal, and Gordon Allport raised the possibility that parents, especially mothers, created "authoritarian personalities" in their children either by coddling them or by being overly strict. These frustrated children then turned to aggression to acquire the sense of control they could not achieve at home.[41]

Thus, in the 1950s American child-rearing advice literature, and religious sources in particular, emphasized the social ramifications of a positive emotional upbringing. Good parenting, never an easy task, was now a higher-stakes effort than ever before. "Happy children," as a Methodist author explained, "grow up with a free and spontaneous acceptance of other people." Declaring that "prejudice begins at home," she warned that parents could either preserve their children's innocence or corrupt it through their own carelessness.[42] Another Methodist writer admonished that any "offhand remark" or "an expression of prejudice toward a particular race or creed will be picked up by the child."[43] Religious educators encouraged parents to maintain regular contacts with "persons of other racial and national groups," for, as one ICRE bulletin declared, "Your children have no natural prejudices." Interracial encounters were valuable learning experiences and moments in which parents could demonstrate their personal tolerance. "Your Christian attitude toward others," the pamphlet admonished, "helps your children learn that real worth is not based on physical appearances. Watch for and plan occasions that will help them begin early to understand the spirit of brotherhood within God's family."[44]

Still, in its best sense Protestant domesticity did not necessarily require political naïveté. One of the most successful efforts against black poverty and southern racism of this era was the Child Development Group of Mississippi, started by the National Council of Churches Delta Ministry in 1965. Although surrounded by threats of harassment, the mainline Protestants who staffed this initiative excelled at encouraging economically deprived parents and children to interact with deeper "personal sensitivity." As one of the mothers in the program reported, the trainers "have taught me how to teach my kids at home," and the Delta program gave her an "experience of how different children react and how to solve their problems." Through her participation she had learned "to love kids more and more." The poverty-stricken participants in the Child Development Group Ministry, according to historian James Findlay, "perceived the program as theirs, not something imposed on them," and were ready to defend it, "fiercely and enthusiastically." These testimonies suggest one strikingly positive result of mainline churches' investment in the child-centered ethos of the 1950s.[45]

The Family Altar

Protestant educators of the postwar era were ambivalent about the family altar, despite its hallowed role in domestic piety. Some continued to insist that regular devotions were a spiritual necessity, an important "talisman" to ward off external evil. As one writer warned, "Many judges, who daily deal with criminals, say that a background of church and Sunday school attendance, religious training, and home devotions are not to be found in the cases brought before them. . . . We, as parents, cannot afford to let our children grow up in a materialistic, selfish world without the source of comfort, strength, and oneness with God that home worship helps to develop."[46]

To ward off such evils, Christian family magazines continued to publish devotional curricula, written by professionals but intended for use in homes. These guides typically followed a time-honored format that included a brief Bible reading and a paragraph of reflection on the passage, a short prayer, and a suggested activity. Although the format assumed regular parental leadership, it also encouraged children's participation, since even the very young could offer a brief prayer or read a short passage of Scripture. In every case the lessons were practical and aimed at real-life situations each family member might encounter—a bout with jealousy, the need for patience.[47]

Yet, despite the uniformly upbeat tone of family devotional literature, a growing majority of Protestant lay people and clergy knew that the "old-fashioned" family altar was probably beyond recovering. At best, they concluded, most families used devotional materials only hurriedly and sporadically.[48] A 1958 survey of Presbyterian parents, for example, found that, although almost 70 percent of parents reported regular table grace (vs. 43 percent of the national population), only 4.3 percent held daily worship at home. Another 12 percent of families met weekly, but nearly 35 percent admitted to interviewers that they never held devotions. As one, probably typical, parent explained to researchers, "We tried three or four times to have this little family worship hour just before bedtime, and either John gets mad at David or David gets mad at John when it is John's turn to read": "He can't read anyway so he tries to improvise with the picture and he tells a little story of what this means to him, and Dave gets bored because this is so elementary to him. Then Carol who is 12 is off wandering somewhere else in her mind." Presbyterian parents reported similar failures around the much-touted "family council." Most had tried it at least once but none successfully. One father candidly explained that, though his younger children were still basically compliant, with the fourteen-year-old "I've got to hit him right between the eyes with a two by four to get his attention. You can't go around in a family circle." Nearly all the parents in the survey reported guilt about such failures, but few expressed much interest in trying again.[49]

One solution was more parent education programming, a movement that was intensifying by the end of World War II.[50] In 1950 eighty delegates from seventeen denominations met together with "a sense of deep devotion to a common urgent mission" to create a "grand strategy for Protestantism" to "reach all families with the Gospel of Jesus Christ."[51] The National Council of Churches provided volumes of printed materials for congregations seeking to become "family-centered." (They were apparently not daunted by the fact that their own survey of Christian education literature found at least fourteen hundred separate publications already available to parents.) The new materials would help individual churches attract new members and help shore up inadequate families with a rigorous schedule of monthly meetings, family-centered worship services, Sunday school programs for everyone from toddlers to grandparents, and "careful guidance" of parents in family devotions.[52] One Baptist program guide, built on the conviction that "every church needs a program of Christian family life education," laid out nine steps for congregations to follow, each one bolstered by a list of supplementary books, filmstrips, leaflets, plays, and magazines. Each month of the year required a different activity, including a January family open house, a May family tea (in conjunction with National Family Week), a June children's day, a July family festival and picnic, and August family visits to "places of historic or religious interest, including denominational camp sites."[53]

Christian Faith and Life

The most important of all these efforts was the Presbyterian Church U.S.A.'s publication of "Christian Faith and Life: A Program for Home and Church" in 1948. Although Presbyterians were by no means the only denomination offering comprehensive family programming, I have focused on their efforts, since they offer some crucial insights into the rise—and decline—of family religion in the 1950s. Their groundbreaking religious education curriculum promised a fully integrated vision of spiritual formation, emphasizing the home as the primary site of religious training. Supporters of the new approach happily referred to it as "Christian Education—Family Style."[54]

The goal of the curriculum was to eradicate "religious illiteracy" among Presbyterians. Traditional Sunday school materials, the denomination's educators argued, tended to fragment or intellectualize biblical content. "One of the greatest problems in Christian teaching," the Christian education board's 1947 report contended, "is that, while there is a great emphasis upon the Bible and attention to it in the Church School, few Christians seem to be able to read the Bible for themselves with understanding even after . . . fifteen years under the Church's instruction."[55]

The new curriculum sought to be simple but comprehensive. Aimed at both teachers and parents, it followed a three-year cycle of graded lessons on the life of Christ, the story of the Bible, and the history of the church. Children and adults received a series of attractively packaged materials designed for classroom study and follow-up discussion around the dinner table. The magazines provided weekly "home-teaching plans," meant to be follow-through reinforcement rather than advance preparation for the Sunday lesson.[56]

The heart of the curriculum, however, was its reading list. During the 1940s and 1950s the Board of Christian Education published a "whole series of hard-cover, four-color-illustrated home reading books [which] were carefully prepared to convey to children and youth panoramic visions of the three great themes of the curriculum: Jesus Christ, the Bible, and the Church." These books were intended to provide occasions for informal parent-child reading and, as an alternative to easily discardable weekly flyers, a durable collection of Christian literature. As one father enthused, "After our children have completed fourteen years of Sunday school they will each have a permanent religious library of thirty-two books, to which, with their Bibles, they can turn again and again for answers to the questions their lives raise for them."[57]

The new curriculum's designers sought parental involvement at every stage of its planning and execution. The first organizing conference in 1941 brought together forty representative pastors, theologians, educators, and parents. Individual churches also convened mothers and fathers for quarterly meetings, with what supporters declared were "spectacular" results. In Santa Fe meetings brought in fifty-four out of a potential seventy-four homes, and in Denton, Texas, 65 percent of parents attended a yearly series of consultations.[58]

Praise descended from all quarters. In 1951 the *Christian Century* referred to Christian Faith and Life as "probably the best church school literature available in America today."[59] Even more telling, other denominations soon adapted the Presbyterian approach into their own curriculum planning, so that it became a model for post–World War II Sunday schools.

Presbyterian congregations apparently agreed. By 1951 over 6,000 churches had adopted the new curriculum, 70 percent of the denomination's Sunday schools. By 1953 those numbers were still growing, swelled by some 1,500 non-Presbyterian church users as well as 135 churches outside the United States, from Japan to Switzerland. Presbyterian educators credited the curriculum with reversing the Sunday school decline of the prewar decades. In 1949 Sunday school attendance grew by nearly 9 percent, the largest increase for any decade in the twentieth century.[60]

In many ways the Christian Faith and Life curriculum was an attempt to respond to the neoorthodox critique of religious education. In its 1947 report to the General Assembly the Board of Christian Education argued that "when attention is concentrated primarily on character development there is a tendency for Christian education to become purely moralistic, neglecting the deeper aspects of Christian faith. It produces then, in the main, religious people with an inclination toward complacency about their own goodness and religiousness but with little inclination toward those disciplines which are necessary for able, intelligent, and aggressive Christian discipleship."[61] The new curriculum, board members hoped, would create these new disciples by emphasizing revelational truth, the church's witness in the world, and the necessity of a life-altering commitment to Christ. Simple role modeling was deemed no longer adequate; as the board report put it, "even as we ourselves would have no knowledge of the Christian gospel had we not learned of it from other people, so the present and future generations will remain ignorant of it unless Christian people accept the responsibility of Christian teaching."[62]

Although they worried about the dangers of religious indoctrination, advocates of the Presbyterian program argued that propaganda could work both ways. As one supporter warned parents, "if you don't indoctrinate your children, somebody else will. And you won't like the result." Similarly, Paul Calvin Payne warned his denomination in 1951 that neglecting the denomination's children was "the most effective way to cooperate with the Russian plot to demoralize the world by blotting out religious life." "We can be sure of one thing," he declared, "the world is not going to 'go pagan' or Christian by some unhappy or happy chance. It will go to those who care most."[63]

Still, the architects of the Christian Faith and Life program attempted to go beyond pragmatic or psychological arguments to create a theological warrant for the family-church partnership. Echoing Bushnell, leading Presbyterian educator James Smart reminded his fellow Calvinists that the covenant family was a divinely ordained reality, instituted through the pledges of infant baptism. Church and family partook equally of covenant promises and responsibilities, and failure was a serious matter in both settings. Thus, as Smart reminded parents, "Unfaithfulness in this ministry is a breaking of vows made solemnly before God and is of a gravity equal to the offense of a minister of the Church when he deliberately disregards his ordination vows." Religious indifference in covenant families "is not the loss merely of a single function by the home, but the loss of the divine order of the home."[64] This understanding made home and church theoretically equal in their tasks; neither was simply an instrument of the other. "Beginning with the family as a unit of the Christian fellowship," the Christian education board contended, "there should be an unfolding of ever wider perspectives until one knows himself a member of a mighty community of faith which circles the earth and binds the Church of the ages into one."[65]

Conclusion

By the late 1950s, even the most enthusiastic supporters of the Christian Faith and Life Program were forced to admit that it was foundering, largely because of indifferent and inconsistent support from parents. In 1959 William A. Morrison, general secretary of the Christian Education board, admitted that the family-based approach had been "naive, sentimental, and superficial" in the face of rampant "theological confusion" within the denomination's membership.[66] The 1958 merger and formation of the United Presbyterian Church U.S.A. necessitated a curriculum evaluation and overhaul. The result was a new model, Christian Faith and Action, which shifted emphasis from both the family's role and neoorthodox theology. This was perhaps a pragmatic recognition of the denomination's increasing theological and social diversity; as Presbyterians turned to discussions of racism, war, and sexual ethics in the 1960s and 1970s, however, they did so without the awareness of the family that had shaped the conversation of the previous decade.[67]

Clearly, the bright, happy picture of Protestant domesticity and the equally bright hopes of church leaders for the family fell far short of reality. Protestant homes proved no more cohesive or orderly than those of their pagan next-door neighbors. Nor did they bring about any spiritual revival. Instead of training their children in Christian theology, Protestant parents waffled around matters of religious truth; their children spent many more hours at Little League games or in front of the ubiquitous television set than they did at the family altar. Even worse, the suburban parents interviewed in surveys had little sense of participation in an ongoing tradition. As one mildly distressed Presbyterian father admitted, "I don't have any sense of carrying on anything."[68]

This should not have been a surprise to anyone. By the late 1950s many mainline Protestant church officials knew from a variety of surveys, publishers' statistics, and their own personal experience that the Christian family ideal was no longer workable. A 1959 survey of parents and churches, sponsored by the National Council of Churches, found "massive confusion" about the task of Christian formation. The format asked parents and Sunday school teachers to report children's frequently asked religious questions—a transaction that, to church officials, attested to woeful levels of theological ignorance on both sides. What emerged was a picture of parents using God "to help in day to day discipline problems," as a cosmic nanny from whom no child could ever escape. The God of the parents and children in this survey appeared chiefly interested "in how quickly children can get to bed at night and how successful they are in keeping their hands and faces clean."[69]

Other observers had reached a similar conclusion. Sociologist Peter Berger, writing in 1961, described Protestant nurture as "a process of religious inoculation, by which small doses of Christianoid concepts and terminology are injected into consciousness. By the time the process is completed, the individual is effectively immunized against any real encounter with the Christian message."[70] Putting matters in a slightly more optimistic light, Disciples of Christ official Richard Lentz concluded in 1960 that "nearly all church families admit that being Christian has not made them perfect. Christian faith has not eliminated problems for them, but in fact has created some additional ones."[71]

By the mid–1950s some insiders had already begun to lose faith in a "family piety that appeals only to the convinced, and reflects the concepts of a former generation."[72] In 1955 the Presbyterian Office of Family Education commissioned a comprehensive research project "to examine the place of the family in the whole life of the Church, and particularly in the teaching task of the home." Members of the research subcommittee (subsequently renamed the Committee on the Christian Home) affirmed the traditional importance of "atmosphere" in Christian nurture, but they worried that parents were not equipped to fulfill this task. In fact, they were beginning to wonder just how many Presbyterian families actually fit the intact nuclear model—indeed, they questioned whether, as one member confessed, "our assumptions about the family are valid." The committee even entertained the possibility that Presbyterians were "in some danger of overstating our conviction about the family."[73]

Three years later the survey data confirmed their doubts. On the one hand, statistics showed that Presbyterian families were doing well: they were considerably more stable, well-educated, and financially comfortable than the average, with 93 percent of those surveyed still in intact marriages.[74] But church officials still had reason to worry. When asked "what kinds of things do you want your children to remember about your family life when they grow up?" 86.2 percent of the parents' responses emphasized togetherness. "To me," one parent explained, "a good family life is a family which does things together, is happy while doing [them]." Only 17 percent made any reference to specifically Christian training. Most "identify Christian faith with congenial personal relationships," the interviewers reported unhappily. "One-hundred suburban parents, active church members, told us that the *family activities* which helped them grow *as Christians* were in order: recreation together and vacations, grace at meal time, and discussion of behavior problems in the family. Placed far down the list (in 12th and 15th place) were the activities which would lead a person to grasp the specific and historic events of the Christian faith." "Whatever the value of rituals," the report concluded, "it is apparent that, to these parents, passing a family tradition is far less important than freeing the children to create their own unique patterns of life which they might develop more fully when they are married." The group most likely to emphasize Christian "character training" were salesmen, who perhaps for occupational reasons valued the formation of disciplined habits.[75]

Most distressing to the researchers was the parents' pragmatic, instrumental view of the institutional church. To most of them faith was basically a means of achieving other ends: individual peace of mind, career success, social status, or family togetherness. As one parent struggled to articulate, "If you can have faith that things are going to work out all right, I think you can work toward better things." "There has to be a balance," another parent explained. "You can't be one-sided on anything . . . especially in modern-day living. You have to have some religion; you have to have some sports; you have to have some activities of all kinds and try to keep the thing balanced. That's our biggest problem, I think, trying to keep the children in things but not too much."[76]

Not surprisingly, the Committee on the Christian Home found the report deeply disheartening. Two family experts who examined the results described the parents in the survey as a "mildly depressed group . . . whose goals are confused, [and] who feel guilty about not achieving."[77] The committee might have used this evidence to reconsider the effectiveness of its past programs, though it did not. Members were most troubled about the administrative response to their report. At the Board of Education meeting in March 1959 the Office of Family Education Research presented twenty-one recommendations, including a request for a permanent family education office. After sitting on the report for nearly three years, however, the board approved only eight of the measures and another five partially. (One critic commented that all of the rejected proposals would have required extra travel or staff training.) Westminster Press also passed on an opportunity to publish the study, worrying that it might not sell.[78]

In fact, the report found an audience. Published by the Association Press in 1961, it sold eight thousand copies in its first two years. Heralded as a "major milestone in religious research," *Families in the Church* was adopted as a bonus book by the Religious Book Club and became the center of a gathering conversation among mainline Protestants about the viability of domestic religion.[79]

Within a very short time Protestant domesticity appeared to have reached its apotheosis and entered a sharp decline. By the early 1960s the private doubts of church officials had become a common perception. The time-honored Christian family rather suddenly became an idol, "an unsatisfactory god, too small and too disappointing," as one Baptist author declared. "Worship of the family is disastrous, worse than no worship at all."[80] Reasons for the reversal were complex, and many of them were obviously born of the rapidly changing social ethos of the 1960s. But the impetus for change was also rooted in the past, growing out of the complicated and contradictory array of Protestant notions about the family. By the mid–1950s some mainline Protestants had already concluded that this heritage was simply untenable. The events of the 1960s would help deepen that conviction.

	Mainliners, Evangelicals,
Chapter 6	and Family Religion

B‌Y THE EARLY 1960s scattered rumblings of doubt among Protestant denominational officials were clearly audible within the larger church, echoing the louder
reverberations of a culture in the throes of rapid transformation. Mainline Protestants' stance toward the family changed with dramatic swiftness. Once the hope
of American democracy, by the mid–1960s the middle-class home was the subject of Protestant lament, bearing the unwelcome stigma of a chronic social problem. Family relationships, at one time the solution to personal pain or spiritual
doubt, came to be seen as the underlying source of all such troubles. "The se-
verest test of Christian conduct," Roger Crook wrote in 1963, "is always within
the home." A Methodist seminary professor agreed, citing Karl Marx in support
of his observation that "the family has never given a very impressive demon-
stration of its willingness to prepare individuals for the broadest forms of cooperative social living." In his view the togetherness ethic had spawned a host of
neurotic, totalitarian, and hedonistic spinoffs, including a marauding tribalism
that "maintains strict togetherness as an expedient for mounting ever more effective exploitive raids on the outside community."[1]

Some critics took issue with the family orientation of the 1950s for being
escapist or politically reactionary. "In some instances," National Council of
Churches family life specialist William Genné wrote in 1966, "we are forced to
suspect that a 'family-centered' church uses this emphasis as an escape from involvement in other equally critical areas of Christian concern," including the
call to social action. "In other words," Peter Berger wrote, "to say that the
churches are linked intimately with the institution of the family to the exclusion

of other institutions is but another way of saying that the churches are impotent in our society."[2]

During the early 1960s a note of weary cynicism began to invade even the cheery pages of Christian family magazines. Writing in 1965, a Baptist woman perhaps spoke for many when she confessed: "Our pastors urge us to pray as families. Billboards glare at us as we drive by: 'The family that prays together, stays together.' All this adds to our frustration, and we keep our awful secret—our family does *not* pray together and we feel guilty."[3]

But by the 1970s even the awful secret was common knowledge. By then the *Christian Home* referred to the traditional family altar as simply "Family Night at Home." The Shalom Curriculum, introduced in 1972 into *A.D.* magazine (a joint United Presbyterian–United Church of Christ publication), offered a monthly lesson plan involving "election projects, posters, music, films, celebrations, toys, gifts, games, newspapers, TV, travel and stories."[4] "Most families find the old patterns of Bible reading and prayer, with everyone in his place, are impossible today," a Methodist laywoman declared in 1971, arguing that "the unsuitability of the inherited pattern for most people should not be a handicap" but "a chance for imagination and creativity." She advised a relaxed approach, letting religious talk arise naturally and without guilt or advance scheduling, with the parents providing "opportunities for discussion and clarification." A Baptist parent agreed: "Prayer is not a habit. It is an experience. When a family prays together it should be a spiritual adventure, not a routine obligation."[5]

At the denominational level institutional investment in the family was disappearing just as quickly as the venerable family altar. By 1975 the Methodist Church was devoting less than 3 percent of its annual budget to evangelistic and educational ministries, a category that included family programs. Other mainline Protestant institutions followed suit. The National Council of Churches did not hold any family life conferences between 1960 and 1991, and, according to one study, the percentage of articles in the *Christian Century* devoted to family-related topics (young people, marriage, divorce, and parenthood) fell by 55 percent between 1955 and 1995.[6]

An Elusive Diagnosis

Why did the family seem to drop so suddenly from mainline Protestant concern? Although even today many mainline congregations continue to emphasize the importance of families in their memberships, they may be acting more out of nostalgia for the 1950s than reflecting demographic reality. As sociologist Penny Marler argues, the golden era of family religion no longer exists, either spiritually or statistically.[7]

This change echoes in many ways a larger and more familiar tale, the precipitous decline of mainline church membership in recent decades. The numbers are sobering: between 1965 and 1985 United Methodist numbers dropped by 17 percent and membership in the United Church of Christ by 19 percent. The two largest Presbyterian bodies lost 28 percent of their members, and American Baptists 37 percent. Mainline decline looked even more alarming in comparison to the growth of evangelical churches. During the 1960s, 1970s, and 1980s smaller conservative denominations grew as quickly as mainline churches were shrinking: between 1960 and 1970, for example, the Assemblies of God grew by almost 23 percent.[8]

Describing these membership changes is much easier than diagnosing them. Sociologist Dean Kelley's influential book, *Why Conservative Churches Are Growing* (1977), argued that the lax membership standards and fuzzy doctrine of mainline churches were the source of their demise. Conservative churches prospered, Kelley argued, because they made challenging demands of their members, whereas joining a mainline church seemed hardly worth the trouble. But, as a growing number of sociological studies have pointed out, mainliners were not necessarily to blame for all of their problems; as the churches of the educated middle class, they bore the full brunt of decades worth of cultural upheaval.

Mainliners' shift from a domestic strategy certainly seems tied to the general disenchantment with the nuclear family in the decades after the 1960s. The statistics of family dissolution during the late 1960s and 1970s are now distressingly familiar. Between 1966 and 1976 the divorce rate doubled, reaching 50 percent. By the early 1970s the marriage rate began to plummet, reflecting decisions to delay marriage or to avoid it entirely; by 1980 the average age at marriage was two years higher than it had been in the 1950s. The birthrate declined accordingly and by 1973 fell below replacement levels, remaining low for the rest of the decade. By 1975 the typical family of the 1950s sitcom, with two parents, two children, and a nonworking mother, accounted for only 7 percent of all households. By 1980, 23 percent of all households were composed of single people. Mainline churches today dramatically reflect these changes: they are composed of more "empty nesters," single adults, and widows than the general population.[9]

And, of course, to a large degree these upheavals in family life were symptomatic of much larger, long-term problems. Robert Putnam and other scholars have uncovered a broad anti-institutional trend in the post–World War II generations, affecting membership levels in religious groups but also the rosters of Democrats, Republicans, Masons, Parent-Teacher Associations, and, as we now know, even bowling leagues. Institutional loyalties of every kind suffered as civic consciousness attenuated under the individualizing glare of television and computer screens. In contrast to their more civic-minded parents, the children of the 1950s, many of them raised in brand-new suburban neighborhoods and taught in large, impersonal high schools and colleges, did not create the same network of social loyalties that had sustained prewar generations.[10]

Within this context, the mainliners' strategic retreat from 1950s-style familism should hardly come as a surprise. They would have been hard-pressed to continue the child-centered ethos of the 1950s in the "Age of Aquarius." The suburban nuclear family—or, in Tom Wolfe's memorable dismissal, "Mom&Dad& Buddy&Sis, dear but square ones"—was both source and symbol of all that was wrong with conformist American society.[11] And, indeed, mainline church leaders did not need trained experts to point out the contradictions between the nuclear family ethos of suburban churches and the larger realities of family life in American society. Although in the 1950s more than 70 percent of American families were headed by a working father and a stay-at-home mother, by the 1980s only 15 percent of them fit that pattern. Some 40 percent of children born in the 1970s experienced their parents' divorce; by the 1980s one in every seven households with children were headed by at least one divorced and remarried parent. Mainliners could not fail to see that the divorced, blended, and extended families of the 1970s and 1980s no longer fit the old nuclear paradigm—and that the families of the poor never had. Social concern and family piety began to look nearly irreconcilable. When, in the wake of Lyndon Johnson's War on Poverty, mainliners began to venture into urban ghettos and rural Appalachian hollows, they faced the utter irrelevance of evening church programs for parents and children or cheerily phrased family devotionals. Suddenly, the realities of economic and political injustice—external givens that had never factored into Protestant discussions of family life—grew impossible to ignore.[12]

Perhaps the cruelest realization of the 1960s and 1970s was the apparent failure of 1950s-style family religion to produce a new crop of adult church members. During the 1960s and 1970s mainline churches were particularly vulnerable to the rising tide of American individualism within the culture of higher education. Colleges and universities grew exponentially in the 1960s: enrollment figures increased by 139 percent during that decade, as the proportion of young adults in college grew from 22.3 percent in 1960 to 35.2 percent by 1970. Social consequences soon followed. Opinion polls soon revealed that this "new class" of college-educated Americans was discernibly more liberal on moral and social questions than the general public. They were more skeptical about religious truth claims and were reluctant to join churches. Typically, mainline churches boasted higher proportions of college-educated members than the general population and certainly more than conservative denominations; in the 1960s, however, this trend began to change. Increasing numbers of evangelical Protestants begin to attend college, tripling their proportional share between 1960 and 1972, when they arrived at virtual parity with the general public. And the college-educated children of the mainliners were less and less likely to return.[13]

During the late 1960s and 1970s religious loyalties declined the most sharply among the college educated. Many of these were cradle roll members of mainline churches who had dropped out of any religious affiliation whatsoever. By the 1990s only 39 percent of children raised in mainline churches had stayed active in them.[14] The changing demographic of mainline churches was soon evident: by the late 1980s, 43 percent of members in the United Church of Christ were age fifty or older, and only 21 percent were under thirty-six. Other mainline denominations reported similar figures, particularly startling alongside the fact that by this time nearly 40 percent of the U.S. adult population was between eighteen and thirty-four years of age.[15]

Was the growing restlessness among mainliners, particularly the young, attributable to the impact of second-wave feminism? Certainly, moderate to liberal Protestant support for the women's movement, including women's right to ordination, was markedly higher than that among conservative Protestant bodies. By the 1980s over half the students at many mainline seminaries were female, and, as they graduated, they began to make slow but increasingly visible inroads into their profession.[16] Feminism quickly became a lightning rod for religious disagreements and for the gathering perception that conservative churches were both antifeminist and pro-family and mainline Protestants were not. Indeed, within the "culture wars" ideology of the 1980s, support or opposition for feminism seemed to predict an individual's theological beliefs on a range of other issues. As one conservative churchwoman declared, "'Having a woman as pastor generally indicates a liberalism which denies the authority of Scripture.'"[17]

But, however true this perception of feminist influence in mainline churches, the movement did not bring about the downfall of the family. Although the number of families in mainline congregations dropped after the 1960s, the proportional share of families within them has not really changed. Moreover, as the previous chapter has shown, discomfort with Protestant familism emanated as much from lay people as it did from denominational officials. Mainline parents were restless about their churches' excessive concern for family religion a decade or more before the advent of second-wave feminism. This restlessness points to the importance of deeper historical reasons behind the decline of family religion in the 1960s. The changes of the 1960s were a long time coming, evidencing not so much a dramatic decline as a "natural, overdue adjustment to the facts of American life"—and several facts in particular.[18]

Mainline Protestants entered the 1960s poorly equipped to maintain their culturally centrist role. One of the first indications of trouble was the 1963 Supreme Court decision against prayer in public schools. For decades Protestants had assumed a close relationship between public school instruction and Christian morality. Students in many districts received regular instruction in "moral guidance" from the Bible, a curriculum that sometimes included daily devotions and Scripture memorization as well. To many parents the *Abington v. Schempp* decision represented a "fantastic nightmare" and certainly a challenge to the long-standing tripartite alliance of Protestant homes, schools, and churches. "Like spoiled children who have seen only one side of a coin," one mother wrote in 1966, "we refused to believe that the other side might be brighter." After thinking things over, however, she decided the separation of church and state was a "priceless gift" and a stimulus to more purposeful religious observances at home. Yet in a real sense the school prayer decision symbolized the changing status of mainline religion in American society and its unmistakable estrangement from the centers of cultural power. As one Presbyterian official mused in 1964, "Only lately has the church been forced to some awareness of this fact and its implications." The election of a Roman Catholic president in 1960 was a "blow to the Protestant ego" that was "repeated with staggering force" by the Supreme Court decision in 1963. "The church as a whole has not yet recovered from these blows," he concluded, "and yet the blows themselves did nothing more than make vividly clear the facts of the situation."[19]

In spite of its rosy public image, 1950s-style Protestant domesticity was never as strong as it appeared. If anything, the Christian family ideology was one of the more vulnerable parts of the mainline Protestant consensus, overburdened with expectations and constantly susceptible to changing cultural norms, new social science categories, and the latest views on middle-class child rearing. Protestant domesticity proved particularly sensitive to cultural change, at least partly because of its relatively weak ties to theological or biblical church traditions. Although Bushnell's Christian nurture theology had initially provoked intense theological discussion, once the ideal became absorbed into middle-class Protestant culture, it passed beyond serious dispute. For a century or more the Christian family ideal bobbed along like a cork on modern social currents, with no natural protection from rough seas. The rapid changes in the 1960s brought a long-overdue, perhaps inevitable, day of reckoning.

Evangelicals appeared to profit from the 1960s ethos—and mainliners did not—largely for historical reasons. To begin with, the times demanded a new language, one that unapologetically addressed two seemingly disparate concerns—in simple terms, theology and sex. In both of these areas mainliners were at a historical disadvantage, unused to addressing either head-on. But evangelicals, long attuned to both of these issues, were uniquely poised to benefit from the rapid cultural changes brought on by the 1960s ethos.

THEOLOGY

The story of Presbyterians in the late 1950s and early 1960s is especially helpful here. The previous chapter left them engaged in serious soul-searching, their concern prompted by the distressing results of the research the Committee on the Christian Home had sponsored in the late 1950s. In October 1957 the Office of Family Education Research sponsored a small, three-day symposium for nineteen participants on "theology and the family." The group of leading Protestant theologians heard presentations by Gibson Winter and Robert Lynn, already emerging critics of Protestant family piety, as well as a paper on "The Doctrine of the Church and the Contemporary Family" by Robert Clyde Johnson and Walter E. Wiest, two theologians from Western Seminary.[20]

The wide-ranging discussion that accompanied the presentations revealed significant areas of doubt about the Christian family ideal. It soon became apparent that the group could neither agree on a definition of a Christian family nor locate crucial differences with non-Christian ones. The conferees agreed that churches still needed to maintain the support of homes to reinforce lessons taught in Sunday school, but they were not sure which institution held the primary responsibility for nurturing children. A discussion of biblical material on families proved similarly inconclusive: the conferees agreed that, although the Old Testament seemed to value family relationships within the nation of Israel, the

New Testament material seemed to imply that family ties were less important than those between fellow Christians. The group's concern for biblical texts even led them into a long and intense discussion of the role of women, in light of Paul's New Testament directives to husbands and wives. Although they were not all ready to uphold a norm of wifely subordination, the group could hardly be accused of sympathy to feminist concerns, agreeing that the "50–50" democratic family model was both impractical and unscriptural.[21]

But the last paper, by Johnson and Wiest, proved the most consequential to the ongoing Presbyterian discussion about families. It opened with the authors' startling assertion that they could find no theological justification for the entire edifice of Protestant family religion. Their historical survey of Protestant thinkers had not unearthed any serious theological reflection about the family or its "intended structure, its problems and values, its proper relationship to the church and state, and its function in the drama of redemption." Many theologians past and present had written on marriage and its sacramental nature, but very few had looked at the family. "The truth of the matter," Johnson and Wiest argued, "is that it is by no means self-evident that there is, or that there should be, a direct theological connection between the church qua church and the family qua family." They were willing to posit the family as a divinely ordained "order of creation," a medium in which Christians might live out their faith in the world, but they did not see the family as in any sense redemptive, and certainly not as an instrument of the church. In other words, Johnson and Wiest found no theological warrant for deputizing the family in any task that rightfully belonged to the institutional church, including the religious education of children.[22]

Over the next several months the Committee on the Christian Home struggled to assimilate what it had heard. A meeting in January 1958 found them in serious discussion, ready to conclude that their past emphasis on family ministries had been entirely wrongheaded. "We have idolized marriage and family life in this Board," one of the members declared. "This is our Baalism!"[23] In April the Committee on the Christian Home met again with Johnson and Wiest. Johnson urged them to "frankly acknowledge that the family is outside the Church" and to "be prepared to accept all of the theological and practical consequences of this acknowledgement no matter how many cherished twentieth century American feelings for sentimentality it has trampled on. We cannot . . . assume in any covert unspoken way that the family mediates, or the family conveys salvation or some unique grace." The committee members were quick to see the practical implications of this position, especially as it challenged the privileging of family religion over individual experiences of the sacred. One member, who was prepared to broaden the definition of a family to include "any human relationship," even suggested that the best religious formation probably occurred outside of a child's home experiences. "Family education," he suggested, might even require that parents stop trying to influence a child's religious beliefs. "In radical terms," Wiest agreed, "it's part of your function to help him lose his faith," or, as Johnson put it, "to let the family disintegrate."[24]

Spurred by their growing uneasiness, in 1961 Presbyterians appointed a task force to revise the Christian Faith and Life Curriculum. The church-home collaboration was at the center of the task force's concern, for its members immediately saw, as one report phrased it, that "it is no longer realistic to see the family as a dependable agent of the church's teaching." "Every time we attempt to define the Christian way of family life," another member agreed, "it has gotten us into trouble because we live in a diverse period of culture—there are different styles and patterns of family life."[25]

The unavoidable conclusion, publicized in an official bulletin in November 1964, was that "the church cannot delegate the responsibility for the teaching of its members to any other group or agency, including the family." Memorandum correspondence between two Presbyterian officials about this statement is revealing: one objected to the statement for "writing off" the family "as a viable source or agency for church education" and expressed his desire to redouble existing efforts to "bring home and church into a more meaningful partnership." In reply his colleague argued that not only was the Christian Faith and Life model of family involvement unnecessarily cumbersome, but "the picture of the family in CFL" was "crashingly middle class" and hardly relevant to "the lower class Negro subculture in our society." If Presbyterians wanted to have any integrity in their social witness, their attitudes about the family would have to change. His colleague was forced to agree.[26]

The dissonance between Presbyterian family life education and the direction of society was difficult to ignore. As one Presbyterian official admitted in 1964, "Everytime we attempt to define the Christian way of family life it has gotten us into trouble." The curriculum was "simply impossible" to apply in diverse cultural settings, "even when the language is not a problem," as in "the inner city or in Southern Appalachia."[27]

After a century or more of placing faith in Christian parents, Presbyterians seemed finally resigned to the fact that they needed professionals to step in and do the job correctly. In January 1965 Lee Edwin Walker, assistant general secretary

of the Board of Christian Education, addressed the Presbytery of Pittsburgh on
"Church Education in the Decade of the Seventies," arguing that the Christian
Faith and Life model was in need of fundamental revision. At best, he observed,
only 30 percent of parents had participated in the program. "Maybe the time
has come for the church to say in effect the same thing that public school education has said. . . . 'Don't bother to teach your children the new math, for you
will only confuse them. We will teach them.'"[28]

By early February 1966 the Board of Christian Education was confident in
its conclusion that "the home should *not* be used as an agency in a process of
formal instruction." The board's report began with Johnson and Wiest's argument that "nothing in Scripture or in traditional theological literature would
seem to demonstrate that the family is related to the church except through the
baptism and faith of the individual members of the family." Family was not, therefore, to be a special means of grace but one aspect of a Christian believer's life
in the larger world. It was thus the responsibility of the church, not parents, to
provide "regular and systematic instruction about the Christian faith." Indeed,
the family could not even act as a partner in such instruction but was, more
properly, "a recipient of the church's ministry." As part of this new allocation of
responsibilities, the church would also deal with larger social issues affecting families, including "sexual ethics, marriage and divorce" and "the relationship of the
family to the community."[29]

In the 1960s the focus of concern in mainline churches passed from children to adults. Caught in a world posing increasingly complex and difficult questions about the Christian faith, religious educators wanted to guide students
toward more sophisticated critical thinking. "It is an adult search," one Presbyterian official explained, "although children also share in it. But seen in its adult
character, the search is a challenge to those who are prepared to be adults, and
to engage in every discipline and enter into every inquiry." The times required
freedom of thought, not child-oriented didacticism, even in its most inoffen-
sive forms. "The teacher does not talk *about* Bible or theology," the official
continued, "but initiates the student into the material itself—with complete
openness toward the questions, problems, and meanings. This eliminates the element of the doctrinaire, or of propaganda or even propagation. Instead, matters Christian are to be studied with complete freedom."[30]

When Presbyterians began to investigate the theological basis behind their
family programs and came up empty-handed, they did not, as they might have,
immediately begin constructing one. Part of the reason was a lack of organiza-

tional follow-through, perhaps occasioned by the institutional changes wrought by the 1958 merger and the formation of the United Presbyterian Church U.S.A. But the memos, correspondence, and meeting minutes themselves communicate a growing sense of weariness around family programs, fast becoming an institutional war horse, as in the outside world, the times continued to press swiftly forward.

SEX

The early 1960s were important for mainline Protestant families in another way: the children of the baby boom were becoming teenagers. Between 1960 and 1970 the number of eighteen- to twenty-four-year olds in the United States grew by over 50 percent, more than all the previous decades of the twentieth century combined. The new generation came of age in a world very different from the one their parents had known. Whereas only 38 percent of the pre–World War II generation graduated from high school, 75 percent of baby boomers did so; half of those high school graduates went on to college, even though two-thirds of their fathers had not. Anthropologist Margaret Mead compared the baby boomers and their parents to immigrants arriving in a new country. Change had occurred so rapidly after World War II that both generations were struggling to adapt to a world of televisions and Sputnik satellites. But, even so, the children, the firstborn in the new country, experienced change far differently than their parents. The post–World War II generation had never known any other kind of life, and those born before the war may have wondered what knowledge they possessed that their children would ever find useful.[31]

Protestant family magazines recorded some of the growing intergenerational confusion. In 1960 a mother writing in *Hearthstone* magazine confidently declared, "You Can Talk with Your Teenager!" "Every young person needs to feel important in his own home," she explained, urging parents to "fashion a permissive household atmosphere so their teenagers can feel free to discuss values and doubts, and be counseled calmly, slowly, and understandingly by loving parents." Indeed, a conjoining article on teenage independence advised: "If parents fight this, they will be fighting the young people and their growth. They will become part of the teen-ager's problem rather than a trusted partner to whom he can come for understanding of and help with his problems."[32]

But within a few years even such a limited parent-child consensus seemed all but impossible. *Hearthstone* began to run articles urging parents to give their teenagers maximum freedom in matters of faith, without even the most limited forms of parental oversight. "Young persons need to find and be themselves," a parent wrote in 1963, "and do what seems to them consistent with their own integrity. About things like smoking and churchgoing, wise parents will explain alternatives and set an example rather than give orders. They will invite and assist, but not coerce." "For us to deny our children their freedom and the chance to look at the world with their own eyes," another father agreed, "is to thwart God, who may want that child to see what his parents have refused or cannot see." He urged parents to love their children unconditionally, as Christ loved humanity, not denying a child "his right to be, up to a point, self-centered and independent." The problematic nature of this advice was not hard to detect. "One gets the impression," an academic observer noted in 1965, "that . . . theological liberalism has been so individualistic, so hesitant to impose rules and regulations upon people, that the youth in these churches get little guidance at all. Much of the literature written from this perspective is fuzzy, ambiguous, and couched with so many qualifications that one is not always sure what conclusion, if any, is intended."[33]

Few parents reported much success with the hands-off approach. A Methodist couple's story, written in 1976, suggests some of its increasingly tragic difficulties. Ten years earlier their "happy, well-adjusted" fraternal twins, Don and Marilyn, had left for college at California universities. "Gradually it became evident that our two bright and energetic 18-year-olds were adopting the garb, language, and habits of what was then called the 'hippie' culture," their mother recalled. "Charles and I felt certain that the transformation was temporary—a campus fad." But these changes were to be permanent and also a source of painful domestic conflict. Don and Marilyn's visits home became occasions for criticisms of their parents' "ticky-tacky" house and "8–5 employment trap" and "usually ended in heated arguments and abrupt departures." After years of conflict the family finally agreed to disagree. The parents took up new hobbies, plumbed the Bible for wisdom, and worked toward acceptance of their children's unconventional lifestyles. Of course, as the mother admitted, "Our new attitudes towards the twins are rarely tested directly, since we see them only occasionally." But those visits were generally successful, since "keeping the conversation on a positive key no longer requires the effort it used to take." "I am sure," she concluded, "that both Marilyn and Don sense our sincerity and realize that our attitudes have changed."[34]

The element of parental risk that Christian nurture theology had been designed to mitigate now appeared to be returning in force. "We learn about hundreds of Hippies who have come from some of the 'better' homes," one parent exclaimed, wondering how children from such painstakingly loving Christian families could fall so deeply between the cracks. Indeed, mainline parents in the 1960s and 1970s, who watched their children's rapid departure from traditional religion, might have felt a certain kinship with the nineteenth-century family of the doomed Aaron Burr.[35]

Clearly, the traditional focus in mainline Protestant child rearing on young children and infants did not serve the churches well in dealing with teenagers. Nor did the assumption that religious faith grew naturally, needing only quiet parental encouragement to blossom; by the mid–1960s the seed metaphor seemed exactly wrong. In the popular imagination, if not in reality, adolescence had become a time of wrenching transitions, when well-adjusted children transformed overnight into rude and hostile strangers.[36]

The inherent tensions within mainline Protestant nurture, already evident in Bushnell's day, became impossible to ignore in the 1960s and 1970s. Middle-class families had long served as incubators of American individualism but within an atmosphere of togetherness. "Like other core elements of culture," Robert Bellah wrote, "the ideal of a self-reliant individual leaving home is nurtured within our families, passed from parent to child through ties that bind us together in solitude as well as love." Parents who had urged their children to find their own spiritual paths could hardly object when they did exactly that.[37]

The Bushnellian focus on young children had also prevented mainline Protestants from dealing with the rigors of adolescent sexuality. To be sure, marital advice books often included discussions on sex, however euphemistically. As one booklet on "The Christian Family," advised in 1924, "Like the first flight around the world, marriage must be the great adventure; manifestly it cannot so become if the flying equipment is hopelessly ruined on its trial trip."[38] But the subject of "adolescent temptations" rarely surfaced in sermons or church literature. In 1931, following publication of an interdenominational study guide that appeared to encourage exchange of ideas by young people on sex-related topics, General Secretary of the Federal Council of Churches Samuel McCrea Calvert issued a quick public denunciation. "The idea that young people should be encouraged to make problems of sex the subject of public discussion or debate," he indignantly declared, "is one which I emphatically repudiate."[39]

The 1950s brought a growing awareness of adolescent sexuality within American culture, if not in mainline Protestant churches. Unsettling images of juvenile delinquency, Elvis Presley, and teenage boys in tight jeans and T-shirts

stalked the middle-class imagination, reinforcing the reality that the mobile entertainment culture of the postwar era was removing young people from regular
parental oversight.[40]

In 1958 John Charles Wynn, chairman of the National Council of Churches
Committee on Family Life, called for a national conference to "boldly cut
through traditional silences" among American Protestants and to open a
long-overdue discussion on sex. Under his leadership the North American Conference on the Church and Family Life, held in the spring of 1961, included
over five hundred invited participants, nearly all of them representing local and
national church committees on family life. Three months before convening, the
delegates received a conference workbook, "Sex Ways in Fact and Faith: Bases
for Christian Family Policy," which contained sixteen chapters written by family life specialists; in his own preparation for the conference Wynn amassed sixty
years worth of church pronouncements about sexuality and assembled them as
an additional chapter in the workbook.[41]

In his conference presentation Wynn summed up his findings. He reported
no shortage of church literature about family life, dating, child rearing, and the
family altar—but precious little about birth control, sexual ethics, or family conflict. Wynn characterized the multitude of pamphlets, resolutions, and pronouncements as "depressingly platitudinous," assuring "ad nauseam that the
family that prays together stays together, without a glimmer of criticism to that
claim. Yet every pastor who does any marriage counseling at all (and that means
all pastors) knows of families who have prayed earnestly and still have come
apart." Wynn was openly critical of what he termed the heretical "works-
righteousness" of Christian family literature: "You know how it runs—if only
the family will accomplish the following works: daily Bible reading, prayer and
mealtimes, tithing, and kindness to stray dogs, then their household will be as-
suredly Christian!" While Wynn allowed that the subjects before the conference were "distasteful" to many, he urged more openness. "If we are ever to move
beyond the comfortable, often dull, discussions we have about table graces and
family recreation to the place that we can deal in Christian concern with the
problems that affect our people, the week before us will be of real aid." Wynn's
hope for candid discussion rested on some changes already in process, including
new theological attention to sexuality, insights from the field of social psychology, and dialogue between Catholics and Protestants about contraception. Wynn
also cited a range of denominational pronouncements on birth control, abortion, homosexuality, and divorce. "Some of you here take for granted a rather

easy communication on the subjects that others find taboo," he continued. "But without an open inquiry of the problems that plague our times, the church could grow even less relevant than it is."[42]

The conference proceedings promised, and provided, a full and frank discussion of difficult topics. During the daytime delegates heard reports on mixed marriages, pregnant brides, illegitimacy, masturbation, homosexuality, family planning, and abortion. In the evening they participated in hymn sings and heard more presentations on family camping, marriage counseling, moving pictures, and sex education. Nevertheless, by the end of the week the undoubtedly weary delegates produced a number of joint statements and suggestions for the larger church. They defined the role of the church as a "redemptive fellowship— friendly, non-judgmental, forgiving, accepting"; they urged including sex education in the Christian education curriculum, greater acceptance of single people, and a reevaluation of marriage and sex "in light of biblical theology and scientific findings," issuing in a "positive Christian ethic on sexual behavior which will be relevant to our culture."[43]

Paralleling the shift in religious education, the family life agenda was moving imperceptibly but steadily from a primary focus on the needs of young children to the concerns of adults. The many denominational pronouncements of the late 1960s and 1970s on divorce, homosexuality, and premarital sex rarely included children in the ethical equation but emphasized adult self-expression and personal fulfillment. The shift in focus opened the way for increasingly radical conclusions. In 1970 a controversial Presbyterian report concluded that "sexual expression with the goal of developing a caring relationship is an important aspect of personal existence and cannot be confined to the married and the about-to-be-married." Although the committee affirmed celibacy as a "valid option for those who adopt it voluntarily," they questioned "whether society has the right to impose celibacy or celibate standards on those who do not choose them." The sexuality study emphasized the church's "obligation to explore the possibilities of both celibate and non-celibate communal living arrangements as ethically acceptable and personally fulfilling alternatives for unmarried persons."[44] Although the average pew sitter hardly shared these conclusions, most had difficulty articulating their objections. Moderate mainliners were hardly more tolerant of premarital and extramarital sex, homosexuality, and abortion than the general population, though levels were discernibly higher among the most liberal of the mainline, the United Church of Christ, Episcopalians, and Presbyterians.[45]

The sexual anarchy of the 1960s challenged mainline Protestants where they were most vulnerable. Decades of careful attention to parents and young children, and a relatively unquestioned faith in the middle-class home, left a void around more complex theological issues of sex and family life. Mainline Protestants came into the 1960s open to charges of simplistic familism and a decided ineptitude with teenagers. Educators and parents rushed to atone for these omissions but within a growing atmosphere of cultural panic over the dissolution of families and a spiraling sexual revolution. In the rising din their voices began to falter and very nearly disappear.

The Pro-Family Movement

In January 1978, President Jimmy Carter announced his intention to begin a "national dialogue" on the state of the American family. The conversation was to center in a series of three regional White House conferences in Baltimore, Minneapolis, and Los Angeles. Discussion was to be civil and constructive, presenting delegates with a variety of concerns and engaging representatives from a wide array of American families.[46] Reality, however, turned out differently. By the time of the Baltimore conference, in the summer of 1980, trouble was already brewing. Conservative Protestant and Catholic groups, led by a core of new leadership from the nascent Christian Right, had begun organizing their members for a confrontation. Even before the delegates met, conservative groups had emphatically objected to a change in the conference title from a singular noun ("A White House Conference on the American *Family*") to a plural noun, arguing that only the two-parent nuclear model fit the true definition. In their view unmarried parents, cohabiting couples, and, in particular, homosexual partnerships did not constitute families. Conservative delegates were also convinced that the conference was stacked in favor of a liberal agenda of substituting government initiatives for the traditional functions of the family in child raising, education, and health care. Many were also deeply concerned about abortion, to the point that conference leaders feared that the issue would co-opt the rest of the proceedings. But this never happened. On the second day of the conference some thirty delegates from conservative groups walked out of the meeting to dramatize their anger and to demonstrate their unity.

Later that summer the American Family Forum convened the first national gathering of the "pro-family movement" in Washington, D.C., marking the emergence of evangelical Protestants as the new protectors of the Christian home.

Although the New Right agenda included many Roman Catholics and conservative Jews, evangelicals rushed to embrace family issues with particular enthusiasm. In 1982 the National Association of Evangelicals celebrated its fortieth year with a three-day convention entitled "Save the Family." The delegates passed a resolution decrying the rising incidence of single-parent families, teenage pregnancies, and rootless, undisciplined children—all "the fruits of a 'secular humanism' that teaches 'self-gratification as life's highest goal'" and encourages a "moral relativism that leaves parents unable to teach their children moral and spiritual absolutes."[47] By the end of the 1980s few contested their leadership; preservation of the family had become a rock-bottom conservative issue and central to a constellation of other hot-button concerns, including abortion, homosexuality, and feminism. Conservative evangelicals became known for their devotion to parenting, homeschooling their children in increasing numbers, subscribing to Christian family magazines, and supporting a growing alternative "Christian" market of toys, games, music, and entertainment videos.[48]

Certainly, evangelicals were not the first to politicize the middle-class family or to recognize its power as unifying national symbol. Late-nineteenth-century Protestant missionaries, temperance reformers, and social purity campaigners had already done so with considerable success. During the 1940s and 1950s the Christian family occupied a hallowed position in American civil religion. But the emergence of an evangelical pro-family movement was riddled with historical ironies. To a large degree evangelicals became pro-family to demonstrate that they were no longer cultural outsiders. Although they employed a familiar rhetoric of alienation and conflict, they had no intention of resuming a fundamentalist-style separatism. Evangelicals recognized, correctly, that, as protectors of the Christian family, they might well assume a central role in the larger civilizing mission of American culture. The problem, of course, was in the timing. Evangelicals assumed the pro-family mantle just as demographic and social pressures began to destroy the very notion of a mythic Christian family. The cultural spotlight they sought soon became an arena of intense and bitter controversy.

Still, the fact that such issues generated powerful emotional reactions was not necessarily a deterrent to many evangelical leaders. In the 1970s and 1980s the controversial pro-family agenda provided the movement with something it had consistently lacked—clear boundary markers. Throughout the twentieth century religious conservatism had proved to be an unstable mixture, frequently rent by disputes over eschatology and biblical interpretation. Although the modern evangelical movement that emerged in the 1950s was partially rooted in old-style fundamentalism, it was not a single denomination, nor did it share a common heritage. As a loose coalition of cobelligerents, evangelicalism had no central core constituency, incorporating reconstructed fundamentalists as well as Pentecostal and holiness groups and an array of conservative Baptist and Presbyterian churches. Not surprisingly perhaps, the late 1970s saw an intensifying debate about the exact definition of *evangelical*, in many cases pitting Reformed and Wesleyan conservatives into two seemingly irreconcilable camps. Pillar doctrines such as biblical inerrancy failed to unite, especially as the infrastructure of evangelical parachurch institutions grew rapidly in many different directions. In the 1980s the pro-family agenda promised, and provided, evangelicals new unity and purpose: in an astonishingly short time conservative Christians flocked toward a consensus around family-related matters such as abortion and feminism. To be evangelical was no longer just to believe certain doctrines but to follow a distinctive social and moral agenda.[49]

The rapid rise of the evangelical pro-family movement was, of course, a bit counterintuitive. Despite the quick progress of pro-family rhetoric among evangelicals, public concern for the family was not normative for conservative Protestants.[50] Although evangelicals and even some fundamentalists had happily participated in 1950s-style Protestant domesticity, they had viewed the family as primarily a moral issue, not a political or social one. Moreover, as heirs of American fundamentalism, evangelicals had tended to take a fairly shallow view of the family, especially in the face of more pressing eschatological concerns.

Before World War II, fundamentalist and evangelical parents had relatively little family advice literature; that which existed was by and large fairly wooden in approach, emphasizing the importance of order and submission to authority. Family was important as a hedge against secularism and early religious training of children largely a means of protecting them from temptations in later life. "In only a few short years," a fundamentalist mother of a young toddler wrote in 1938, "you and I shall have to send our boys and girls out into a world with all sorts of temptations, where they will meet a pagan philosophy of life. If they ever needed good, early training it is at present." "Surely," she concluded, "if we have followed the plan laid down in the Word of God we shall have nothing to fear" (see fig. 4).[51]

One of the first sources of advice for fundamentalist parents was evangelist John R. Rice, who published a popular handbook on the Christian home in 1948. Rice advised a strictly hierarchical approach to family interaction, in vivid contrast to the relational emphasis among mainline Protestants. (He was perhaps

Figure 4. The fundamentalist home under siege (Sunday School Times, 8 December 1934).

best known for his previous book, *Bobbed Hair, Bossy Wives, and Women Preachers* (1941), in which the title captured the essence of his argument.) "All sin," Rice argued repeatedly in his periodical, *The Sword of the Lord,* "can be traced to rebellion against authority, the authority of parents, the teacher, the husband, the boss, the government, and the authority of the Bible and God." Rice advised parents not to be afraid to employ corporal punishment, for "the child will get far tougher treatment at the hands of the world."[52]

In the mid–1960s Rice's heir, evangelist Bill Gothard Jr., began conducting a series of public lectures on family relationships that eventuated in a popular seminar series on "Basic Youth Conflicts." Both Rice and Gothard emphasized the importance of obedience and submission, on the part of both children and wives. Gothard, in particular, preached a "chain of command" extending from God through husbands to their families. In an age of widespread teenage rebellion Gothard stood firm on the need for obedience to all forms of authority, pointing out that "Jesus could have forsaken His parents at the age of 12 on the basis of needing to be about His Father's business. Instead He became subject to His parents until His public ministry began at the age of 30."[53]

In 1977 Church of the Nazarene child psychologist James Dobson began the Focus on the Family organization to provide a Christian alternative to secular child-rearing literature. Dobson's approach emerged in response to the egalitarian, interactive models of child discipline popular in the 1970s. In his popular book *The Strong-Willed Child*, he explicitly rejects the nonauthoritarian approach of secular experts such as John Holt, Benjamin Spock, and Haim Ginnott: "I find no place in the Bible where our little ones are installed as co-discussants at a conference table deciding what they will and will not accept from the older generation."[54] After his first book, *Dare to Discipline*, appeared in 1970, Dobson became convinced of the need for Christian families to take a stand and organize. During Focus on the Family's early days his "greatest encouragement," Dobson said, came from "wives and mothers who believed in traditional values, and yet were not hearing the things I was saying within the books they were reading and the television shows they watched."[55] By the time of the White House conference in 1980 Dobson's organization was sponsoring a popular series of films based on his books (which reached ten million viewers) and airing a daily radio program going out to one hundred stations, soon to be four hundred. *Dare to Discipline* had sold over a million copies. Office staff answered some fifty thousand letters a week and offered referrals to a network of twelve hundred professional therapists. In 1994 Focus on the Family began an outreach to single parents (*Single Family Magazine*) while networking with family organizations around the world, from Japan to Central America.[56]

Dobson's leadership in New Right causes, which followed on the heels of his organizational success, has often obscured his more mundane role as a prominent evangelical father figure. His radio program and monthly newsletters have exerted vast influence over popular evangelical approaches to euthanasia, abortion, and homosexuality. Still, Dobson's phenomenal success in shaping an evangelical family agenda reflects the way in which evangelical strengths have neatly complemented mainline Protestant weaknesses. By the 1980s Dobson and a host of other conservative Protestants had no difficulty using theological language to talk about the family, and they also had no problem addressing issues around sex.

THEOLOGY

Evangelical theologizing about families originated in a long-standing concern about the role of women. In the early twentieth century, old-style fundamentalists may have felt few affinities with domestic Christianity, but they did care deeply about gender differences. Maintaining clear standards of masculine and feminine identity was part of an ongoing quest for ordered certainties in an increasingly relativistic age.[57] While the fundamentalist tradition did not sentimentalize motherhood, it did insist that women were intrinsically better suited to bear primary responsibility for the home. Mothers, far more than fathers, were the final moral line of defense against secularism. "The Christian home needs constant, prayerful guarding against the infiltration of materialism and worldliness," a fundamentalist mother wrote in 1960, "and this is the mother's God-given task. It is she who should know what her children are reading, who should encourage them to form strong, pure, Christian character, and zealously guard them from the flood of salacious literature that endangers the morals of our nation."[58]

The evangelical movement of the 1970s and 1980s inherited a moralistic preoccupation with gender roles from its fundamentalist predecessors. Indeed, the late 1950s marked an intensifying of concern about hierarchy and order; in response to the growing formlessness of middle-class sexual mores, conservative Protestants began to insist all the more on the necessity of a wife's submission to her husband's authority. They had no doubt that this order was scriptural. "The normal Christian home," Charles Ryrie wrote in 1952, "consists of husband, wife, and children, each with his or her own particular place and responsibility." The husband was the head of the home, and thus "decisions concerning the Lord's will belong ultimately in the realm of the husband's authority; and although he may be guided along *with* his wife, he should not be guided *by* her."[59]

Fundamentalist and evangelical authors of the 1950s and 1960s were similarly convinced that the Bible offered clear theological guidelines for raising children. Good parenting required daily Bible reading, accompanied by "obedience to what the Scriptures teach."[60] Ryrie, for example, argued that Christian parents were obligated to follow the biblical model of physical punishment: "It is a very serious thing to tamper with these clear principles of the Word of God." Indeed, he declared, "as long as natural psychology and progressive education refuse to recognize the biblical teaching of the total depravity of every person born into the world, their guiding principles cannot be safe. . . . The Christian homemaker must be very careful to examine every principle of natural psychology he may intend to use, in the light of the revealed truth in the Word of God."[61]

From the 1940s onward, conservative Protestants uniformly insisted on the need for a family altar, primarily as a means of instilling biblical content. Thus, the Christian Home League, formed in 1946, enlisted volunteer teams of men to persuade church groups to hold home devotions. Through personal testimonies and evangelistic presentations they successfully enlisted thousands of pledges in the postwar era.[62] Fundamentalist periodicals were more interested in the family altar as an evangelistic tool than as a means of togetherness. Parents who spoke about God to their children "regularly, consistently, devotionally, earnestly, and daily" might hope to see that child saved. Moreover, parental demonstrations of obedience to God's commands were an important model to their children. "The Word in the hearts of the parents and the Word diligently taught the children," one author wrote, "form the substantial rock-bottom basis of disciplined, obedient children."[63]

Regular corporate devotions were not a requirement for truly Christian families. In the 1970s and 1980s evangelical family advice literature continued to insist on the importance of family worship, even though the advice itself took on a more jovial, fun-loving tone. Knowledge and daily application of the Bible's teachings remained the distinguishing characteristic of family truly devoted to God. "You would not think of letting your family go an entire day without food," a Baptist pastor admonished in 1976. "Surely it is even more vital that your family have daily spiritual food, for if your children are spiritually healthy, your grandchildren will also receive a proper spiritual diet. Yes, there is no better way to avoid 'a famine . . . of hearing the words of the Lord' than to establish daily family worship, and no better time to begin than now!"[64]

Fundamentalist and evangelical talk about families tended to be heavily rule oriented and simplistic, yet it was at the same time a popular theology, adding a much-needed religious dimension to the basically secular discourse of family life experts. Evangelical family literature also enabled religious conservatives to begin to take the lead in the escalating social debate, gaining at last the riveted attention of a culture they had once attempted to reject.

SEX

Despite the popular stereotype of fundamentalists as terrified of sex, their insistence on moralistic standards of behavior required them to address the topic frequently and explicitly. Beginning in the 1930s, fundamentalists also directed serious attention to the spiritual and physical needs of teenagers. Advice columns in fundamentalist periodicals regularly fielded questions from both men and women about a variety of sexual matters, albeit in appropriately veiled terms. The standard response was a warning against the "lust of the flesh" and the need for separation from the world. Even the most innocent forms of popular music, as one fundamentalist author explained, introduced the temptation "to dance, to drink, to be impure morally, or to sin in some other way." "If we are commanded to abstain from fleshly lusts (inordinate desires)," he counseled, "then by all means let us abstain from anything that would tend to excite or arouse such desires!"[65] In similarly exhaustive terms John R. Rice issued a popular broadside against the movies, arguing that "one who learns to delight in the murders, the embraces, the lewd scenes, the witty but dirty sayings, the love triangles, the bedroom scenes, the illicit romances, the drinking, the smoking, the unbelief, the divorces of the picture screen, will some day find the Word of God dull and dry and tasteless!"[66]

By the mid–1940s some fundamentalists had also begun a crusade to win the hearts of American teenagers. The Youth for Christ movement proved immensely important to the revitalization of old-style fundamentalism into a broader evangelical coalition. Recognizing the moral vulnerability of young people, postwar religious entrepreneurs adapted the jazzy rhythms of popular music into a national evangelistic crusade. Huge and entertaining youth rallies attracted thousands of American teenagers; by 1945 Youth for Christ leaders estimated a weekly attendance at rallies at 300,000 to 400,000. Youth for Christ proved not only a huge success with American teenagers; it also propelled separatist fundamentalism into a full-scale engagement into American culture.[67]

Not surprisingly perhaps, evangelicals came into the 1970s convinced that they held a distinct advantage over their secularized mainline cousins. "With the obvious crumbling of the foundations of the American home so visible today," Wheaton College president V. Raymond Stedman wrote in 1977, "thousands of young mothers and fathers are begging for help."[68] Indeed, in the absence of any alternatives, books by evangelical authors such as James Dobson soon appeared in the advertisement columns of liberal Protestant magazines and found their way into the libraries of mainline churches.

EVANGELICAL NURTURE

Upon closer inspection, however, many of these evangelical family experts were far closer to Bushnell than they might have realized. Even the most determined advocates of parental authority emphasized the importance of a healthy "Christian atmosphere" and pleasant childhood associations with evangelical religion. Like their mainline cousins, evangelicals still tended to define Christian living in terms of values rather than behavior and often came perilously close to equating godly living with proper etiquette. Beverly LaHaye, for example, reminded her readers that "there is a great need in the home to create an atmosphere where everyone's dignity is respected and where everyone's thoughts are listened to and valued." Moreover, she advised that "authoritarian statements should be used only as a last resort when all the reasons and explanations have failed."[69] Even a book entitled God, the Rod, and Your Child's Bod, appearing in 1982, described the Christian family as "that place where parents so live the Christian life and so practice the presence of Christ that the children grow up to naturally accept God as the most important fact in life."[70]

In many ways James Dobson has played a role similar to Bushnell's among twentieth-century evangelicals. While certainly not rejecting the necessity of conversion, Dobson has alerted evangelical parents to the environmental and psychological forces behind a mature religious faith. Most mainline Protestants, steeped for generations in a theology of human agency, would find much of Dobson's therapeutic talk relatively commonplace, yet, within an evangelical tradition dominated by John R. Rice and Bill Gothard, Dobson's child-centered approach came as a distinct step forward. In the 1970s evangelical child-rearing literature developed against a background of profound suspicion toward social science professionals, an attitude slowly mitigated by the increasing income and education levels of conservative Protestants. Thus, as one evangelical commentator grudgingly conceded in 1974, "None of the experts are dangerous in themselves. They only become problematic as they are distorted."[71]

Dobson's domestic theology employs therapeutic insights on behalf of religion in the home. Indeed, the whole thrust of Focus on the Family is to "turn hearts toward home" and to create early associations with evangelical Christianity that are warm and pleasant. Focus on the Family magazine regularly features attractive, well-groomed moms and dads, all relentlessly clean and brimming with good health. The virtues of self-denial and redemptive suffering do not figure as prominently as self-esteem and self-help. Indeed, a recent article entitled "Believe Well, Live Well" offered the somewhat startling claim that great sex "begins in church!" Christianity, the author declared, allows parents to "be emotionally supportive, [and] to communicate effectively," and it contributes to a "stable power structure" in the home. Supporting her conclusion with numerous opinion surveys drawn from secular self-help literature, the author echoed themes that, a half-century earlier, no liberal religious educator would have disagreed with.[72]

American middle-class parenting has always been suffused with a yearning for certitude, for greater spiritual control within a system governed by arbitrary chance. If anything, in the decades between 1840 and 1960 the number of random variables had increased dramatically: the stable tripartite alliance of church, home, and school had been gradually reduced to a thin partnership between home and church, both beset by moral and spiritual challenges from a rapidly decentralizing culture. In the 1970s and 1980s the evangelical child-rearing model offered a clear and compelling alternative to randomness, a trustworthy set of spiritual guidelines that promised demonstrable results. In a sense this evangelical literature was resuming a conversation about parenting initiated a century and a half before. At that time Bushnell's model of Christian nurture promised a more sure outcome than evangelical conversion could offer; now, however, in an increasingly "post-Christian" culture, certainty lay in a therapeutic reworking of the didactic, moralistic model that Bushnell's heirs had long ago decided against.

Yet in many ways evangelicals are also very much the heirs of Bushnell. Despite their often vehement disagreements with mainliners, evangelical child-rearing literature echoes many of the old themes within the mainline Protestant tradition—the redemptive value of Christian domesticity, the spiritual power of properly godly parents. Indeed, present-day evangelicals often appear to conflate Christian formation with middle-class socialization, and, like mainliners, they tend to construe the family's social agenda in very narrow terms. Evangelicals certainly share the anti-institutional bias of their more liberal Protestant cousins, and they have much the same difficulty articulating the purpose of the church-family partnership. Evangelicals tend to locate family issues within a highly complex array of parachurch organizations—lobby groups, social service outreach, and therapeutic agencies. Against this complicated background, parents and children are sometimes clients, sometimes constituents, sometimes themselves agents of outreach. Within this complex institutional tangle they might well ask a question that might have occurred to Protestants a century earlier: what, then, are churches for?

Chapter 7   Alternatives and Possibilities

THE STORY OF WHITE mainline Protestants is only one among many twentieth-century accounts of family and religious life. Without doubt it is an important one, if only by virtue of its proximity to significant theological and cultural themes of change in our time. But, told in isolation, the white mainline Protestant story too easily ends up as a simplistic cautionary tale, a moral lesson about the pitfalls of the past that sensible people in the present must take action to avoid. That is not my intention. I close with two brief, historically specific, alternative accounts of religion and the family, one from the Roman Catholic tradition and another African American Protestant. Stories from the past rarely offer unambiguous lessons, and most historians, myself included, do not offer moral applications eagerly. My purpose is not to valorize these groups at the expense of white mainliners nor to suggest that Catholics and black Protestants necessarily hold the best answers to the questions behind this book. The Roman Catholic and African American families discussed here were not necessarily more moral or statistically happier than those of white liberal Protestants. But "decentering" the mainline narrative opens the possibility for some illuminating comparisons, some of which may prove useful to future considerations of the church and family problem among white Protestants, of all theological persuasions.

For most of the twentieth century both Catholics and African American Protestants were decidedly nonmainstream religious groups, sidelined by various forms of social prejudice. An African past, as well as the twin ordeals of slavery and racial discrimination, shaped black American religion into an alternative form of spiritual consciousness. In less dramatic fashion Catholics were outsiders as well. Although they vastly outnumbered individual Protestant denominations and numerically dominated various regions of the country, years of Protestant domination had left a lingering sense of spiritual marginality: Roman Catholics thought and acted like a minority group even when demographics told them otherwise.

For both of these groups family played into a sense of otherness. The domestic ideology of white mainline Protestants was a complicated mixture of religious formation, middle-class socialization, and patriotic, civilizing ideals; groups outside the mainstream, however, had much more limited access to these cultural projects. Their domestic ideals could not, as with mainline Protestants, imperceptibly merge sacred into secular space; home in many ways remained a special location where both children and parents assembled necessary theological and spiritual equipment for engaging life's struggles. Family life could nurture an awareness of difference and teach both children and parents to maintain an authentic center within a morally contradictory or aggressively secular world.

The Christian Family Movement

The Christian Family Movement (CFM) in postwar Roman Catholicism aimed at nothing less than the "re-christianization of family life" and, by extension, American society itself. "Families not only must learn *how* to live a Christian life," as Gerard Weber wrote in 1951, "but something must be done to make it possible to live without demanding heroic sanctity."[1]

The goal of CFM was to reeducate the Catholic laity on the social dimensions of Christian family life. "An authentic lay spirituality," wrote William Nerin, Oklahoma state chaplain for CFM, "is simply this—to get a layman to see *all* of the world in which he lives, to see it as Christ does, and to act upon the world, as each man has some responsibility for it. . . . CFM tries to develop real *lay* people committed to this world."[2]

The Christian Family Movement emerged in the 1940s, alongside the Presbyterian Faith and Life Curriculum but within the larger framework of Catholic Action, a constellation of lay organizations pursuing Pope Pius X's exhortation to "restore all things in Christ." CFM began as a network of men's discussion groups in Chicago, headed by the well-known social reformer Monsignor Reynold Hillenbrand; women's groups formed alongside it, and eventually both merged into a couple's movement. Although the decision to discard the gender-segregated pattern was unprecedented, it followed logically from the members' commitment to bring their Christian allegiance to the smallest details of daily life.[3] In 1949 the Chicago groups joined with others from Notre Dame to form a national organization, headed by a young professional couple, Patty and Pat Crowley.[4] If numbers are any indication, the Christian Family Movement clearly met a need. By 1955 it had grown to include over six thousand couples in the United States and beyond. It would peak in the mid–1960s, numbering some forty to fifty thousand families.[5]

CFM was first and foremost a couples' movement but also committed to family renewal. Interestingly, CFM literature is relatively silent about the Christian formation of children, though it has much to say about marriage as a vehicle of spiritual growth. No doubt, this reflects the sacramental orientation of Catholic theology but perhaps also a conscious protest against the familism of the 1950s; the contrast with typically Protestant concerns is immediately obvious. For example, an article listing "Ideas for a Happier Family Life," written in 1957, devoted only a brief section to parent-child interaction and as much or more to sections on husband-wife and family-neighborhood-community relationships as well as the cultivation of Christian spirituality.[6]

CFM offered an experience of community to socially mobile young Catholics, and an occasionally radical sense of Christian purpose. Ralph Weissert, a veteran of the first chapter in South Bend, Indiana, stayed in the movement for over forty years because, as he said, it brought "a new awakening to what being a Christian really was."[7] CFM challenged Catholic parents and children to extend concern for family piety to a comprehensive vision of social justice. The heart of the movement was the parish-based couples group, which met biweekly to worship, to study, and to discuss ways in which each member could effect change on his or her own doorstep. Each meeting followed a set pattern, outlined in the CFM handbook, *For Happier Families*, emphasizing reading and study of the Scriptures and the liturgy and an open-ended, participatory discussion known as the "Inquiry."

The Inquiry adapted an educational philosophy and method from the work of Canon Joseph Cardijn, the Belgian leader of the Young Christian Worker movement in the 1920s and 1930s. Cardijn believed that social transformation happened most often "from like to like," through natural human associations, rather than through broad-based attempts to inform and inspire. He organized his workers into small homogeneous cell groups in which they followed a three-part process of social inquiry: first, studying the nature of the problems confronting them; second, realistically assessing the best means of immediate action; and, third, pressing for mutually agreed upon goals as a group. Hillenbrand, an admirer of Cardijn, helped popularize this educational method among American Catholics in the 1930s and 1940s.[8]

The "Jocist" method (taken from the French title of Cardijn's book *Jeunesse Ouvrière Chrétienne* [1938]) and its shorthand process, "observe, judge, act," proved a natural way of involving relatively well-educated and increasingly homogeneous suburban Catholics in social action. As Leo Ward explained, the cell group principle "means that people of like interests and like needs work together to Christianize each others' lives and (they hope) their environment."[9] Thus, one's suburban, middle-class associations, normally considered a telltale sign of religious indifference, could actually form the context for Christian acts of mercy.

CFM leaders believed that authentic religious formation of both individuals and families came about through actions motivated by Christian compassion. Spiritual reflection was important but not as an end in itself, nor was it a higher form of religious endeavor than work for social justice. As historian Jeffrey Burns explains: "The lay person grew spiritually, not by renouncing the world, but by accepting his or her position in the world, and performing faithfully the ordinary tasks of daily living. . . . An action carried out in an area of lay responsibility was a holy action and contributed to the personal holiness and formation of the lay man or woman who performed it."[10]

The theological underpinning of CFM, and of the larger Catholic Action movement, drew from an understanding of the church as the mystical body of Christ. Imported from European Catholicism and introduced to Americans in the intellectual renaissance generated by the Catholic publishing house of Sheed and Ward, the doctrine affirmed the integral role of the "lay apostolate" in the liturgy and in the work of the church in society. It also emphasized the need for Christian community as a counterforce to the selfish thrust of American materialism. "The enemy to be destroyed is individualism," Dennis Geaney wrote in a piece on CFM in 1956. "It can only be destroyed by a corporate spirituality, corporate worship, and a passionate desire to build real community at every level of life."[11] As Father Reynold Hillenbrand declared in 1945, "People the world over are sick of individualism, of being sundered from others, of the tragic loss which comes from thinking and acting alone. They are sick of individualistic, subjective piety because it lacks depth and vision. They are sick of the individualism that has undone so many homes."[12]

In the burgeoning world of postwar Catholic family and social outreach,

CFM was unique. It was the first national Catholic organization for husbands and wives together (who were traditionally separated into male and female sodalities), and, as Debra Campbell argues, it "represented a new phenomenon, an apostolate based in the homes of married Catholic couples."[13] American Catholicism, at least in comparison to mainline Protestantism, had invested relatively little in the family as a site of religious formation; godly Catholic parents were primarily expected to send their young to parochial schools for a sound religious education. Domestic spirituality tended to be private and devotional, often symbolized in the enshrinement of the Sacred Heart or a family rosary.

CFM, however, chose to tackle the problem of family irreligion in its larger, increasingly complicated social context. As the program book *The Family in a Time of Change* (1966) noted, most church publications on family life were "commendable but cozy, not addressed to the crucial questions but only to the 'trimmings'—charming customs, more togetherness for already secure families."[14] By the 1960s CFM leaders had begun to criticize not only national social welfare policy but church statements on birth control and what they saw as an irresponsible encouragement of large Catholic families. Although this stance exacerbated existing tensions with church hierarchy and kept the movement outside the Catholic mainstream, most CFM leaders saw it as the logical extension of their basic concern for family unity and spirituality.[15]

During the postwar era Catholicism was hardly in a mood for social critique. As Burns writes, "To Catholics the atmosphere of the 1950s seemed a Godsend—no one was more anti-communist or pro-family than [they were]."[16] Never before had the traditional social conservatism of Catholic subculture seemed so up-to-date and almost fashionable. To a rising generation of Roman Catholics entering the suburban middle classes for the first time, rocking the boat on social issues hardly seemed advisable.

CFM, however, prodded and pushed those Catholics most invested in the status quo to question its secular assumptions. The movement's potential weakness, but also its greatest strength, lay in its primarily middle-class constituency. CFM encouraged suburban couples to know their neighborhoods and to enjoy non-Catholic friendships; it also, however, provided a critical and compassionate stance for evaluating the surrounding, still hostile Protestant culture. As Burns argues, echoing an analysis by Catholic sociologist John L. Thomas, CFM "enabled the couple to withstand the assault being made on their Catholicism by providing them with a sense of solidarity with other Catholic families and assisted the couple in adjusting and accommodating to the culture in which they found themselves without betraying their distinctive Catholic subculture.'"[17]

A decade or more before concerns for social justice surfaced in the Protestant mainstream, CFM families campaigned for racial equality, aid for learning-disabled children, urban renewal, and better treatment for migrant workers. "CFM members were Don Quixotes," a 1979 article recalled, "who jousted with inner-city poverty in Chicago, New York and Oakland, protested the war in Southeast Asia, confronted racism in Los Angeles, hunger in American Indian communities and injustice in California's San Joaquin fields. CFM families adopted Korean War orphans, read Adele Davis, baked whole wheat bread and integrated white neighborhoods."[18]

CFM succeeded in measurable ways. In the mid–1960s a three-year study of CFM families showed that they were "more than twice as active in social, civic and community affairs as similar couples of comparable background." The survey also documented "a salutary effect" on familial relationships.[19] As a "training ground for many middle-aged Catholic liberals," CFM also created a permanent legacy of social awareness.[20] And, as Jeffrey Burns comments, "In the final analysis, the fact that CFM enabled middle class Catholics to overcome their own self-interests to even the smallest degree must be applauded and seen as a triumph of the Human Spirit."[21]

The Christian Family Movement also raised possibilities for family life that, even today, remain largely unexplored. As Robert Coles mused in his published conversation with Daniel Berrigan, *The Geography of Faith* (1971), "I wonder whether the most radical challenge to the values in a particular society hasn't been made when families begin to reorder their living arrangements and the way they bring up their children."[22] For most of us that possibility remains open; the work of the Christian Family Movement suggests that it still could happen.

Beloved Communities

"My parents taught me something very early," Martin Luther King Jr. told an audience of Mississippi blacks in 1966. "Somehow they instilled in me a feeling of somebodyness, and they would say to me over and over again that you're just as good as any child in Atlanta, Georgia."[23] Doubtless, many parents across the United States recited that maxim to their children in the 1930s when King was a young boy, but among African American families in the segregated American South the lesson was difficult to teach and hard to remember.

Still, many of them succeeded and in amazing ways. An impressive array of African American leaders and intellectuals—from Howard Thurman to Zora Neale Hurston, bell hooks, and Henry Louis Gates—have acknowledged their "beloved communities" of origin in the segregated South. In doing so, they are by no means romanticizing the past. These were places that provided safety and refuge but also, just by existing, challenged the social status quo. "[When] a people no longer have the space to construct homeplace," as hooks explains, "we cannot build a meaningful community of resistance. Throughout our history, African-Americans have recognized the subversive value of homeplace."[24]

In the wake of the Daniel Patrick Moynihan's much-disputed report on *The Negro Family: The Case for National Action* (1965), the "tangle of pathology" image has been hard to shake; in a longer historical perspective, however, the kind of family King represents has proven remarkably durable. "As the statistics reveal," one study reports, "Afro-Americans were battered, but not destroyed by slavery and oppression." Two-parent households not only survived slavery but also war, emancipation, and migration to the North. In the early twentieth century, as many historians have demonstrated, the majority of African American families fit a broadly middle-class pattern of two-parent households within a network of extended kin. The well-known problems of black families in recent decades reflect the economic decay of city neighborhoods and the effects of urban sprawl, not simply an incipient flaw in household structure.[25]

Martin Luther King's family provides an outstanding, and well-documented, example of the potential for moral education within African American households. Like all families, of course, his was far from perfect—as, for that matter, was King himself. His adult life, as much as anyone else's, demonstrates the need to challenge and transcend the assumptions that frame one's upbringing. In one sense King's great achievement was his refusal to accept the racial caste system that formed the boundaries of his childhood world. Yet, at the same time, the complex moral lessons he learned from parents and extended family clearly formed the basis of King's vision of the revolutionary power that resides within families.[26]

Martin Luther King's parents, Martin Sr. and Alberta, modeled a strong ethic of community responsibility. "Dad led, fought and taught us through his proud example," Christine King Farris, Martin's older sister, wrote in 1986. "Before Black people in Atlanta had access to City Hall—much less occupied it—Dad was a voice for the voiceless."[27] Daddy King grew up a sharecropper's son who was, as James Cone describes him, "a classic example of a person who pulled himself up by his own boot straps, thereby becoming a persuasive symbol of the merits of thrift, service, responsibility and sacrifice." As pastor of Ebenezer Baptist Church, King Sr. was also a board member of the local branch of the National Association for the Advancement of Colored People (NAACP) and of Morehouse College. He was active in the Negro Voters' League, and led the fight for equity in black and white public school teachers' salaries.[28]

King's parents did not flinch from the difficult realities their children confronted in segregated society. When Martin was six, two neighborhood friends, sons of a white local store owner, stopped playing with him because, as their father explained, Martin was "colored." From this painful school-age snub King's mother took the opportunity to explain the "color problem" to her son and reminded him never to allow racism to determine his self-worth. As King later recalled: "[She] took me on her lap and began by telling me about slavery and how it had ended with the Civil War. She tried to explain the divided system of the South—the segregated schools, restaurants, theaters, housing, the White and Colored signs on the drinking fountains, waiting rooms, lavatories—as a social condition rather than a natural order. Then she said the words that almost every Negro hears before he can yet understand the injustice that makes them necessary: 'You are as good as anyone.'"[29] Still, despite the comforting words, this new knowledge left a deep and painful impact. Alberta's unflinching explanation of the South's racial history filled her young son with outrage—and righteous anger. "I was shocked," King later remembered, "and from that moment on I was determined to hate every white person."[30]

Raising morally sensitive children in pre–World War II Atlanta was clearly no easy task. The difficulty was compounded by the economic and social powerlessness of African American parents outside their own neighborhoods. Once, when Martin and his father asked for service in a shoe store, the clerk refused to help them unless they moved to the back of the room. Daddy King left in protest, but he could not prevent the damage being done to his son's sense of moral order. "This was the ridiculous nature of segregation in the South," the elder King later observed. "A grown man could make no sense of it to a very bright six-year-old boy."[31] But on other occasions King's father refused to back down before a racial insult. When a white patrolman pulled him over and demanded, "Boy, show me your license," Daddy King snapped back, pointing at young Martin: "Do you see this child here? That's a *boy* there. I'm a *man*. I'm Reverend King."[32]

Resisting racism required toughness on the part of both parents and children. Not surprisingly, homes such as King's were far more patriarchal and strict than their white counterparts.[33] Daddy King rarely negotiated with his children. As Stephen Oates comments, "Reverend King ruled his home like a fierce Old Testament patriarch, certain that he alone knew what was best for the children and intolerant of dissent or rival viewpoints."[34] Although Martin, as the middle child of three, eventually learned to accommodate both his father's will and his own need for independence, the youngest child, nicknamed A.D., eventually foundered on his father's authoritarianism.

Parental toughness, whether in the form of a patriarchal father or a matriarchal mother, reflected the tough lessons in reality that African American children needed to learn for their own survival. As a New Orleans mother told psychologist Robert Coles in the early 1960s: "It's like with cars and knives, you have to teach your children to know what's dangerous and how to stay away from it, or else they won't live long. White people are a real danger to us until we learn to live with them. So if you want your kids to live long, they have to grow up scared of whites; and the way they get scared is through us. . . . So I make them store it in the bones, way inside, and then no one sees it."[35]

But, as King's example suggests, even negative emotions could have a positive moral effect. Anger, the great bane of middle-class civility, helped to bond his household. "As my children grew," Daddy King later reminisced, "I became more familiar with what Mama and Papa had been talking about when they'd seemed a little harsh with us. To prepare a child for a world where death and violence are always near drains a lot of energy from the soul. Inside you, there is always a fist balled up to protect them."[36] Anger was in one sense a necessary tool in a black child's education, despite the risks entailed. As James Cone writes, "The person most responsible for my deep resentment against oppression was my father," noting at the same time that "the tenacity with which he defended his rights and spoke the truth, regardless of the risks, earned him much respect among some blacks and the label 'crazy' among others."[37]

Within a socially isolated nuclear family, like many of the white Protestant ones described in this book, anger on this scale could be frightening and destructive; in King's experience, however, an extended family of concern distributed the pain of negative emotions that would have broken a single household. "It was quite easy for me to think of God as love," he once recalled, "mainly because I grew up in a family where love was central and where lovely relationships were ever present."[38] King's religious autobiography, written during his years at Crozer Seminary, begins with a lengthy description of his community and neighborhood playmates, both "highly significant in determining my religious attitudes."[39] King's sister described how their Aunt Ida Worthem "spent hours reading to us from newspapers, books and encyclopedias."[40] Jennie C. Parks, the children's maternal grandmother, was, in the words of King biographer Lewis Baldwin, "a strong spiritual force, a bearer of culture, and a pillar of strength," who gave young Martin "a strong sense of identity, self-esteem, and mission." Baldwin continues: "The family history, tales, and vivid Biblical stories shared by Aunt Ida, Grandmother Jennie, and Alberta, all of whom stood in the best tradition of black storytellers in the South, served a didactic purpose in that the King children were informed of the values of family, church, and the larger black community."[41]

The extended family in King's household was not simply the product of economic necessity. Nor did it signal, as many whites assumed, family "disorganization." Instead, the presence of these elderly women in the King home reinforced the moral dimensions of family life. Patricia Hill Collins, for example, argues that the "othermother" in black family life may symbolize the spiritual dignity behind the daily tasks of child rearing. "By continuing community-based child care," she writes, "African-American women challenge one fundamental assumption underlying the capitalist system itself: that children are 'private property' and can be disposed of as such."[42]

In the segregated South extended families encompassed not just blood relatives but entire communities with the responsibility for helping to raise "other people's children." To a degree such closeness simply made a virtue of necessity. As one expatriate southerner explained, "We were a little more together down South. You had to be. All the Negroes were in one community. Everything they did, they did it together. You went to the same schools. You couldn't go and eat dinner downtown at a white restaurant. It was you on one side of town and whites on the other side."[43]

But strong community identity also provided children with a potent mixture of safety and freedom. As Samuel Proctor writes, "My block was populated with at least thirty adults who had absolute control over me, and the earliest experience of moral choice was whether or not to meet their expectations. . . . In my early years it was common for a neighbor to take special interest in a favorite child and make available special trips to shops, to the farms out of town, and to curious places like the naval base and the huge coal pier at Lambert's Point, where foreign ships were loaded with coal for West Virginia and Kentucky."[44] Similarly, Charles Willie recalled the example of his Sunday School superintendent, who "organized Christmas parties at the church for the children and Labor Day picnics in the country for the teenagers and young adults. He gave neckties to boys who graduated from high school and went on to college. He saved cereal box tops for the young. . . . He was never thought of as a janitor. To the children in the community he was the Reverend J. I. Farrar—a decent, kind, and courteous gentleman, a man interested in children to whom one could always turn for help. He loved his community and he loved his church. It was the Rev. Farrar's love for the children in his community, in part, which taught them how to love others, despite the presence of racism."[45]

Adults, in fact, provided parents with a variety of spiritual resources, for in African American communities the lines between home and church often blurred. As theologian J. Deotis Roberts explains, "there have been times when the church has been a family for the homeless and times when the family altar has been a domestic church." But, in contrast to the Victorian ideal of the home as a private refuge from society and to the modern family without walls, the black church and community extended the nuclear family's sacred space beyond its physical boundaries.[46] As members of an extended moral family, black children naturally received a variety of adult mentors. Howard Thurman, for example, recalled his tutelage by two members of his church who showed him how to "raise a hymn, pray in public, [and] lead a prayer meeting." "With each learning step," Thurman wrote, "your sense of your own worth as a Christian was heightened. Your sponsor reinforced this by reminding you of your confession of faith whenever your behavior warranted it."[47]

Prayer was also an effective teaching tool between parents and children, as "the gift of prayer was learned at the feet of others."[48] "I learned how to pray from my mother," Baptist pastor C. L. Franklin confided to his Detroit congregation in the late 1950s. "I never knew what prayer was until I learned it from her. And her faith in God was contagious for me."[49] Hearing his mother pray was also a formative experience for Howard Thurman. "She spread her life out before God, telling him of her anxieties and dreams for me and my sisters, and of her weariness. I learned what could not be *told* to me."[50] Many of the lessons black children received were simply too complex to be put into didactic language and required a bit of moral imagination to understand. When James Cone's mother sang her favorite song, "This Little Light of Mine," her son knew that "she was affirming much more than what was apparent in the lines. . . . The 'light' was what illuminated her existence, an alternative view of life, different from the current estimations of her being in the world. It was her attempt to make a

statement about her life and to say to the world that she is who she is only because of the presence of God in her world."[51]

Parents had to add an important, and often contradictory, subtext to Sunday school truisms about love and cooperation. Black children growing up in a
racist culture had to internalize two systems of morality, one abstract and often
distant and another distressingly real. In King's case, however, the community
of which he was a member helped to mediate the contradictions. Concerned
adults cushioned vulnerable children with physical care and affection and by
personal example provided alternative interpretations for the negative messages
that young boys and girls were bound to receive from the outside world.

The past strengths of African American families, when placed alongside
modern statistics of family distress and dissolution among urban blacks, suggest
the deeper and more spiritual costs of poverty and unemployment: the loss of a
community of concern. "My heart bleeds for children today," Samuel Proctor
writes, "who live in neighborhoods where life is so cramped and there is so little
trust that children do not have . . . linkages with adults that are safe and
unthreatening and through which they could ease their way without trauma into
a stronger sense of self."[52] The recent history of African American families also
underscores the inherent weaknesses of the domestic strategy utilized in white
mainline and now evangelical churches. Robert O. Dulin concluded in 1971
that "the possibility of a program of Christian education based upon the home
is valid only for those families that have sufficient resources and time to provide for [their] offspring the necessary protection and tools needed to find one's
way in society. Among those families equipped with such resources, the masses
of Black families are not numbered. . . . [Their] energies are exhausted in the
rudiments of basic momentary survival. Thus, there is little energy and time left
for imbuing one's offspring with the understandings and disciplines to counter-
act the evil influences of society."[53]

King's story does not, of course, suggest simple solutions to the black family
crisis, nor, as we have seen, was his upbringing without ambiguities of its own.
What it does suggest, however, is a powerful precedent for Christian nurture in
black families, an alternative American Protestant tradition that is capable of
producing not just good citizens but Old Testament–style prophets. As King's
own example attests, his parents did not aim to produce a pliable, well-adjusted
child—the stated goal of much white mainline Protestant advice literature. Instead, King's parents taught him to insist on a single standard of justice in a world
full of moral contradictions, a costly lesson he learned well. "There are some

things in our social system to which I am proud to be maladjusted," King later declared in one of his most memorable speeches, "and to which I suggest that you too ought to be maladjusted. I never intend to adjust myself to the evils of segregation and the crippling effects of discrimination. . . . I call upon you to be maladjusted; for it may be that the salvation of the world lies in the hands of the maladjusted."[54]

Implications

One of the most difficult tasks now facing mainline churches—and American institutions more generally—is that of transforming their people from consumers into members.[55] The "market economy" of American church life has long encouraged the view that congregations are service providers whose wares may be refused or accepted at will; Americans shop for churches as they do for cars and television sets. This consumeristic mind-set has been particularly acute in regard to families, which, as we have seen, have been alternately cast as clients in need of church programming and as a highly prized commodity whose support is essential to the survival of religious institutions. As a result, the relative roles of parents and churches lack clear definition. Breaking this cycle is not easy: it requires confronting some deeply established assumptions about the nature of church and the role of parents—two important issues that both of the examples described here address in novel ways.

The Catholic Family Movement demonstrates the importance of a clear and compelling understanding of the church's institutional identity. The Catholic Action Movement taught believers to see the active Christian community as a manifestation of the mystical body of Christ. This powerful unifying metaphor provided a bulwark against endemic American individualism and a supernatural means and purpose for lay people to undertake tasks in the outside world. When members of CFM cell groups held a meeting, they were not helping the church or demonstrating personal loyalty to a congregational program—they *were* church.

This understanding meant, first of all, that family relationships did not need to be primary conduits of grace. Parental example was still important, as was a godly marriage—but good relationships were not an end in themselves. Emotionally positive homes were not necessarily closer to God than their more fragile counterparts. In the Catholic Family Movement divine grace was mediated through the institutional church; thus, theological and therapeutic language stayed relatively separate from each other, and socialization remained distinct from spiritual formation.

Although a Roman Catholic ecclesiology is not a live option for Protestants, it helps highlight a pervasive anti-institutionalism and its impact on Protestant understandings of family life. Although Bushnell insisted that church and family were to be close partners in the Christian nurture of children, domesticity clearly held the upper hand in the relationship. Indeed, Bushnell's contemporary critic John Nevin worried that this scheme really placed the onus of salvation on parents and ignored the supernatural role of the institutional church. Nevin emphasized the other resources available to parents; he underscored the importance of infant baptism as the beginning point of a child's journey toward faith within the bounds of the Church, a process with a "supernatural basis" but still "objective and real." Yet, despite Nevin's concerns, by the end of the nineteenth century the Christian home was well on its way toward becoming a surrogate congregation, a church in miniature that nurtured the faith of children, provided regular worship, and worked to spread the Gospel in the surrounding world.

This momentum proved difficult to stop. Families drifted away from churches in part because they had no reason not to. In the 1940s neoorthodox critics of liberal pedagogy echoed Nevin's analysis of Bushnell, but their critique led to the formation of yet another family-related church program, the Christian Faith and Life curriculum. It took another decade before mainline Protestants began to realize the complete dearth of theological warrant for family-based religion.

The events of the next several decades left that insight hanging. Even the recently renewed discussion among mainliners about religion and families has tended to follow old patterns, emphasizing the pragmatic value of faith in maintaining healthy family relationships and the importance of larger social policy issues. The middle ground—the place where families and churches meet—still awaits more definition. Yet without a clear theological rationale for the family's role within the church, and the church's role within the family, the mistakes of the past seem all too real.

The story of Martin Luther King's family shows parents acting as moral teachers. In the King household parents had a pressing mandate to help their children deal with daily life in an immoral society. Their responsibility was not to be ministers of grace through example but to tell the truth whatever its costs. A surrounding network of concerned adults cushioned the emotional complexities of this task, and they allowed harried parents room even to make a mistake now and then. But, in fact, relationships themselves were secondary, for family life had a didactic purpose that could not be set aside. Parents had a knowledge of the world that their children needed to learn for their own survival.

In the mainline Protestant tradition the lines of parental responsibility are far less clear. Part of the reason is theological, since an optimistic view of the child's moral nature has subtly rendered direct parental intervention slightly superfluous. If children were spiritual seedlings, requiring only a bit of watering to grow, then parents need not hover constantly with garden hose and fertilizer. In fact, as a growing chorus of religious education professionals warned, good parents always made sure to consult the horticulturalist first.

The theological definition of "good" parenting is an elusive one. Bushnell emphasized the influence of parents' behavior on children, and Progressive educators advised parents to provide the proper environment—but neither defined their pedagogical role or, more particularly, the question of content in religious formation. Do mainline Protestant parents have a knowledge of the world, and of the larger Christian tradition, that their children need to know for their survival? Family is not just a set of social issues that require a solution, but, as the examples in this chapter suggest, a series of ongoing theological and cultural questions. What is a good parent? Where does parental responsibility end and the church's begin? And where are children responsible agents, and where are they not? There are, of course, no simple answers to any of these queries nor any clear end to the task of addressing them. But that does not make the challenge less pressing or less worth long and careful pursuit.

Notes

Introduction

1. The term *mainline* is, of course, problematic in that it assumes that all other religious groups are somehow marginal. Especially in recent years, as evangelical and Pentecostal groups have grown rapidly, terms such as *old line* or *religious establishment* seem like better descriptions. Historians use *mainline* to describe a tradition that has been shaped by theological liberalism and emphasizes ecumenism and tolerance, social witness, and Christian nurture—this in contrast to more evangelical groups that emphasize personal salvation and evangelism. I use the term *mainline* throughout this book to identify an emerging tradition based around a Christian nurture theology, even though the differences between mainline and evangelical did not clearly emerge until the early twentieth century; before that they are best understood as different emphases within a generalized Protestant consensus. My study deals with mainliners in their denominational settings, although, as recent studies have pointed out, these categories are hardly consistent indicators of difference. On defining *mainline*, see, for example, Wade Clark Roof and William McKinney, *American Mainline Religion: Its Shape and Future* (New Brunswick, N. J.: Rutgers University Press, 1987); Robert Wuthnow, *The Restructuring of American Religion* (Princeton, N. J.: Princeton University Press, 1988); William R. Hutchison, ed., *Between the Times: The Travail of the Protestant Establishment in America, 1900–1960* (Cambridge, Mass.: Harvard University Press, 1989); and Randall Balmer, *Grant Us Courage: Travels along the Mainline of American Protestantism* (New York: Oxford University Press, 1996).
2. The major study of religion in the family is Colleen McDannell, *The Christian Home in Victorian America, 1840–1900* (Bloomington: Indiana University Press, 1986). The main texts on twentieth-century American family life (for example, Steven Mintz and Susan Kellogg, *Domestic Revolutions: A Social History of American Family Life* [New York: Free Press, 1988]; Stephanie Coontz, *The Way We Never Were: American Families and the Nostalgia Trap* [New York: Basic Books, 1992]; Elaine Tyler May, *Homeward Bound: American Families in the Cold War Era* [New York: Basic Books, 1988]) do not mention religion, except in passing. Studies of American childhood are also predominantly secular, especially as they deal with white Protestant children in the twentieth century. See, for example, *American Childhood: A Research Guide and Historical Handbook*, ed. Joseph M. Hawes and N. Ray Hiner (Westport, Conn.: Greenwood

Press, 1985); Elliot West and Paula Petrik, eds., *Small Worlds: Children and Adolescents in America, 1850–1950* (Lawrence: University of Kansas Press, 1992). Much recent sociological literature on families does not, however, exhibit this lack of interest in religion. See, for example, Wuthnow, *Restructuring of American Religion;* Nancy Ammerman and Wade Clark Roof, eds. *Work, Family, and Religion in Contemporary Society* (New York: Routledge, 1995); Gerald Moran and Maris Vinovskis, *Religion, Family, and the Life Course* (Ann Arbor: University of Michigan Press, 1992); William D'Antonio and Joan Aldous, *Families and Religions: Conflict and Change in Modern Society* (Beverly Hills, Calif.: Sage Publications, 1983).

3. Carolyn Osiek and David Balch, *Families in the New Testament World: Households and House Churches* (Louisville, Ky.: Westminster John Knox Press, 1997).
4. Clarissa Atkinson, *The Oldest Vocation: Christian Motherhood in the Middle Ages* (Ithaca, N.Y.: Cornell University Press, 1991).
5. Steven Ozment, *When Fathers Ruled: Family Life in Reformation Europe* (Cambridge, Mass.: Harvard University Press, 1983), 132–177. Luther's emphasis was similar to Erasmus' positive view of marriage and parenthood. See Rosemary O'Day, *The Family and Family Relationships, 1500–1900: England, France and the United States of America* (New York: St. Martin's Press, 1994), 39–44.
6. O'Day, *Family and Family Relationships*, 46–49.
7. McDannell, *Christian Home in Victorian America*, 5; John Demos, *A Little Commonwealth: Family Life in Plymouth Colony* (New York: Oxford University Press, 1970), 104–105.
8. John Cotton, *The Way of Life* (London, 1641), quoted in Charles Hambrick-Stowe, *The Practice of Piety: Puritan Devotional Disciplines in Seventeenth-Century New England* (Chapel Hill: University of North Carolina Press, 1982), 143–144.
9. Witold Rybczynski, *Home: A Short History of an Idea* (New York: Penguin Books, 1986).
10. One good example is Robert Wuthnow, *Growing Up Religious: Christians and Jews and Their Journeys of Faith* (Boston: Beacon Press, 1999). The most useful analysis of secularization I have encountered is found in Christian Smith et al., *American Evangelicalism: Embattled and Thriving* (Chicago: University of Chicago Press, 1998). This study emphasizes the symbiotic relationship of religious groups with modernity. Those that thrive best do not simply oppose or capitulate to it; rather, they adapt to its pressures in strategic ways.
11. The series on Family, Religion and Culture, edited by Don Browning and Ian Evison, is a good example of this. See, for example, Don Browning, Bonnie Miller-McLemore, Pamela Couture, K. Brynolf Lyon, and Robert Franklin, *From Culture Wars to Common Ground: Religion and the American Family Debate* (Louisville, Ky.: Westminster John Knox Press, 1997). See also the literature on Christian practices, for example, Dorothy Bass, *Practicing Our Faith: A Way of Life for Searching People* (San Francisco: Jossey-Bass, 1997); Craig Dykstra, *Growing in the Life of Faith: Education and Christian Practices* (Louisville, Ky.: Geneva Press, 1999); Robert Wuthnow, *After Heaven: Spirituality in America since the 1950s* (Berkeley: University of California Press, 1998).
12. Wade Clark Roof, *Spiritual Marketplace: Baby Boomers and the Remaking of American Religion* (Princeton, N. J.: Princeton University Press, 1999), 236–239, 247–253; Nancy Ammerman, "Golden Rule Christianity: Lived Religion in the American Mainstream," in *Lived Religion in America: Toward a History of Practice*, ed. David Hall (Princeton, N. J.: Princeton University Press, 1997), 196–216.

Chapter 1   Christian Nurture and Victorian Domesticity

1. Joseph A. Collier, *The Christian Home, or Religion in the Family* (Philadelphia: Presbyterian Board of Publication, 1859), 8, 169. For a similar argument, see Erastus

Hopkins, *The Family a Religious Institution; or, Heaven Its Model* (Troy, N.Y.: Elias Gates, 1840).

2. I. W. Wiley, *Religion of the Family* (Cincinnati: Hitchcock and Walden, 1872), 7.

3. Boardman, *The Bible in the Family; or, Hints on Domestic Happiness*, 13th ed. (1852; rpt., Philadelphia: American Sunday-School Union, 1887), 209.

4. Steven Mintz and Susan Kellogg, *Domestic Revolutions: A Social History of American Family Life* (New York: Free Press, 1988), 45. For a relatively recent summary of some complex historical debates on this subject, see Steven Ruggles, "The Transformation of American Family Structure," *American Historical Review* 99 (February 1994): 103–128. For an engaging overview, see Witold Rybczynski, *Home: A Short History of an Idea* (New York: Penguin Books, 1986).

5. Seal Wilentz, "Society, Politics, and the Market Revolution," in *The New American History*, ed. Eric Foner (Philadelphia: Temple University Press, 1990), 51–68.

6. Edward Shorter, *Making of the Modern Family* (New York: Basic Books, 1975); Carl Degler, *At Odds: Women and the Family in America from the Revolution to the Present* (New York: Oxford University Press, 1980).

7. Norbert Elias, *The Civilizing Process*, trans. Edmund Jephcott (New York: Urizen Press, 1978).

8. "One of the Blessings of 'Sweet Home,'" *Advocate and Guardian* 19 (February 1853): 20–21.

9. Clifford Edward Clark, *The American Family Home, 1800–1960* (Chapel Hill: University of North Carolina Press, 1986), 29; Jane Nylander, *Our Own Snug Fireside: Images of the New England Home, 1760–1860* (New York: Knopf, 1993).

10. Jack Larkin, *The Reshaping of Everyday Life, 1790–1840* (New York: Harper and Row, 1988), 105–148; Margaret Marsh, *Suburban Lives* (New Brunswick, N. J.: Rutgers University Press, 1990), 21–56.

11. "Editor's Table," *Godey's Ladies' Book* 21 (September 1840): 142–143.

12. Ellen M. Plante, *Women at Home in Victorian America: A Social History* (New York: Facts on File, 1997).

13. Ellen Rothman, *Hands and Hearts: A History of Courtship in America* (New York: Basic Books, 1984).

14. The perception of the United States as a youthful nation was true both chronologically and statistically. For most of the nineteenth century the American population was predominantly young, with a median age below 20; in 1850, 41 percent of the population was younger than 15. By the 1970s the median age of the population was 28.7. See David Hackett Fischer, *Growing Old in America* (New York: Oxford University Press, 1978), 224; Priscilla F. Clement, *Growing Pains: Children in the Industrial Age* (New York: Twayne Publishers, 1997), 1.

15. Fischer, *Growing Old in America*, 86–90; Karen Calvert, "Children in American Family Portraiture, 1670–1810," *William and Mary Quarterly* 39 (1982): 87–113.

16. Robert V. Wells, *Revolutions in Americans' Lives: A Demographic Perspective on the History of Americans, Their Families, and Their Society* (Westport, Conn.: Greenwood Press, 1982), 91–100; Frances Kobrin, "The Fall in Household Size and the Rise of the Primary Individual in the United States," in *The American Family in Socio-Historical Perspective*, ed. Michael Gordon, 2d ed. (New York: St. Martin's Press, 1978), 69–81.

17. Philip Greven, *Four Generations: Population, Land, and Family in Colonial Andover, Massachusetts* (Ithaca, N.Y.: Cornell University Press, 1970).

18. See Viviana Zelizer, *Pricing the Priceless Child: The Changing Social Value of Children* (New York: Basic Books, 1985).

19. Michael B. Katz, *The People of Hamilton, Canada West: Family and Class in a Mid-Nineteenth Century City* (Cambridge, Mass.: Harvard University Press, 1975).

20. Carroll Smith Rosenberg, "The Female World of Love and Ritual: Relations between Women in Nineteenth-Century America," *Signs* 1 (1975): 1–29.

21. Barbara Welter, "The Cult of True Womanhood, 1820–1860," *American Quarterly* 18 (1966): 151–74; Ruth Cowan, *More Work for Mother: The Ironies of Household Technology from the Open Hearth to the Microwave* (New York: Basic Books, 1983), 40–45; Glenna Matthews, *"Just a Housewife": The Rise and Fall of Domesticity in America* (New York: Oxford University Press, 1987).

22. Deborah White, *Ar'n't I a Woman? Female Slaves in the Plantation South* (New York: Norton, 1985); Herbert Gutman, *The Black Family in Slavery and Freedom, 1750–1925* (New York: Pantheon Books, 1976).

23. Christine Stansell, *City of Women: Sex and Class in New York, 1789–1860* (New York: Knopf, 1986).

24. Catherine Brekus, "Restoring the Divine Order to the World: Religion and the Family in the Antebellum Women's Rights Movement," in *Religion, Feminism and the Family*, ed. Anne Carr and Mary Stewart Van Leeuwen (Louisville, Ky.: Westminster/John Knox Press, 1996), 166–182; Carolyn Johnston, *Sexual Power: Feminism and the Family in America* (Tuscaloosa: University of Alabama Press, 1992).

25. Stephen Frank, *Life with Father: Parenthood and Masculinity in the Nineteenth-Century American North* (Baltimore: Johns Hopkins University Press, 1998).

26. Horace Bushnell, *Christian Nurture* (1861; rpt., Cleveland: Pilgrim Press, 1994), 63.

27. Ibid., 10.

28. See *Horace Bushnell*, ed. H. Shelton Smith (New York: Oxford University Press, 1965), 375–378; and Robert Edwards, *Of Singular Genius, of Singular Grace: A Biography of Horace Bushnell* (Cleveland: Pilgrim Press, 1992). Helpful sources on Bushnell also include Glen A. Hewitt, *Regeneration and Morality: A Study of Charles Finney, Charles Hodge, John W. Nevin, and Horace Bushnell* (Brooklyn, N. Y.: Carlson Publishing, 1991), 125–158; and Ann Taves, "Mothers and Children and the Legacy of Mid-Nineteenth-Century American Christianity," *Journal of Religion* (1987): 203–219.

29. Nancy Schrom Dye and Daniel Blake Smith, "Mother Love and Infant Death, 1750–1920," *Journal of American History* 73 (1986): 329–353; Sylvia Hoffert, *Private Matters: American Attitudes toward Childbearing and Infant Nurture in the Urban North, 1800–1860* (Urbana: University of Illinois Press, 1989), 169–187. See also Samuel H. Preston and Michael R. Haines, *Fatal Years: Child Mortality in Late Nineteenth-Century America* (Princeton, N. J.: Princeton University Press, 1991).

30. Thomas Schlereth, *Victorian America: Transformations in Everyday Life* (New York: HarperPerennial, 1991), 273–274.

31. Dye and Smith, "Mother Love and Infant Death," 346.

32. Peter Slater, *Children in the New England Mind* (Hamden, Conn.: Archon Books, 1977).

33. H. Shelton Smith, *Changing Conceptions of Original Sin* (New York: Charles Scribner's Sons, 1955); Nathan Hatch, *The Democratization of American Christianity* (New Haven, Conn.: Yale University Press, 1989).

34. Harry S. Stout, *Divine Dramatist: George Whitefield and the Rise of Modern Evangelicalism* (Grand Rapids, Mich.: Eerdmans, 1991); Mary Ryan, *Cradle of the Middle Class: The Family in Oneida, New York, 1790–1865* (Cambridge, U. K.: Cambridge University Press, 1981); Paul Johnson, *A Shopkeeper's Millennium: Society and Revivals in Rochester, New York, 1815–1837* (New York: Hill and Wang, 1978).

35. Christine Heyrman, *Southern Cross: The Beginnings of the Bible Belt* (New York: Knopf, 1997), 125.

36. Palmer, quoted in Ann Loveland, "Domesticity and Religion in the Antebellum Period: The Career of Phoebe Palmer," *Historian* 39 (May 1977): 455–471.

37. Karen Calvert, *Children in the House: The Material Culture of Early Childhood, 1600–1900* (Boston: Northeastern University Press, 1992), 19–38.
38. See, for example, *A Treatise on the Proceedings of a Camp-Meeting, Held in Bern, N.Y., County of Albany: By a Spectator* (Albany: Webster and Skinner, 1810), 5, 6, 10.
39. J. G. Pike, *Persuasives to Early Piety, Interspersed with Suitable Prayers* (New York: American Tract Society, 1830); Pike, *A Guide for Young Disciples of the Holy Savior, in Their Way to Immortality* (New York: American Tract Society, 1830).
40. David Morgan, *Visual Piety: A History and Theory of Popular Religious Images* (Berkeley: University of California Press, 1998), 78–93.
41. William Mosely, *The New Token for Children; or, a Sequel to Janeway's; Being an Authentic Account, Never before Published, of the Conversion, Exemplary Lives and Happy Deaths of Twelve Children*, 3d ed. (Philadelphia: William W. Woodward, 1808), v, 118, 18, 63–66.
42. Mosely, *New Token for Children*, v. See also *Juvenile Piety; Or, the Happiness of Religion, Exemplified in the Joyful Deaths of Pious Children* (Boston: Lincoln and Edmonds, 1819); *Accounts of the Happy Deaths of Two Young Christians* (Boston: Willis, 1819).
43. Abbott, *The Young Christian; Or, a Familiar Illustration of the Principles of Christian Duty* (New York: American Tract Society, 1832), 3.
44. Joseph Kett, *Rites of Passage: Adolescence in America, 1790 to the Present* (New York: Basic Books, 1977), 11–37.
45. *To a Child* (Andover, Mass.: New England Tract Society, 1815), 3.
46. *Philadelphia Female Tract Society, no. 7* (Philadelphia: Bailey, 1816), 7, 9.
47. Lucy Larcom, *A New England Girlhood* (1889; rpt., Corinth Books, 1961), 63, 50, 74.
48. Philip Greven, *The Protestant Temperament: Patterns of Child-Rearing, Religious Experience, and the Self in Early America* (New York: New American Library, 1977); on Wayland, see William McLoughlin, "Evangelical Child-Rearing in the Age of Jackson," *Journal of Social History* 9 (1975): 35–39.
49. E. Bickersteth, *Domestic Portraiture; or, the Successful Application of Religious Principle in the Education of a Family, Exemplified in the Memoirs of Three of the Deceased Children of the Rev. Legh Richmond. With a Few Introductory Remarks on Christian Education* (New York: Robert Carter and Brothers, 1849), xiv, 42.
50. Collier, *Christian Home*, 195.
51. Bushnell, *Christian Nurture*, 74.
52. Phoebe Palmer, *The Way of Holiness, with Notes by the Way* (New York: Palmer and Hughes, 185–), 275–288. Appreciation to James Bratt for this citation.
53. Charles Hambrick-Stowe, *Charles G. Finney and the Spirit of American Evangelicalism* (Grand Rapids, Mich.: Eerdmans, 1996), 274–275.
54. On Bushnell's supernaturalism, see Robert Bruce Mullin, "Horace Bushnell and the Question of Miracles," *Church History* 58 (1989): 460–473.
55. Norman Pettit, *The Heart Prepared: Grace and Conversion in Puritan Spiritual Life*, 2d ed. (Middletown, Conn.: Wesleyan University Press, 1989). Theodore Munger's influential biography of Bushnell similarly argued that he was attempting to recover an older orthodoxy, not impose a new one. See Munger, *Horace Bushnell: Preacher and Theologian* (Boston and New York: Houghton, Mifflin, 1899), 67–97.
56. Ann Boylan, *Sunday School: The Formation of an American Institution, 1790–1880* (New Haven, Conn.: Yale University Press, 1988), 141–146.
57. Lydia Maria Child, *The Mother's Book* (Boston: Carter, Hendee and Babcock, 1831), 9.
58. Porter, "Bushnell on Christian Nurture," *New Englander* 6 (1848): 131.
59. Bushnell, *Christian Nurture*, 252.
60. Ibid., 233.
61. Ibid., 244–245.

62. See G. W. Burnap, "Bushnell on Christian Nurture," *Christian Examiner* (November 1847): 435–451.

63. Bushnell, *Christian Nurture*, 9–64.

64. Bennett Tyler, *Letter to the Rev. Horace Bushnell, D.D., Containing Strictures on His Book, Entitled "Views of Christian Nurture, and Subjects Adjacent Thereto"* (Hartford, Conn.: Brown and Parsons, 1848), 25, 35, 64.

65. Bushnell, *Christian Nurture*, 338–407, 271–293.

66. James Bratt, "The Reorientation of American Protestantism, 1835–1845," *Church History* 67 (March 1998): 52–82; Ryan, *Cradle of the Middle Class*.

67. "Early Training," *Mother's Magazine* 8 (1845): 4.

68. Collier, *Christian Home*, 24–25, 123; S. S. Pugh, *Christian Home Life: A Book of Examples and Principles* (New York: American Tract Society, 1864), 120–121.

69. See Colleen McDannell and Bernhard Lang, *Heaven: A History* (New Haven, Conn.: Yale University Press, 1988), 264–269.

70. Collier, *Christian Family*, 172.

71. Lawrence Foster, *Religion and Sexuality: Three American Communal Experiments of the Nineteenth Century* (New York: Oxford University Press, 1981), 239.

72. John Hyde, *Mormonism: Its Leaders and Designs* (New York: W. P. Fetridge and Co., 1857), 52, 77.

73. *Emile*, trans. Barbara Foxley (London: Everyman Library, 1998), 264.

74. Alexis de Tocqueville, *Democracy in America*, ed. Richard D. Heffner (New York: New American Library, 1956), 228–229.

75. Bernard Wishy, *The Child and the Republic: The Dawn of Modern American Child Nurture* (Philadelphia: University of Pennsylvania Press, 1968), 17.

76. E. Anthony Rotundo, *American Manhood: Transformations in Masculinity from the Revolution to the Modern Era* (New York: Basic Books, 1993), 31–55; Rotundo, "Boy Culture: Middle-Class Boyhood in Nineteenth-Century America," in *Meanings for Manhood: Constructions of Masculinity in Victorian America*, ed. Mark Carnes and Clyde Griffen (Chicago: University of Chicago Press, 1990), 15–36.

77. Collier, *Christian Home*, 51.

78. Pugh, *Christian Home Life*, 162.

79. Bushnell, *Christian Nurture*, 59.

80. "The Lost Son—The Submissive Father," *Mother's Magazine* 8 (1845): 293.

81. Collier, *Christian Home*, 109.

82. Pugh, *Christian Home Life*, 64.

83. "Maxims for Family Peace," in *Home Scenes; or, Lights and Shadows of the Christian Home* (New York: American Tract Society, 1865), 134–135.

84. Peter N. Stearns, "Girls, Boys, and Emotions: Redefinitions and Historical Change," *Journal of American History* 80 (June 1993): 36–74.

85. G. Stanley Hall, *Life and Confessions of a Psychologist* (New York: D. Appleton and Co., 1924), 36–44.

86. Karen Halttunen, *Confidence Men and Painted Women: A Study of Middle-Class Culture in America, 1830–1870* (New Haven, Conn.: Yale University Press, 1982); John F. Kasson, *Rudeness and Civility: Manners in Nineteenth-Century Urban America* (New York: Hill and Wang, 1990); Stuart M. Blumin, "The Hypothesis of Middle-Class Formation in Nineteenth-Century America: A Critique and Some Prospects," *American Historical Review* 90 (April 1985): 299–338.

87. George Winfred Hervey, *The Principles of Courtesy: With Hints and Observations on Manners and Habits* (New York: Harper and Brothers, 1852), xiv–v.

88. Sarah Hale, *Manners, or, Happy Homes and Good Society All the Year Round* (Boston: J. E. Tilton, 1868), 17–18.

89. Bushnell, *Christian Nurture*, 248–249.

90. Howard A. Barnes, *Horace Bushnell and the Virtuous Republic* (Metuchen, N. J.: ATLA and Scarecrow Press, 1991), 39.
91. Bushnell, *Christian Nurture*, 91.
92. Bushnell, *God's Thoughts Fit Bread for Children: A Sermon Preached before the Connecticut Sunday-School Convention* (Boston: Nichols and Noys, 1869), 36.
93. Bushnell, *Christian Nurture*, esp. 194.
94. Hodge, "Bushnell on Christian Nurture," *Biblical Repertory and Princeton Review* 19 (October 1847): 526, 534, 533.
95. Nevin, "Educational Religion," *Weekly Messenger of the German Reformed Church*, 23 June 1847. See also the essay by Nevin's colleague at Mercersburg, Philip Schaff, "The Influence of Christianity on the Family," *Mercersburg Quarterly Review* 5 (October 1853): 473–491.
96. Nevin, "Educational Religion," *Weekly Messenger*, 14 July 1847.
97. "Last Home of Christianity," *New York Observer*, 2 August 1855, 244.

Chapter 2 **Protestant Homes and Christian Civilization**

1. "Men's Part in Home Making," *Baptist Visitor* (April 1878): 2.
2. Colleen McDannell, "Parlor Piety: The Home as Sacred Space in Protestant America," in *American Home Life, 1880–1930: A Social History of Spaces and Services*, ed. Jessica H. Foy and Thomas J. Schlereth (Knoxville: University of Tennessee Press, 1992), 162–189.
3. Wiley, *Religion of the Family* (Cincinnati: Hitchcock and Walden: n.p., 1872), n.p.; J. P. Newman, "Sermon: Religious Education the Safeguard of the Nation," in *Christian Educators in Council*, ed. J. C. Hartzell (New York and Cincinnati: n.p., 1883), 216.
4. Samuel Phillips, *The Christian Home, as It Is in the Sphere of Nature and the Church* (New York: G. and F. Bill, 1860), 20, 31.
5. Boardman, *The Bible in the Family: Or, Hints on Domestic Happiness*, 13th ed. (1852; rpt., Philadelphia: American Sunday-School Union, 1887), 2, 32.
6. Boardman, *Bible in the Family*, 41, 204.
7. R. Mallary DeWitt, *Family Worship* (Boston and Chicago: Congregational Sunday School and Publishing Society, 1891), 15, 18.
8. Heman Humphrey, *Domestic Education* (Amherst, Mass.: J. S. and C. Adams, 1840), 16.
9. "Woman's Place and Work in the World: A Lecture Delivered in Meadville, PA, April 4th, 1880 by the Rev. T. L. Flood, A.M.," *Chautauqua Assembly Herald* 5 (June 1880): 2.
10. Glenna Matthews, *The Rise of Public Woman: Woman's Power and Woman's Place in the United States, 1630–1970* (New York: Oxford University Press, 1992).
11. Nancy Cott, *The Bonds of Womanhood: "Woman's Sphere" in New England* (New Haven, Conn.: Yale University Press, 1977).
12. "The Woman's Hour: An Address Delivered in the Amphitheatre Tuesday, August 1, 1882, by Mrs. Emily Huntington Miller, of Evanston, Illinois," *Chautauqua Assembly Herald*, 3 August 1882, 2.
13. Mary Livermore, *My Story of the War: A Woman's Narrative of Four Years Personal Experience* (Hartford, Conn.: n.p., 1888), 133; Lucius Brockett and Mary C. Vaughan, *Woman's Work in the Civil War: A Record of Heroism, Patriotism and Patience* (Philadelphia: n.p., 1867), 538.
14. Bushnell, *The Reform against Nature* (New York: Scribner and Co., 1869). Bushnell, quoted in Catherine Brekus, "Restoring the Divine Order to the World: Religion and the Family in the Antebellum Women's Rights Movement," in *Feminism and*

the Family, ed. Mary Stewart Van Leeuwen and Anne Carr (Louisville, Ky.: Westminster/John Knox Press, 1996), 173–174.

15. Catherine E. Beecher and Harriet Beecher Stowe, American Woman's Home or, Principles of Domestic Science; Being a Guide to the Formation and Maintenance of Economical, Beautiful and Christian Homes (1869; rpt., Hartford, Conn.: Harriet Beecher Stowe Center, 1998), 49–50. See also Kathryn Kish Sklar, Catherine Beecher: A Study in American Domesticity (New Haven. Conn.: Yale University Press, 1973).

16. Mary Mann, Christianity in the Kitchen: A Physiological Cook-Book (Boston: Ticknor and Fields, 1857), 2.

17. Catherine E. Beecher, Woman's Profession as Mother and Educator, with Views in Opposition to Woman Suffrage (Philadelphia and Boston: George Maclean, 1872), 181, 458–459.

18. Bushnell, Christian Nurture, 221.

19. May Wright Sewall, "Domestic Legislation," National Citizen and Ballot Box 6 (September 1881):1.

20. Minutes of the 4th Convention of the NWCTU, Held in Chicago, 1877 (Chicago: n.p., 1889), 142, 175.

21. Willard, "Woman Represents the Home," Annual Address of Miss Frances E. Willard, President, before the 19th Annual W.C.T.U. Convention, Denver, Co., 1892 (Chicago: n.p., 1892), 28.

22. See Ruth Bordin, Woman and Temperance: The Quest for Power and Liberty, 1873–1900 (1981; rpt., New Brunswick, N. J.: Rutgers University Press, 1990), 3–14.

23. Colin Goodykoontz, Home Missions on the American Frontier, with Particular Reference to the American Home Missionary Society (1939; rpt., New York: Octagon Books, 1971), esp. 360. Wiley, quoted in Elizabeth Rust, "Women's Home Missionary Society," in Isaac W. Wiley, Late Bishop of the Methodist Episcopal Church, ed. Richard S. Rust (Cincinnati: n.p., 1885), 149. See also Evelyn Brooks Higginbotham, Righteous Discontent: The Women's Movement in the Black Baptist Church, 1880–1920 (Cambridge, Mass.: Harvard University Press, 1993).

24. "Women's Work," Hope 4 (June 1888): 3; Mary Burdette, "Baptist Home Missionary Society," in Transactions of the National Council of Women of the United States, Assembled in Washington, D.C., February 22 to 25, 1891, ed. Rachel Foster Avery (Philadelphia: J. B. Lippincott, 1891), 130.

25. Nancy Cott, Public Vows: A History of Marriage and the Nation (Cambridge, Mass.: Harvard University Press, 2000), 77–104.

26. Second Annual Report of the General Assembly's Committee on Freedmen, of the Presbyterian Church of the United States of America, Presented May 1867 (Pittsburgh: n.p., 1867), 10, 11.

27. Joanna Moore, In Christ's Stead: Autobiographical Sketches (Chicago: n.p., 1902), 54, 178–180; Bertha Grinnell Judd, Fifty Golden Years: The First Half Century of the Woman's American Baptist Home Missionary Society, 1877–1927 (Rochester, N.Y.: Du Bois Press, 1927), 1–8, 85–86. See also Grace M. Eaton, A Heroine of the Cross: Sketches in the Life and Work of Miss Joanna P. Moore (n.p.p., n.d.).

28. Second Annual Report of the Board of Managers of the Women's Home Missionary Society of the Methodist Episcopal Church, for the Year 1882–1883 (Cincinnati: n.p., 1884), 26; "An Open Letter," Tidings 3 (October 1883): 2; "The Training School," Tidings 2 (January 1883): 4.

29. Amelia S. Quinton, "Woman's Work in Solving the Indian Problem," in Christian Educators in Council, ed. J. C. Hartzell (New York and Cincinnati: Phillips and Hunt, 1884), 103.

30. Missionary Work of the Woman's National Indian Association and Letters of Missionaries (Philadelphia: n.p., 1885), 1.

31. Judd, *Fifty Golden Years*, 39; *Baptist Missionary Training School Catalog, 1881–1903* (Chicago: n.p., 1903), 14; *Baptist Missionary Training School Catalog, 1881–1891*, 9–10, 12. The Methodist curriculum was very similar. See *Fifth Annual Report of the Board of Managers of the Women's Home Missionary Society of the Methodist Episcopal Church for the Year 1885–1886* (Cincinnati: n.p., 1886), 99–100.

32. See, for example, Higginbotham, *Righteous Discontent*; Vicki Ruiz, "Dead Ends or Gold Mines? Using Missionary Records in Mexican American Women's History," in *Unequal Sisters: A Multi-Cultural Reader in U.S. Women's History*, ed. Vicki L. Ruiz and Ellen Carol DuBois, 2d ed. (New York: Routledge, 1994), 298–315.

33. Cott, *Public Vows*, 117–120.

34. On women's organizations, see Susan Yohn, "'Let Christian Women Set the Example in Their Own Gifts': The 'Business' of Protestant Women's Organizations," in *Women in Twentieth-Century Protestantism*, ed. Margaret Bendroth and Virginia Brereton (Urbana: University of Illinois Press, 2002); Roger Finke and Rodney Stark, *The Churching of America, 1776–1990: Winners and Losers in Our Religious Economy* (New Brunswick, N. J.: Rutgers University Press, 1992), 154.

35. See Gregory Schneider, *The Way of the Cross Leads Home: The Domestication of American Methodism* (Bloomington: Indiana University Press, 1993), 196–208.

36. Bushnell, *Christian Nurture*, 385–407.

37. DeWitt, *Family Worship*, 18–22.

38. Preface to Rev. Ashton Oxenden and the Rev. C. H. Ramsden, *Family Prayers* (New York: Anson D. F. Randolph, 1868), n.p.

39. Common practices described in DeWitt, *Family Worship*, 39–46.

40. *The Altar at Home: Prayers for the Family and the Closet. By Clergymen in and near Boston*, 12th ed. (Boston: Walker, Wise, and Co., 1863), v.

41. Alexis McCrossen, *Holy Day, Holiday: The American Sunday* (Ithaca, N. Y.: Cornell University Press, 2000).

42. Tarbell, *All in the Day's Work: An Autobiography* (New York: Macmillan, 1939), 16.

43. "The Cotter's Saturday Night," in *Home Scenes; Or, Lights and Shadows of the Christian Home* (New York: American Tract Society, 1865), 136–138.

44. Charles F. Deems, *The Home Altar: An Appeal in Behalf of Family Worship; with Prayers and Hymns, and Calendar of Lessons from Scripture, for Family Use*, 4th ed. (New York: Funk and Wagnalls, 1867), 34. For a more complete discussion of this topic, see Colleen McDannell, *The Christian Home in Victorian America, 1840–1900* (Bloomington: Indiana University Press, 1986), 77–85.

45. Deems, *Home Altar*, 31. See also John H. Power, *Discourse on Domestic Piety and Family Government, in Four Parts* (Cincinnati: L. Swormstedt and A. Poe, 1852), 15–24. This practice was clearly declining in the late nineteenth century, especially in urban areas where the majority of domestic servants were Irish-Catholic. See DeWitt, *Family Worship*, 41–42.

46. Colleen McDannell, *Material Christianity: Religion and Popular Culture in America* (New Haven, Conn.: Yale University Press, 1995), 67–102.

47. DeWitt, *Family Worship*, 31.

48. Lyman Abbott, *For Family Worship* (New York: Dodd, Mead, 1883), iii.

49. Ann M. Boylan, *Sunday School: The Formation of an American Institution, 1790–1880* (New Haven, Conn.: Yale University Press, 1988), 147–152.

50. David Morgan, *Visual Piety: A History and Theory of Popular Religious Images* (Berkeley: University of California Press, 1998), 3, 5; Wiley, *Religion of the Family*, 148.

51. See, for example, John Heyl Vincent, *The Home Book for Very Little People, Their Brothers and Sisters, Their Mothers and Teachers* (New York: Phillips and Hunt, 1887), 4.

52. See Joseph Kett, *Rites of Passage: Adolescence in America, 1790 to the Present* (New York: Basic Books, 1977), 189–204.

53. Alice Hamilton, *Exploring the Dangerous Trades: The Autobiography of Alice Hamilton*, *M.D.* (Boston: Little, Brown, 1943), 27.
54. Ella Gilbert Ives, *The Evolution of a Teacher* (Boston: Pilgrim Press, 1914), 16–17.
55. James Russell Miller, *Home-Making* (Philadelphia: Presbyterian Board of Publication, 1882), 257.
56. John Hall, *A Christian Home: How to Make and How to Maintain It* (Philadelphia: American Sunday-School Union, 1883), 154–155.
57. Wiley, *Religion of the Family*, 9; Boardman, *Bible in the Family*, 20.
58. Miller, *Home-Making*, 223–224.
59. Frederick W. Dallinger, *Recollections of an Old-Fashioned New Englander* (New York: Round Table Press, 1941), 252.
60. Ray Stannard Baker, *Native American* (New York: Charles Scribner's Sons, 1941), 95–98.
61. William Jennings Bryan and Mary Baird Bryan, *The Memoirs of William Jennings Bryan* (Philadelphia: United Publishing of America, 1925), 44.
62. Steffens, *The Autobiography of Lincoln Steffens* (New York: Harcourt, Brace, 1931), 77.
63. Edgar Lee Masters, *Across Spoon River: An Autobiography* (New York: Farrar and Rinehart, 1936), 32.
64. William R. Hutchison, "Cultural Strain and Protestant Liberalism," *American Historical Review* 76 (1971): 386–411. See also Susan Curtis, *A Consuming Faith: The Social Gospel and Modern American Culture* (Baltimore: Johns Hopkins University Press, 1991), 72–127.
65. George Marsden, *Fundamentalism and American Culture, 1875–1925* (New York: Oxford University Press, 1980).
66. F. L. Chappell, "The Worker's Dispensational Environment," *Christian Alliance and Foreign Mission Weekly*, 20 March 1896, 275; A. J. Gordon, *The Ministry of the Spirit* (New York: Fleming H. Revell, 1894), 165–166. On the women's movement, see "Woman Suffrage," *Watchman*, 7 March 1895, 1–2; and "Women in Politics," *The Truth; or Testimony for Christ* 21 (January 1895): 5–6; and, on the National Reform Association, see "Home, Not National Religion," *Watchman*, 23 February 1888.
67. For a more extended discussion, see Margaret Bendroth, "Fundamentalism and the Family: Gender, Culture, and the American Pro-family Movement," *Journal of Women's History* 10 (winter 1999): 35–54.
68. James H. Brookes, "At Home with the Lord," *Truth; or Testimony for Christ* 2 (December 1876): 5–6.
69. Scofield, quoted in Lang and McDannell, *Heaven: A History*, 337–338.
70. On fundamentalism and the family, see Margaret Bendroth, *Fundamentalism and Gender, 1875 to the Present* (New Haven, Conn.: Yale University Press, 1993), 97–117.
71. "Gems Taken at Random from Dr. Gordon's Utterances," *Clarendon Light* 3 (January 1895): 8; Miss C. C. Murray, "Dying to Self: The Consecrated Life," *Christian Alliance and Foreign Mission Weekly*, 16 March 1894, 286. Paul Boyer finds antisentimentalism endemic to premillennialist thought. See *When Time Shall Be No More: Prophecy Belief in American Culture* (Cambridge, Mass.: Harvard University Press, 1992), 126–127. See also Virginia Lieson Brereton, *Training God's Army: The American Bible School, 1880–1940* (Bloomington: Indiana University Press, 1990), 112–122. The particular form of Keswick piety in fundamentalism emphasized "dying to self" and being willing to relinquish human relationships if necessary. See, for example, Charles Trumbull, "Have You Surrendered All?" in *The Victorious Christ: Messages from Conferences Held by the Victorious Life Testimony in 1922* (Philadelphia: Sunday-School Times, 1923), 106.
72. A. B. Earle, "Trials and Triumphs of Evangelism. Address to Park Street Church Conference, May 29, 1890," *New England Evangelist*, no. 19 (December 1890): n.p.

73. David A. Rausch, *Arno C. Gaebelein, Irenic Fundamentalist and Scholar* (New York: Edwin Mellen Press, 1983), 207. Other examples abound. See, for example, "Dr. R. A. Torrey in His Home: An Address by the Rev. R. A. Torrey, Jr., at the Memorial Service, Feb 5, 1929," *Moody Bible Institute Monthly* (October 1929): 68–69.
74. Harry Ironside, *Random Reminiscences from Fifty Years of Preaching* (1939; rpt., New York: Garland Publishing, 1988), 47–54, 73–85; Ironside's letter quoted in E. Schuyler English, *H. A. Ironside: Ordained of the Lord* (New York: Loizeaux Bros, 1946), 192. Other biographical accounts include: Robert L. Bumner, *A Man Sent from God: A Biography of Dr. John R. Rice* (Grand Rapids, Mich.: Eerdmans, 1959), 233f.; R. K. Johnson, *Builder of Bridges: A Biography of Dr. Bob Jones* (Murfreesboro, Tenn.: Sword of the Lord Publishing, 1969), 58f.
75. Chafer, "The Doctrine of Sin," *Bibliotheca Sacra* 92 (January–March 1935): 16.
76. J. S. Mill, *A Manual of Family Worship with an Essay on the Christian Family* (Dayton, Ohio: W. R. Funk, 1900), 53.

Chapter 3 **From Christian Home to Christian Family**

1. Steven Mintz and Susan Kellogg, *Domestic Revolutions: A Social History of American Family Life* (New York: Free Press, 1988), 107–131. See also discussion in J. S. Mill, *A Manual of Family Worship, with an Essay on the Christian Family* (Dayton, Ohio: W. R. Funk, 1900), 39–40.
2. George Walter Fiske, *The Christian Family* (New York: Abingdon, 1929), 38–40.
3. Ibid., 23, 124–125.
4. Ibid., 108, 35.
5. See, for example, David I. Macleod, *The Age of the Child: Children in America, 1890–1920* (New York: Twayne Publishers, 1998).
6. Paula Fass, *The Damned and the Beautiful: American Youth in the 1920s* (New York: Oxford University Press, 1977), 53–118.
7. Beth Bailey, *From Front Porch to Back Seat: Courtship in Twentieth Century America* (Baltimore: Johns Hopkins University Press, 1988); John D'Emilio and Estelle B. Freedman, *Intimate Matters: A History of Sexuality in America*, 2d ed. (Chicago: University of Chicago Press, 1988; 1997), 239–274; Daniel Scott Smith, "The Dating of the American Sexual Revolution: Evidence and Interpretation," in *The American Family in Social-Historical Perspective*, 2d ed. (New York: St. Martin's Press, 1978), 426–438.
8. James Turner, *Without God, Without Creed: The Origins of Unbelief in America* (Baltimore: Johns Hopkins University Press, 1985), 216.
9. H. L. Mencken, *Prejudices, Fourth Series* (New York: A. A. Knopf, 1924), 78–79.
10. William R. Hutchison, *The Modernist Impulse in American Protestantism* (Cambridge, Mass.: Harvard University Press, 1976), 2; Richard Fox, "The Culture of Liberal Protestant Progressivism, 1875–1925," *Journal of Interdisciplinary History* 23 (winter 1993): 639–660.
11. George Stewart, *Can I Teach My Child Religion?* (Garden City, N.Y.: Doubleday, Doran, and Co., 1929), 65.
12. Luther Weigle, "The Christian Ideal of Family Life as Expounded in Horace Bushnell's 'Christian Nurture,'" *Religious Education* 19 (February 1924): 47, 55.
13. Warren Susman, "'Personality' and the Making of Twentieth-Century Culture," *Culture as History: The Transformation of American Society in the Twentieth Century* (New York: Pantheon Books, 1984), 271–285.
14. On Progressivism, see Steven J. Diner, *A Very Different Age: Americans of the Progressive Era* (New York: Hill and Wang, 1998); John Whiteclay Chambers, *The Tyranny of Change: America in the Progressive Era, 1890–1920*, 2d ed. (New Brunswick,

N. J.: Rutgers University Press, 2000); Morton White, *Social Thought in America: The Revolt against Formalism* (Boston: Beacon Press, 1957).

15. Ronald L. Howard, *A Social History of American Family Sociology, 1865–1940* (Westport, Conn.: Greenwood Press, 1981), 42–47.

16. Mintz and Kellogg, *Domestic Revolutions*, 109. On reformers, see, for example, Samuel Dike, "Some Aspects of the Divorce Question," *Princeton Review* 60 (March 1884): 169–190; "Family," in *The New Encyclopedia of Social Reform*, ed. William D. P. Bliss (New York: Funk and Wagnalls, 1908), 476–485.

17. George Boynton Child, "The Housekeeping Movement," *Independent*, 9 May 1912, 1003–1004.

18. Clifford Edward Clark, *The American Family Home, 1800–1915* (Chapel Hill: University of North Carolina Press, 1986), 163; Candace M. Volz, "The Modern Look of the Early-Twentieth Century House: A Mirror of Changing Lifestyles," in *American Home Life, 1890–1930: A Social History of Spaces and Services*, ed. Jessica H. Foy and Thomas Schlereth (Knoxville: University of Tennessee Press, 1992), 25–48.

19. Ruth Cowan, "Coal Stoves and Clean Sinks: Housework between 1890 and 1930," in Foy and Schlereth, *American Home Life*, 211–224. According to studies, women spent more time with housework in 1940 than they did in 1910. See Joan Vanek, "Time Spent in Housework," *Scientific American* 231 (November 1974): 116–125.

20. Clark, *American Family Home*, 153.

21. Steven L. Schlossman, "Before Home Start: Notes toward a History of Parent Education in America, 1897–1929," *Harvard Educational Review* 46 (1976): 441. See also Hall, "The Content of Children's Minds," *Princeton Review* 11 (1883): 249–272. On women and "experts," see Barbara Ehrenreich and Deirdre English, *For Her Own Good: 150 Years of the Experts' Advice to Women* (New York: Anchor Books, 1978); Sheila Rothman, *Woman's Proper Place: A History of Changing Ideals and Practices, 1870 to the Present* (New York: Basic Books, 1978); Molly Ladd-Taylor, ed., *Raising a Baby the Government Way: Mothers' Letters to the Children's Bureau, 1915–1932* (New Brunswick, N. J.: Rutgers University Press, 1986).

22. Mintz and Kellogg, *Domestic Revolutions*, 120–123.

23. Dorothy Ross, *G. Stanley Hall: The Psychologist as Prophet* (Chicago: University of Chicago Press, 1972).

24. Karen Calvert, "Children in the House, 1890–1930," in Foy and Schlereth, *American Home Life, 1890–1930*, 75–93.

25. John Dewey, "My Pedagogic Creed," in *The Philosophy of John Dewey, vol. 2: The Lived Experience*, ed. John J. McDermott (New York: G. P. Putnam's Sons, 1973), 443, 453–454.

26. Lawrence Cremin, *American Education: The Metropolitan Experience, 1876–1980* (New York: Harper and Row, 1988), 153–372.

27. Ruth Leys, "Mead's Voices: Imitation as Foundation, or, The Struggle against Mimesis," *Critical Inquiry* 19 (winter 1993): 227–307.

28. E. Brooks Holifield, *The History of Pastoral Care in America: From Salvation to Self-Realization* (Nashville, Tenn.: Abingdon Press, 1983), 187f.

29. Charles Lippy, *Being Religious, American Style: A History of Popular Religiosity in the United States* (Westport, Conn.: Praeger Publishers, 1994), 140–165.

30. See, for example, a relevant French parallel: Antoine Prost, "The Family and the Individual," in *A History of Private Life: Riddles of Identity in Modern Times*, ed. Antoine Prost and Gérard Vincent (Cambridge, Mass.: Harvard University Press, 1991), 51–101.

31. See William Leach, *Land of Desire: Merchants, Power, and the Rise of a New American Culture* (New York: Vintage Books, 1993); Richard Ohman, *Selling Culture: Magazines, Markets, and Class at the Turn of the Century* (New York: Verso, 1996).

32. John R. Gillis, *A World of Their Own Making: Myth, Ritual, and the Quest for Family Values* (Cambridge, Mass.: Harvard University Press, 1996).

33. Alice Kessler-Harris, *Out to Work: A History of Wage-Earning Women in the United States* (New York: Oxford University Press, 1983).

34. Mary S. Young, "Mothers and Daughters," *Woman's Work* 30 (July 1915): 163–164; "Women's Society No Longer," *Women and Missions* 1 (February 1925): 430. On missions, see Patricia Hill, *The World Their Household: The American Woman's Foreign Mission Movement and Cultural Transformation, 1870–1920* (Ann Arbor: University of Michigan Press, 1985); Dana Robert, *American Women in Mission: A Social History of Their Thought and Practice* (Macon, Ga.: Mercer University Press, 1996).

35. Lucy Peabody, "Woman's Place in Missions Fifty Years Ago and Now," *Missionary Review of the World* 50 (December 1927): 909–910.

36. *Annual Address of Miss Frances E. Willard, President, before the 19th Annual W.C.T.U. Convention, Denver, Co., 1892* (Chicago: Women's Christian Temperance Publishing Association, 1892), 117–118.

37. George B. Stewart, "Religious and Moral Education through the Home," in *The Religious Education Association: Proceedings of the First Annual Convention, Chicago, February 10–12, 1903* (Chicago: Office of the Association, 1903), 108.

38. Arthur Schlesinger, "A Critical Period in American Religion, 1875–1900," *Massachusetts Historical Society Proceedings* 64 (1930–1932): 523–546; Paul Carter, *The Spiritual Crisis of the Gilded Age* (DeKalb: Northern Illinois University Press, 1967).

39. Dewey, "The Relation of Modern Psychology to Religious Education," quoted in Steven C. Rockefeller, *John Dewey: Religious Faith and Democratic Humanism* (New York: Columbia University Press, 1991), 260; Stephen A. Schmidt, *History of the Religious Education Association* (Birmingham, Ala.: Religious Education Association, 1983), 33.

40. George A. Coe, *Education in Religion and Morals* (Chicago: Fleming H. Revell, 1904), 26. See also Coe, "What Does Modern Psychology Permit Us to Believe in Respect to Regeneration?" *American Journal of Theology* 12 (July 1908): 353–368.

41. Fox, "Culture of Liberal Protestant Progressivism," 651f. See also Heather Warren, "The Shift from Character to Personality in Mainline Protestant Thought," *Church History* 67 (September 1998): 537–555.

42. A. J. William Myers, *Horace Bushnell and Religious Education* (Boston: Manthorne and Burack, 1937), 105, 123, 134.

43. Coe, *Education in Religion and Morals*, 39–40.

44. Clyde Votaw, *The Progress of Moral and Religious Education in the American Home* (Chicago: Religious Education Association, 1911), 16, 13.

45. Sherrill, *Family and Church* (New York: Abingdon, 1937), 12.

46. Freudianism did not, however, appreciably affect popular child-rearing manuals or, I would add, theological views of children. See Geoffrey H. Steere, "Freudianism and Child-Rearing in the Twenties," *American Quarterly* 20 (winter 1968): 759–767.

47. Sophia Lyon Fahs, "The Beginnings of Religion in Baby Behavior," *Religious Education* 25 (1930): 896–897.

48. Samuel Wells Stagg and Mary Boyd Stagg, *Home Lessons in Religion: A Manual for Mothers*, vol. 1: *The Three-Year-Old* (New York: Abingdon Press, 1923), 10, 11.

49. Anna Freelove Betts, *The Mother-Teacher of Religion* (New York: Abingdon, 1922), 149–152; Stagg and Stagg, *Home Lessons in Religion*, 1:39–41.

50. Stagg and Stagg, *Home Lessons in Religion*, 1:13.

51. On parent education, see *Recent Social Trends in the United States: Report of the President's Research Committee on Social Trends* (New York: McGraw-Hill,1933), 1:705–707; Imogene M. McPherson, "Trends in Parent Education," *Religious Education* 29 (January 1933): 62–69.

52. Blanche Carrier, *Church Education for Family Life* (New York: Harper and Brothers, 1937), 7–8.

53. Regina Westcott Weiman, *The Modern Family and the Church* (New York: Harper and Brothers, 1937), 314–316.

54. L. Foster Wood, *Building Spiritual Foundations in the Family* (Philadelphia: Judson Press, 1936), 70–71; International Council of Religious Education, *Organization and Administration of Christian Education in the Local Church* (Chicago: ICRE, 1935), 60.

55. William Clayton Bower and Percy Roy Hayward, *Protestantism Faces Its Educational Task Together* (Appleton, Wis.: C. C. Nelson, 1949), 139–141.

56. Carrier, *Church Education for Family Life*, 16–21.

57. George Walter Fiske, *Problems of Christian Family Life To-Day* (Philadelphia: Westminster Press, 1937), 14.

58. Weiman, *Modern Family and the Church*, 321.

59. Sherrill, *Family and Church*, 22.

60. Stewart, "Religious and Moral Education through the Home," 117–118.

61. Henry F. Cope, *Religious Education in the Family* (Chicago: University of Chicago Press, 1915); Speer and Hallock, *Christian Home Making* (New York: Round Table Press, 1939), 16.

62. Wood, *Growing Together in the Family* (New York: Abingdon, 1935), 108.

63. Stewart, "Religious and Moral Education through the Home," 112, 118.

64. Frances M'Kinnon Morton, "The Prayer-Life of the Family," *Home Department* 17 (January–March 1934): 21.

65. Regina Westcott Weiman, *The Family Lives Its Religion: Creating the Family and the Creative Family* (New York: Harper and Brothers, 1941), 216.

66. Dorothy Clarke Wilson, *Christian Family Brown* (Boston and Los Angeles: Baker's Plays, 1936), 27–29.

67. Ibid., 2.

68. Ernest Burgess, "The Family as a Unity of Interacting Personalities," *Family* 7 (March 1926): 3–9; Robert Griswold, *Fatherhood in America: A History* (New York: Basic Books, 1993), 93.

69. Howard, *Social History of American Family Sociology*, 63, 73.

70. Ruth S. Cavan and Katherine H. Ranck, *The Family and the Depression: A Study of 100 Chicago Families* (Chicago: University of Chicago Press, 1938).

71. Speer and Hallock, *Christian Home Making*, 3, 38.

72. J. H. Montgomery, *Christian Parenthood in a Changing World* (New York: Methodist Book Concern, 1933), 12–13.

73. Wood, *Building Spiritual Foundations in the Family*, 31–41.

74. A. D. Mayo, "The New Education—Christian Education," *Education* 19 (May 1899): 552, 548.

75. Mary A. Johnson, "When Does the Home Get Its Chance?" (letter to the editor), *Christian Century*, 23 April 1930, 532.

76. David Nasaw, "Children and Commercial Culture: Moving Pictures in the Early Twentieth Century," in *Small Worlds: Children and Adolescents in America, 1850–1950*, ed. Elliott West and Paula Petrik (Lawrence: University Press of Kansas, 1992), 14–25; Alice Miller Mitchell, *Children and Movies* (Chicago: University of Chicago Press, 1929), 42–47, 161 (table 13).

77. "Good Citizenship and the Movies," *Christian Century*, 26 February 1930, 264.

78. Winthrop Hudson, *The Great Tradition of the American Churches* (1953; rpt., New York: Harper Torchbooks, 1963), 212.

Chapter 4   Protestant Families in Wartime

1. "Building the Christian Family: A Program for the Churches" (New York: Committee on Marriage and the Home of the Federal Council of the Churches of Christ in America, 1934), 2; *Home and Church Working Together* (New York: Federal Council of Churches of Christ in America and ICRE, 1940), 8; "From the Creed of a Religious Educator," in Florence M. Taylor, *Their Rightful Heritage: Home and Church Working Together for the Christian Nurture of Children* (Boston: Pilgrim Press, 1942), n.p.
2. Frederick C. Grant, "Presenting Religion to Youth," *Religion in Life* 6 (1937): 384.
3. Willard Sperry, *What You Owe Your Child: The Problem of Religion and Morals in the Modern Home* (New York: Harper and Row, 1935), 20–21, 27; Louis I. Newman, "How Shall 'We Moderns' Teach Our Children Religion?" *Religious Education* ([hereafter *RE*] 27 [1932]: 311–317) offers a Jewish parallel.
4. Ames, "Can Religion Be Taught?" *RE* 25 (1930): 42–50.
5. Sperry, *What You Owe Your Child*, 39.
6. *Recent Social Trends* (Washington, D.C.: U.S. Government Printing Office, 1930), 1:674.
7. Albert C. Wildman, "An Experiment in Aiding Religious Education in the Homes of the Congregation of the Prestonia Presbyterian Church, Louisville, Kentucky, December 30, 1928 to February 10, 1929" (Th.M. diss., Louisville Presbyterian Seminary, 1929), 14.
8. Robert Lynd and Helen M. Lynd, *Middletown: A Study in Contemporary American Culture* (New York: Harcourt, Brace, 1929), 178.
9. Ibid., 337–338.
10. Ibid., 338.
11. Ibid., 342.
12. James H. S. Bossard and Eleanor S. Boll, *Ritual in Family Living: A Contemporary Study* (Philadelphia: University of Pennsylvania Press, 1950), 120, 176, 26–27.
13. Robert Wuthnow, *Growing Up Religious: Christians and Jews and Their Journeys of Faith* (Boston: Beacon Press, 1999), xxvii–xxix.
14. Lippman, *Preface to Morals* (1929; rpt., New York: Time-Life Books, 1964), 56, 76, 104.
15. In 1932 the REA solicited letters from religious education professionals and published their responses. See P. R. Hayward, "What the Depression Is Doing to the Cause of Religious Education," *RE* 27 (1932): 873–886. On this period, see William R. Hutchison, "Protestantism as Establishment," in *Between the Times: The Travail of the Protestant Establishment in America, 1900–1960*, ed. William Hutchison (Cambridge, Mass.: Harvard University Press, 1989), 3–18.
16. Robert W. Lynn, "Family–Sunday School Partnership: A Chapter in the History of Protestant Educational Strategy" (Th.D. diss., Union Theological Seminary, 1962), 61.
17. Nevin C. Harner, *The Educational Work of the Church* (New York: Abingdon, 1939), 222, 217; *Organization and Administration of Christian Education in the Local Church* (Chicago: ICRE, 1935), 60.
18. Blanche Carrier, *Church Education for Family Life* (New York: Harper and Brothers, 1937), 22–23.
19. *Organization and Administration of Christian Education in the Local Church*, 60.
20. *A Church Program for Promoting Christian Family Life* (Philadelphia: Board of Christian Education of the Presbyterian Church in the U.S., 1934), 5, 9.
21. Reinhold Niebuhr, *Moral Man and Immoral Society* (New York: Charles Scribner's, 1932), xxii. See also Paul A. Carter, *The Decline and Revival of the Social Gospel: Social and Political Liberalism in American Protestant Churches, 1920–1940* (Ithaca, N. Y.:

Cornell University Press, 1956); Charles C. Brown, *Niebuhr and His Age: Reinhold Niebuhr's Prophetic Role in the Twentieth Century* (Philadelphia: Trinity Press International, 1992), 36–67.

22. Reinhold Niebuhr, *Does Civilization Need Religion? A Study in the Social Resources and Limitations of Religion in Modern Life* (1927; rpt., New York: Macmillan, 1941), 129–130.

23. Niebuhr, *Leaves from a Notebook of a Tamed Cynic* (1929; rpt., Louisville, Ky.: Westminister/John Knox Press, 1980), 127–128.

24. H. Shelton Smith, *Faith and Nurture* (New York: Charles Scribner's Sons, 1942); see also H. Shelton Smith, "Christian Education," in *Protestant Thought in the Twentieth Century: Whence and Whither?* ed. Arnold S. Nash (New York: Macmillan, 1951), 225–246; Lynn, "Family–Sunday School Partnership"; and, to a lesser extent, Paul H. Vieth, *The Church and Christian Education* (St. Louis, Mo.: Bethany Press, 1947).

25. Smith, *Faith and Nurture*, 42.

26. Ibid, 44.

27. Ibid., 46.

28. Ibid., 48.

29. Ibid., 87.

30. Ibid., 49.

31. Ibid., 102, 104.

32. Ibid., 103.

33. Ibid., 113.

34. Ibid., 120, 121.

35. Ibid., 165, 139.

36. William Clayton Bower, "Some Points of Tension between Progressive Religious Education and Current Theological Trends," *RE* 34 (1939): 166–167; George A. Coe, "Religious Education is in Peril," *International Journal of Religious Education* (hereafter *IJRE*) (January 1939): 9–10; Bower, "Creative Religious Education," *Religion in the Making* 2 (November 1941): 5–19.

37. Steven A. Schmidt, *History of the Religious Education Association* (Birmingham, Ala.: Religious Education Association Press, 1983), 124–129.

38. "Men against Stars," in *Minutes of the General Assembly of the PCUSA*, pt. 2: *Reports of Boards* (Philadelphia: Office of the General Assembly, 1946), 11–12, 18f.

39. *White House Conference on Children in a Democracy* (Washington, D.C.: U.S. Government Printing Office, 1940), 181–188.

40. Steven Mintz and Susan Kellogg, *Domestic Revolutions: A Social History of American Family Life* (New York: Free Press, 1988), 165–167.

41. Paul M. Dennis, "Between Watson and Spock: Eleanor Roosevelt's Advice on Child-Rearing from 1928 to 1962," *Journal of American Culture* 18 (spring 1995): 41–50.

42. Stassen, "Challenges Facing Religious Education," *IJRE* (April 1943): 3.

43. J. Edgar Hoover, "Crime and the Sunday School," *Sunday-School Times*, 7 February 1948, 107–108; Edward R. Elson, "J. Edgar Hoover—Churchman," *Presbyterian Life*, 27 November 1948, 4–5.

44. William McGuire King, "The Reform Establishment and the Ambiguities of Influence," in Hutchison, *Between the Times*, 122–140.

45. "National Family Week Inaugurated," *IJRE* (March 1943): 4, 35; William Clayton Bower and Percy Roy Hayward, *Protestantism Faces Its Educational Task Together* (Appleton, Wis.: C. C. Nelson, 1949), 140–147.

46. "Advance in Home Cooperation," *IJRE* (April 1943): 15.

47. William M. Tuttle Jr., *"Daddy's Gone to War": The Second World War in the Lives of*

America's Children (New York: Oxford University Press, 199), 13. See Anna Freud and Dorothy Burlingham, *War and Children* (New York: Medical War Books, 1943); John Bowlby, *Attachment and Loss* (New York: Basic Books, [1969]).

48. Tuttle, *"Daddy's Gone to War,"* 31.
49. *Christian Family Life Education* (New York: ICRE, 1940), 18–32.
50. Taylor, *Their Rightful Heritage,* 2.
51. "Fireside Chat," *Hearthstone* 1 (October 1949): n.p.; Daniel A. Poling, "The Christian Home in a Warlike World," *Religion in Life* 9 (1940): 609–615.
52. "The Study of Christian Education; V: The Family," IJRE, MS, 18, 20.

Chapter 5   Praying to Stay Together in the 1950s

1. James Hudnut-Beumler, *Looking for God in the Suburbs: The Religion of the American Dream and Its Critics, 1945–1965* (New Brunswick, N. J.: Rutgers University Press, 1994), 31–40.
2. Steven Mintz and Susan Kellogg, *Domestic Revolutions: A Social History of American Family Life* (New York: Free Press, 1988), 178–179; Elaine May, *Homeward Bound: American Families in the Cold War Era* (New York: Basic Books, 1988), 3–9. For a more complete overview, see Landon Y. Jones, *Great Expectations: America and the Baby Boom Generation* (New York: Ballantine Books, 1981). For a recent summary of the debate about the 1950s, see, in *Journal of Marriage and the Family* 55 (August 1993): David Popenoe, "American Family Decline, 1960–1990: A Review and Appraisal," 527–542; Norval Glenn, "A Plea for Objective Assessment of the Notion of Family Decline," 542–544; Judith Stacey, "Good Riddance to 'The Family': A Response to David Popenoe," 545–547; Philip A. Cowan, "The Sky *Is* Falling, but Popenoe's Analysis Won't Help Us Do Anything about It," 548–553; and Popenoe's response, "The National Family Wars," 553–555.
3. Dennison Nash and Peter Berger, "The Child, The Family, and the 'Religious Revival' in Suburbia," *Journal for the Scientific Study of Religion* 1–2 (October–April 1961–1963): 85–93; Annie Dillard, *An American Childhood* (New York: Harper and Row, 1987), 195. See also William Whyte, *The Organization Man* (New York: Simon and Schuster, 1956).
4. Msgr. Raymond J. Gallagher, Rabbi Marc H. Tanenbaum, and the Rev. Dr. William J. Villaume, "The Place of Religion in American Life," in *The Nation's Children*, vol. 1: *The Family and Social Change,* ed. Eli Ginzberg (New York: Columbia University Press, 1960), 208–226.
5. Tuttle, *"Daddy's Gone to War": The Second World War in the Lives of America's Children* (New York: Oxford University Press, 1993), 24–26; Irene Tauber and Conrad Tauber, *People of the United States in the Twentieth Century* (Washington, D.C.: GPO, 1971), 156.
6. May, *Homeward Bound;* Clifford Edward Clark, *The American Family Home, 1800–1960* (Chapel Hill: University of North Carolina Press, 1986), 209f.
7. Tom Engelhardt, *The End of Victory Culture: Cold War America and the Disillusioning of a Generation* (New York: Basic Books, 1995), 133–149; Ella Taylor, *Prime-Time Families: Television Culture in Postwar America* (Berkeley: University of California Press, 1989).
8. May, *Homeward Bound,* 16–20; Thomas Hine, *Populuxe* (New York: Knopf, 1987), 130.
9. Spock, quoted in Michael Zuckerman, "Dr. Spock: The Confidence Man," in *The Family in History,* ed. Charles E. Rosenberg (Philadelphia: University of Pennsylvania Press, 1975), 179–207.
10. "Report of the Family Life Committee," *Journal of the 1956 General Conference of the*

Methodist Church (Nashville, Tenn.: Methodist Publishing House, 1956), 1853–1855. See also C. A. Bowen, "A Regenerative Force," *Christian Home* 10 (November 1951): 1.

11. George Buttrick, "Religion and the Home," in *Sermons on Home and Family Life*, ed. John Charles Wynn (New York: Abingdon, 1956), 43.

12. Robert C. Lintner, "Children Deserve Christian Homes," *Christian Home* 10 (May 1951): 2–4; Wilbur E. Hammaker, "'Nothing's Too Good for Our Child,'" *Christian Home* 10 (February 1951): 2–4.

13. Claudia Bushman with Richard L. Bushman, "Latter Day Saints: Home Can Be a Heaven on Earth," in *Faith Traditions and the Family*, ed. Phyllis Airhart and Margaret Bendroth (Louisville: Westminster/John Knox Press, 1998), 23–25.

14. One of the most explicit efforts in this regard was by Yale professor of Christian education Randolph Crump Miller, *Education for Christian Living* (Englewood Cliffs, N. J.: Prentice-Hall,1956), 96–99. For a larger overview of trends in the thinking of religious educators, see Kendig Brubaker Cully, *The Search for a Christian Education—since 1940* (Philadelphia: Westminster Press, 1965).

15. *Education of Christian Parents in America: An Interpretive Digest of the National Conference on Education of Christian Parents* (New York: ICRE, 1950), 15.

16. Lee J. Gable, *Christian Nurture through the Church* (New York: National Council of Churches, 1955), 26.

17. Robert W. Lynn, "Family–Sunday School Partnership: A Chapter in the History of Protestant Educational Strategy" (Th.D. diss., Union Theological Seminary, 1962), 122f.; "The Church Family: Disappearing Dad," *Presbyterian Life* 16 (November 1957).

18. Leonard Brummett, "Mrs. Housewife, Meet the Master," *Hearthstone* 3 (January 1951): 19–21.

19. See Philip Wylie, *Generation of Vipers*, 8th ed. (1942; rpt., New York: Pocket Books, 1965), 184–205; Ferdinand Lundberg and Marynia Farnham, *Modern Women: The Lost Sex* (New York: 1947); May, *Homeward Bound*.

20. Ada Beth and C. Adrian Heaton, *Our Contagious Faith: How Persons Grow through Christian Teaching in Church and Home* (Philadelphia: Judson Press, 1961), 7–8.

21. Jackson Wilcox, "The Marks of a Christian Home," *Hearthstone* 2 (January 1950): 31–32, 44.

22. Donald More Maynard, *Your Home Can Be Christian* (New York: Abingdon-Cokesbury, 1952), 19, 16. See similar list in *Parents: First Teachers of Religion* (1946; rpt., Chicago: ICRE, 1950).

23. Carl Kardatzke, *The Home Christian* (Anderson, Ind.: Warner Press, 1951), 100–103.

24. R. M. Woleruth, "What Is a Christian Home?" *Christian Home* 10 (May 1951): 19.

25. Lawrence P. Fitzgerald, "The Slifers Live Abundantly," *Hearthstone* 2 (May 1950): 2, 4. See also Wouter Van Garrett, "Supper at the Barkers," *Home* 41 (July–September 1958): 9.

26. Hazel A. Lewis, "Your Child *Is* Learning the Christian Way," *Hearthstone* 2 (June 1950): 17.

27. Annie Laurie VonTungelin, "We Have a Happy Family," *Home* 41 (July–September 1958):5.

28. John Brush, "Talk Religion at Home," *Hearthstone* 1 (February 1950): 15.

29. Daniel Beckman, *The Mechanical Baby: A Popular History of the Theory and Practice of Child Raising* (Westport, Conn.: Lawrence Hill and Co., 1977), 173–174; Eric Hoffer, *The True Believer* (New York: Harper and Row, 1951).

30. Harry C. Monro, *Protestant Nurture: An Introduction to Christian Education* (Englewood Cliffs, N.J.: Prentice-Hall, 1956), esp. 105–120.

31. Brooks Holifield, *A History of Pastoral Care in America: From Salvation to Self-Realization* (Nashville, Tenn.: Abingdon Press, 1983), 260f.

32. Smart, *Teaching Ministry of the Church: An Examination of the Basic Principles of Christian Education* (Philadelphia: Westminster Press, 1954), 175.
33. Elizabeth N. Jones, "Family Counselors," *Hearthstone* 1 (October 1949): 35.
34. John R. Seeley, R. Alexander Sim, and Elizabeth W. Loosley, *Crestwood Heights:A Study of the Culture of Suburban Life* (New York: Basic Books, 1956), 218.
35. Carl Zimmerman and Lucius Cervantes, *Successful American Families* (New York: Pageant Press, 1960).
36. Peter Berger, *The Noise of Solemn Assemblies: Christian Commitment and the Religious Establishment in America* (Garden City, N.Y.: Doubleday, 1961), 97; Dan Wakefield, "Slick-Paper Christianity," *The Nation* 185 (1957): 56–59.
37. "Some Parents' and Teachers' Reports of Children's Questions and Comments about and Applications of the Christian Faith," issued by Department of Children's Work, Commission on General Christian Education, National Council of Churches, June 1962, n.p. (RG 112, 19–3, Presbyterian Historical Society, Philadelphia).
38. Margaret Bunel Edwards, "Which Way to Shelter," *Hearthstone* 15 (October 1963): 19. See also Florence Laughlin, "Children and the Bomb," *Hearthstone* 17 (July–August 1965): 3. On civil defense, see Paul Boyer, *By the Bomb's Early Light: American Thought and Culture at the Dawn of the Atomic Age* (New York: Pantheon Books, 1985), 319–333.
39. Robert Wuthnow, *After Heaven: Spirituality in America since the 1950s* (Berkeley: University of California Press, 1998), 19–51; Wade Clark Roof, *A Generation of Seekers: The Spiritual Journeys of the Baby Boom Generation* (San Francisco: Harper, 1993), 151–174.
40. Part of this story is documented in James F. Findlay, *Church People in the Struggle: The National Council of Churches and the Black Freedom Movement, 1950–1970* (New York: Oxford University Press, 1993).
41. Ruth Feldstein, "Antiracism and Maternal Failure in the 1940s and 1950s," in *"Bad Mothers": The Politics of Blame in Twentieth-Century America*, ed. Molly Ladd-Taylor and Laurie Umansky (New York: New York University Press, 1998), 145–168.
42. Elizabeth George, "Prejudice Begins at Home," *Christian Home* 10 (January 1951): 16–17.
43. Jean Louise Smith, "Children Learn Religion at Home," *Christian Home* 10 (January 1951): 5–6.
44. "Parents the First Teachers of Religion," n.p. See also Barbara Faiss, "Teaching World-Mindedness to Children," in *Christian Growth in Family Life*, ed. Richard Lenz (St. Louis, Mo.: Bethany Press, 1959), 50–54, 86.
45. Findlay, *Church People in the Struggle*, 125–131.
46. Lois S. Smith, "A Child's Part in Family Devotions," *Hearthstone* 1 (January 1950): 21. See also Nels Ferre, *Strengthening Spiritual Life through Family Devotions* (Nashville, Tenn.: Upper Room, 1951); Lentz, *Christian Growth in Family Life*, 38–43.
47. See, for example, Nell and Cawthon Bowen, "Devotions for the Family," *Christian Home* (January 1954): 54–58; Anna Laura Gebhard, "At Family Altars," *Hearthstone* (September 1957): 17–19.
48. John Charles Wynn, "The Family Worships Together—Hurriedly," in John Charles Wynn, *How Christian Parents Face Family Problems* (Philadelphia: Westminster Press, 1955), 69–83.
49. Roy Fairchild, "United Presbyterian Parents Speak to the Church," Working Paper No. 8, May 1959, pt. 2: "Problems, Satisfactions, and Religious Perspectives of Parents," Office of Family Education Research, Board of Christian Education, UPCUSA, 60–6, 30 (RG 39, 1–5, Presbyterian Historical Society, Philadelphia).
50. See "The Family in Transition—A Symposium," *Religious Education* 39 (May–June 1944): 131–168.

51. *Education of Christian Parents in America*, 3. The conference was sponsored by the ICRE and included delegates from Germany, Japan, and Canada as well as several Jewish delegates.
52. Gable, *Christian Nurture through the Church*, 27–30.
53. Joseph John Hanson, "Christian Family Life," pamphlet distributed by Department of Adult Work and Family Life, Board of Education and Publication, American Baptist Convention, n.d., esp. 2, 11, 12.
54. Helen R. and Raymond V. Kearns Jr., "Christian Education—Family Style," *Presbyterian Life* 30 October 1948, 18–20. See also Ralph Norman Mould, "These Parents Teach Religion," *Christian Century* 25 January 1950, 111–113.
55. Quoted in David Hester, "The Use of the Bible in Presbyterian Curricula, 1923–1985," in *The Pluralistic Vision: Presbyterians and Mainstream Protestant Education and Leadership*, ed. Milton Coalter, John M. Mulder, and Louis B. Weeks (Louisville: Westminster/John Knox Press, 1992), 215.
56. See description in Craig Dykstra and J. Bradley Wigger, "A Brief History of a Genre Problem: Presbyterian Educational Resource Materials," in Coalter, Mulder, and Weeks, *Pluralistic Vision*, 197.
57. Ibid., 195–196; Gordon Mattice, "Basic Business of the Church: A Review of the Work of the Board of Christian Education," *Presbyterian Life*, 27 May 1950, 24–25; Kearns, "Christian Education—Family Style," 20.
58. Mould, "These Parents Teach Religion," 112. The results of one poll are in J. Gordon Chamberlin, *Parents and Religion: A Preface to Christian Education* (Philadelphia: Westminster Press, 1961), 70–76. See also Roy Fairchild and J. C. Wynn, "As the Family Sees the Church," *Presbyterian Life*, 15 October 1959, 20–23.
59. Quoted in "A Program for These Times," in *Minutes of the General Assembly of the Presbyterian Church in the U.S.A.*, pt. 2: *The Reports of the Boards* (Philadelphia: Office of the General Assembly, 1951), 9. See also Wesner Fallaw, "Religious Education: Coming or Going?" *Christian Century* 9 February 1949, 170–171.
60. "Report on Christian Education," in *Minutes of the General Assembly*, pt. 2, 12–3; "Report on Christian Education," in *Minutes of the General Assembly of the Presbyterian Church in the U.S.A.*, pt. 2: *Reports of the Boards* (Philadelphia: Office of the General Assembly, 1954), 42.
61. Report printed in *Historical Sections of the Digest, United Presbyterian Church of North America and Presbyterian Church in the U.S.A.* (Philadelphia: Office of the General Assembly, 1958), 2331.
62. Ibid., 2328. William Bean Kennedy suggests that the curriculum's neo-orthodox theology was intended to appeal both to conservatives, who would appreciate its emphasis on personal rebirth, and to liberals, who would support its more nuanced reading of the Scriptures. See "Neo-Orthodoxy Goes to Sunday School: The Christian Faith and Life Curriculum," *Journal of Presbyterian History* 58 (1980): 351–352. See also the series of articles, replicated in pamphlet form, by Old Testament scholar Oswald T. Allis in the *Sunday School Times*, 26 June, 3 July, and 10 July 1948, sharply critical of the curriculum's approach to biblical material.
63. Payne, "The Future Comes Creeping In," *Presbyterian Life* 23 June, 1951, 8; Chad Walsh, "If We Don't Somebody Else Will," *Presbyterian Life* 18 February 1950, 34.
64. Smart, *Teaching Ministry of the Church*, 180, 181.
65. *Historical Sections of the Digest*, 2331.
66. Quoted in Report on Christian Education, in *Minutes of the General Assembly of the United Presbyterian Church in the U.S.A.*, pt. 2: *Annual Reports of Major Program Agencies* (Philadelphia: Office of the General Assembly, 1962), 55.
67. See evaluation in Hester, "Use of the Bible in Presbyterian Curricula," 223–226.
68. Lynn, "Family–Sunday School Partnership," 100.

69. "Some Parents' and Teachers' Reports of Children's Questions and Comments about and Applications of the Christian Faith," issued by the Department of Children's Work, Commission on General Christian Education, National Council of Churches, June 1962, n.p. (RG 112, 19–3, Presbyterian Historical Society).
70. Berger, *Noise of Solemn Assemblies*, 116.
71. Richard Lentz, "Your Family and Your Faith," *Hearthstone* 12 (January 1960): 2.
72. Norman Langford, "Policy on Family Participation in the Curriculum," 26 September 1955, 2 (RG 39, 1–3, Presbyterian Historical Society).
73. "Minutes," Subcommittee on the Christian Home, 29 March 1955 (RG 39, 1–2), PHS. The survey included two-hour group interviews of 845 parents (one per family with a fairly even sex ratio) held in 63 different churches recruited by the interviewers, supplemented by 25-item questionnaires administered in group sessions. This resulted in 719 usable questionnaires (responses by parents not using CFL were eliminated), supplemented by 281 additional ones completed in other church settings. See "United Presbyterian Parents Speak to the Church": Working Paper No. 8, May 1959, pt. 1: "Procedures, Purposes, and Participants in the Study, from the Office of Family Education Research" (RG 39, 1–5, PHS).
74. "Presbyterian Family Portrait," *Presbyterian Life*, 15 October 1959, 17–19.
75. Roy Fairchild, "United Presbyterian Parents Speak to the Church," 9–10, 47.
76. Ibid, 47–48.
77. "Consultative Conference with Drs. Pruyser and Bossard," 23 and 24 March, 1959, 3–4 (RG 39, 1–5).
78. Inter-office memorandum, 15 March 1962, from Family Education Advisory Committee to Mr. Morrison, Re. Final Disposition of Family Education Research Proposal (RG 39, 1–14); "Family Education Research United Presbyterian Church in the U.S.A.," remnants of a report, 1963 (RG 39, 1–15).
79. Roy W. Fairchild and John Charles Wynn, eds., *Families in the Church: A Protestant Survey* (New York: Association Press, 1961).
80. Arthur L. Maye, "The Family—Golden Calf," *Hearthstone* 15 (February 1963): 4–6.

Chapter 6   Mainliners, Evangelicals, and Family Religion

1. Roger Crook, "Can Families Commit Murder?" *Hearthstone* 15 (June 1963): 23; Haskell M. Miller, "Beyond the Family Circle," *Christian Home*, n.s. 3 (January 1971): 4.
2. Genné, "Too Much Family?" *IJRE* 42 (April 1966): 8–10; Berger, "The Second Children's Crusade," *Christian Century* 2 December 1959, 1399–1400.
3. Valaria Gaile Shaw, "Family Devotions Any Time," *Hearthstone* 17 (March 1965): 21.
4. John Westerhof, "Into a World of Peace," *A.D.* 1 (September 1972): 62.
5. Mary Anne Cavicchi, "Another Day and Time," *Christian Home* (December 1971): 8–10; Shaw, "Family Devotions Any Time," 21.
6. W. Bradford Wilcox, "For the Sake of the Children? Family-Related Discourse and Practice in the Mainline," in *Quietly Influential: The Public Role of Mainline Protestantism*, ed. Robert Wuthnow and John H. Evans (Berkeley: University of California Press, 2001).
7. Penny Marler, "Lost in the Fifties: The Changing Family and the Nostalgic Church," in *Work, Family, and Religion in Contemporary Society*, ed. Nancy Tamon Ammerman and Wade Clark Roof (New York: Routledge, 1995), 23–60.
8. Mark A. Noll, *A History of Christianity in the United States and Canada* (Grand Rapids, Mich.: Eerdmans, 1992), 468; Roger Finke and Rodney Stark, *The Churching of America, 1776–1990: Winners and Losers in Our Religious Economy* (New Brunswick,

N. J.: Rutgers University Press, 1992), 237–275; C. Kirk Hadaway and David A. Roozen, *Rerouting the Protestant Mainstream: Sources of Growth and Opportunities for Change* (Nashville, Tenn.: Abingdon Press, 1995), 19–35.

9. Peter N. Carroll, *It Seemed like Nothing Happened: America in the 1970s* (1982; rpt., New Brunswick, N. J.: Rutgers University Press, 2000), 278–296; Mintz and Kellogg, *Domestic Revolutions: A Social History of American Family Life* (New York: Free Press, 1988), 203–237; Marler, "Lost in the Fifties."

10. Robert Putnam, *Bowling Alone: The Collapse and Revival of American Community* (New York: Simon and Schuster, 2000).

11. Tom Wolfe, *The Electric Kool-Aid Acid Test* (New York: Bantam Books, 1968), 114. Two other evocative books on the 1960s ethos are Tod Gitlin, *The Sixties: Years of Hope, Days of Rage* (New York: Bantam Books, 1987); and Marty Jezer, *Abbie Hoffman: American Rebel* (New Brunswick, N. J.: Rutgers University Press, 1993). See also Robert Ellwood, *The 60s Spiritual Awakening* (New Brunswick, N. J.: Rutgers University Press, 1994). On the changing value structure of the post–1960s, see Daniel Yankelovich, *The New Morality: A Profile of American Youth in the 1970s* (New York: McGraw-Hill, 1974).

12. Mintz and Kellogg, *Domestic Revolutions*, 203, 225, 227.

13. Robert Wuthnow, *The Restructuring of American Religion: Faith and Society since World War II* (Princeton: Princeton University Press, 1988), 153–164, 187.

14. Wade Clark Roof, *Generation of Seekers: The Spiritual Journeys of the Baby Boom Generation* (New York: HarperCollins, 1993), 177–178.

15. To a degree, of course, the graying of mainline churches reflects the aging of the American population and a declining birthrate among middle- and upper-middle-class Protestants; however, the change also reflects loss of young constituents. In the late 1980s Roof and McKinney reported that 80 percent of those disaffiliating were forty-five or younger. See Wade Clark Roof and William McKinney, *American Mainline Religion: Its Changing Shape and Future* (New Brunswick, N. J.: Rutgers University Press, 1989), 152–155, 170–173.

16. Roof, *American Mainline Religion*, 204–209; Paula Nesbitt, *Feminization of the Clergy in America: Occupational and Organizational Perspectives* (New York: Oxford University Press, 1997), 25.

17. Wuthnow, *Restructuring of American Religion*, 230.

18. William Hutchison, "Discovering America," in *Between the Times: The Travail of the Protestant Establishment in America, 1900–1960*, ed. Hutchison (Cambridge, U. K.: Cambridge University Press, 1989), 307.

19. Jean Spencer, "A Priceless Gift," *Hearthstone* 17 (June 1966): 10–11; Edwin Gaustad, "The Pulpit and the Pews," in *Between the Times*, 42–43; "A United Presbyterian Way of Christian Education," 1964, 10–2 (RG 112, 10–2, Presbyterian Historical Society).

20. Participants included: Marcus Barth, Dora Chaplin, William Graham Cole, Arnold Come, Fred Denbeaux, Joseph Fletcher, Harry Goodykoontz, Joseph Haroutunian, William Hulme, Gordon Jackson, Randolph Crump Miller, Richard McCann, Otto Piper, [Mrs. Ben] Russell, Paul Ramsey, and Presbyterian committee members Roy Fairchild, Dorothy Fritz, George Hunt, Walter Jenkins, Norman Langford, Ben Sissel, Eli Wismer, and J. C. Wynn.

21. "A Compendium of the Discussions from the Consultative Conference on Theology and the Family," sponsored by the Office of Family Education Research, 17–20 October 1957 (RG 39, 1–6, PHS).

22. Robert Clyde Johnson and Walter E. Wiest, "Can There Be a Protestant Theology of the Family?" (RG 112, 10–9, PHS).

23. Committee on the Christian Home, Minutes of Meeting, 10 January 1958 (RG 39, 1–2, PHS).
24. Committee on the Christian Home, Minutes of 21 and 22 April 1958, 2, 18, 27 (RG 39, 1–2, PHS). (The document contains penciled notations from an unidentified committee member that read, in reference to this last set of observations, "here they hit bottom.")
25. "A United Presbyterian Way of Christian Education," 1964, 9. Members of the task force included Eli Wismer, George Allen, Orville Chadsey, Walter Jenkins, Robert Kempes, Norman Langford, Helen Link, John Ribble, Ralph Sundquist, Edward Trefz, and Jack Worthington.
26. *The Growing Edge: An Occasional Bulletin of the Educational Systems Coordinating Committee* 1 (November 1964): A–3; inter-office memorandum to ESCOM, from Jack Worthington, 13 January 1965 (RG 112, 10–9, PHS).
27. "Edited Transcription of Reports of Small Group Discussions of 'A United Presbyterian Way of Christian Education,'" 15 April 1964, 12 (RG 112, 10–2, PHS).
28. "Board Answers Questions about Church Education in the 1970s," MS, 29 January 1965 (RG 112, 10–1, PHS).
29. "The Family and Church Education," Statement of the Present Thinking of the Board of Christian Education Staff, February 1, 1966, 2, 3, 5, 6 (RG 112, 10–9, PHS).
30. Division of Educational Services, Basic Principles, MS, November 1966, 2, 4 (RG 112, 11–8, PHS).
31. Landon Y. Jones, *Great Expectations: America and the Baby Boom Generation* (New York: Ballantine Books, 1980), 95–105. See also Thomas Hine, *The Rise and Fall of the American Teenager* (New York: Avon Books, 1999), 249–273.
32. Alice Edson Cornell, "You Can Talk with Your Teenager!" *Hearthstone* 12 (September 1960): 6–7; Roy Hansen, "Are You Sure You Love Your Teen-Ager?" *Hearthstone* 12 (July 1960): 8.
33. Sherman R. Hanson, "Let Us Make Men," *Hearthstone* 15 (June 1963): 7–9; Norman R. DuPuy, "My Child Does as He Is Told!" *Hearthstone* 17 (January 1965): 7–9; Luther G. Baker Jr., "Changing Religious Norms and Family Values," *Journal of Marriage and the Family* 27 (February 1965): 10. The growing permissiveness of middle-class culture is discussed in Duane F. Alwin, "Trends in Parental Socialization Values: Detroit, 1958–1983," *American Journal of Sociology* 90 (July–November 1984): 359–382.
34. B. Claire Wallace, "Forging Family Friendship," *A.D.* 14 (September 1976): 41–43.
35. Mrs. Lloyd V. Channels, "The Threatened Home," *Hearthstone* 21 (January 1969): 3.
36. Psychological study of adolescents and religion was not new, or course. Studies by Edwin Starbuck and James Leuba date from the turn of the century. There is little evidence, however, that mainline religious educators made much use of such studies, which analyzed conversion experiences of young adults and did not fit the Christian nurture focus on younger children. See Joseph Kett, *Rites of Passage: Adolescents in America, 1790 to the Present* (New York: Basic Books, 1977), 62–85.
37. Robert Bellah et al., *Habits of the Heart: Individualism and Commitment in American Life* (Berkeley: University of California Press, 1985), 62.
38. Quoted in John P. Marcum, "Family, Birth Control, and Sexuality in the Christian Church (Disciples of Christ): 1880–1980," *Encounter* 52 (spring 1991):118.
39. Calvert, quoted in Marcum, "Family, Birth Control and Sexuality in the Christian Church," 120.
40. Beth Bailey, *From Front Porch to Back Seat: Courtship in Twentieth Century America* (Baltimore: Johns Hopkins University Press, 1988).
41. The workbook was subsequently published: E. M. Duvall and S. M. Duvall, eds., *Sex Ways—in Fact and Faith: Bases for Christian Family Policy* (New York: Association

Press, 1961). Conference proceedings are contained in *Foundations for Christian Family Policy*, ed. Elizabeth Steel Genné and William Henry Genné (New York: National Council of the Churches of Christ in the U.S.A.), 1961. See also report in "The Church and Family Life," *Hearthstone* 13 (September 1961): 32.

42. Wynn, "Where the Churches Speak and Where They Are Silent," in *Foundations for Christian Family Policy*, 35–40.

43. "The Task before Us," *Foundations in Christian Family Policy*, 254–258.

44. "Excerpt from the Report 'Sexuality and the Human Community' (1970)," in *The Churches Speak On: Sex and Family Life; Official Statements from Religious Bodies and Ecumenical Organizations*, ed. J. Gordon Melton (Detroit: Gale Research, 1991), 127.

45. On attitudes to the "new morality," see Roof and McKinney, *American Mainline Religion*, 209–217. While mainliners were on the whole more liberal on issues of sexual freedom than evangelicals and Roman Catholics, the authors concluded that they still held to a fairly traditional morality.

46. William M. Martin, *With God on Our Side: The Rise of the Religious Right in America* (New York: Broadway Books, 1996), 171–190.

47. Jean Caffrey Lyles, "NAE's Focus on the Family," *Christian Century*, 1 April 1982, 398–400.

48. James Davison Hunter, *Culture Wars: The Struggle to Define America* (New York: Basic Books, 1991), 176–196; Michael Lienesch, *Redeeming America: Piety and Politics in the New Christian Right* (Chapel Hill: University of North Carolina Press, 1993), 52–93; Colleen McDannell, "Creating the Christian Home: Home Schooling in Contemporary America," *American Sacred Space* (Bloomington: Indiana University Press, 1995), 187–219.

49. David Watt, *A Transforming Faith: Explorations of Twentieth-Century American Evangelicalism* (New Brunswick, N. J.: Rutgers University Press, 1991), 93–136. The publication *The Evangelicals: What They Believe, Who They Are, Where They Are Changing*, ed. John Woodbridge and David Wells (Nashville, Tenn.: Abingdon, 1975), created a host of dissenters, mostly from Wesleyan traditions. The most systematic response is found in *The Variety of American Evangelicalism*, ed. Donald Dayton and Robert Johnston (Downers Grove, Ill.: InterVarsity Press, 1991).

50. Margaret Bendroth, "Fundamentalism and the Family: Gender, Culture, and the American Pro-Family Movement," *Journal of Women's History* 10 (winter 1999): 35–54.

51. Mrs. W. Edson Dutton, "When Shall We Teach Our Children about God?" *Moody Bible Institute Monthly* 38 (May 1938): 462. See also John P. Bartkowski and Christopher G. Ellison, "Divergent Models of Childrearing in Popular Manuals: Conservative Protestants vs. the Mainstream Experts," *Sociology of Religion* 56 (spring 1995): 21–34.

52. John R. Rice, "The Bible on Child Correction and Discipline," *Sword of the Lord* 22 March 1940, 1–4.

53. Bill Gothard Jr., "The Chain of Command," *Faith for the Family* (March–April 1975): 11–12. See also Wilfred Bockelman, *Bill Gothard: The Man and His Ministry: An Evaluation* (Santa Barbara, Calif.: Quill Publications, 1976); Bendroth, *Fundamentalism and Gender: 1875 to the Present* (New Haven, Conn.: Yale University Press, 1993), 97–117.

54. Dobson, *The Strong-Willed Child* (Wheaton, Ill.: Tyndale, 1978), 170–171.

55. "Focus at Fifteen," *Focus on the Family* 16 (March 1992): 10–14.

56. "1994: The International Year of the Family," *Focus on the Family* 18 (July 1994): 2; "Focus at Fifteen"; Rodney Clapp, "Meet James Dobson, His Father's Son," *Christianity Today*, 7 May 1982, 14.

57. For a general discussion, see Helen Hardacre, "The Impact of Fundamentalisms on Women, the Family, and Interpersonal Relations," in *Fundamentalisms and Society: Reclaiming the Sciences, the Family, and Education*, ed. Martin Marty and R. Scott Appleby (Chicago: University of Chicago Press, 1993), 129–150.
58. Mary L. Miles, "Mothers—the Guardians of the Home," *Sunday-School Times*, 6 February 1960, 103; Joseph Edwin Harris, "The Faith of Our Mothers," *Sunday-School Times*, 7 May 1960, 361. Interestingly, mothers have tended to be the more important parent for religious conservatives. See William Hutchison, "Cultural Strain and Protestant Liberalism," *American Historical Review* (1971): 386–411; Wade Clark Roof, *Spiritual Marketplace: Baby Boomers and the Remaking of American Religion* (Princeton, N. J.: Princeton University Press, 1999), 229.
59. Ryrie, "Is Your Home Scriptural?" *Bibliotheca Sacra* 109 (October–December 1952): 346.
60. S. Maxwell Coder, "The Christian Family and the Word of God," *Moody Monthly* 61 (August 1961): 15.
61. Ryrie, "Is Your Home Scriptural?" 350.
62. James A. Bryan, "Building Family Altars," *Sunday-School Times*, 15 March 1958.
63. Norman V. Williams, "Vital Values of a Family Altar," *Moody Monthly* 50 (December 1949): 230–231; Robert Owen, "Family Altars Make a Difference," *Moody Monthly* 62 (March 1962): 25, 38. See also, in a similar vein, James Wesley Baker, "The Children's Liberation Movement: Whose Rights?" *Faith for the Family* 3 (March–April 1975): 5–6f.
64. Ben Strobehn, "Is There a Famine in Your Family?" *Faith for the Family* 3 (January–February 1976): 12–13, 38.
65. Bernard DeRemer, "Popular Music and the Christian Life," *Moody Monthly* 49 (February 1949): 458–459.
66. Rice, *What Is Wrong with the Movies?* (Grand Rapids, Mich.: Zondervan, 1938), 105. The book was republished at least twelve times after it first appeared.
67. Joel A. Carpenter, *Revive Us Again: The Reawakening of American Fundamentalism* (New York: Oxford University Press, 1997), 166.
68. Stedman, foreword to Charles Swindoll, *You and Your Child* (Nashville, Tenn.: Thomas Nelson, 1977), 9.
69. See Beverly LaHaye, *How to Develop Your Child's Temperament* (Irvine, Calif.: Harvest House, 1977), 126–127; "What about Family Devotions?" *Focus on the Family* 18 (August 1994): 14.
70. Larry Tomczak, *God, the Rod, and Your Child's Bod* (Old Tappan, N. J.: Fleming H. Revell, 1982), 39.
71. Diane Cooksey Kessler, *Parents and the Experts: Can Christian Parents Accept the Experts' Advice?* (Valley Forge, Pa.: Judson Press, 1974), 79. See also Richard Mouw, *Consulting the Faithful: What Christian Intellectuals Can Learn from Popular Religion* (Grand Rapids, Mich.: Eerdmans, 1994), 64.
72. Marianne K. Hering, "Believe Well, Live Well," *Focus on the Family* 18 (September 1994): 4.

Chapter 7   **Alternatives and Possibilities**

1. Weber, "For Happier Families," *Homiletic and Pastoral Review* 51 (1951): 623.
2. William Nerin, "What Is CFM? Tapping the Source of Married Apostles," *Homiletic and Pastoral Review* 65 (January 1965): 314, 315.
3. See, for example, Debra Campbell, "The Struggle to Serve," in *Transforming Parish*

Ministry: The Changing Role of Catholic Clergy, Laity, and Women Religious, ed. Jay Dolan et al. (New York: Crossroads, 1990), 246.

4. The history of the Christian Family Movement is thoroughly documented in Jeffrey Burns, *American Catholics and the Family Crisis, 1930–1962: An Ideological and Organizational Response* (New York: Garland Publishing, 1988). On the Crowleys' marriage and role in CFM, see the interview with Patty Crowley, "If She Couldn't Stand the Heat, She Would Have Stayed in the Kitchen," *U.S. Catholic* 47 (May 1982): 25–29.

5. "Growth of CFM," *America*, 9 August 1955, 30; Susan Hansen, "Family Movement Struggles to Survive in 1980s," *National Catholic Reporter*, 14 August 1987, 6. The decline was due to a variety of factors. As a family movement, CFM was in a sense superseded by Marriage Encounter in the 1960s and 1970s and, as a social movement, by organizations more directly involved in social issues. Many CFM members, it appears, graduated into nonreligious forms of community organizing. CFM also encountered internal divisions over the issue of birth control, which the Crowleys began raising in the 1960s.

6. "Ideas for a Happier Family Life," *Ave Maria*, 23 November 1957, 12–14.

7. Hansen, "Family Movement Struggles to Survive in 1980s," 6.

8. Steven M. Arvella, "Reynold Hillenbrand and Chicago Catholicism," *U.S. Catholic Historian* (1990): 353–370.

9. Leo R. Ward, *Catholic Life, U.S.A.: Contemporary Lay Movements* (St. Louis, Mo.: B. Herder Book Co., 1959), 33.

10. Burns, *American Catholics and the Family Crisis*, 300–301.

11. Geaney, "The Christian Family Movement and the Suburban Catholic," *Catholic Mind* 54 (July 1956): 394.

12. Quoted in Stephen M. Avella, "Reynold Hillenbrand and Chicago Catholicism," *U.S. Catholic Historian* (1990): 363.

13. Campbell, "Struggle to Serve," 250.

14. *The Family in a Time of Change* (Chicago: Coordinating Committee of the Christian Family Movement, 1966), 3.

15. See the interview with P. Crowley, "If She Couldn't Stand the Heat," 25–29.

16. Burns, *American Catholics and the Family Crisis*, 157.

17. Ibid., 299.

18. Jeffrey Lewis, "Boom Years Gone, but CFM Lives On," *National Catholic Reporter*, 16 March 1979, 15. See also accounts in Dennis J. Geaney, "Christian Family Movement, 1960," *America*, 7 May 1960, 216–218; John E. Truxaw, "The Luceys Are Different," *Ave Maria*, 17 December 1960, 5–8.

19. James T. McHugh, "Strains of Renewal Show on CFM," *National Catholic Reporter*, 3 September 1969, 5.

20. Rich Casey, "CFM Shows Undefiant Independence of Church," *National Catholic Reporter*, 10 September 1971, 22.

21. Burns, *American Catholics and the Family Crisis*, 324.

22. Coles, *The Geography of Faith: Conversations between Daniel Berrigan, When Underground, and Robert Coles* (Boston: Beacon Press, 1971), 54.

23. Quoted in Lewis V. Baldwin, *There Is a Balm in Gilead: The Cultural Roots of Martin Luther King, Jr.* (Minneapolis, Minn.: Fortress Press, 1991), 91.

24. bell hooks, *Yearning: Race, Gender and Cultural Politics* (Boston: South End Press, 1990), 47.

25. Mary Frances Berry and John W. Blassingame, *Long Memory: The Black Experience in America* (New York: Oxford University Press, 1982), 80–81; Herbert Gutman, *The Black Family in Slavery and Freedom, 1750–1925* (New York: Pantheon Books, 1976).

26. J. Deotis Roberts, *Roots of a Black Future: Family and Church* (Philadelphia: Westminster Press, 1980), 87.
27. Christine King Farris, "The Young Martin: From Childhood through College," *Ebony* 41 (January 1986): 57.
28. James Cone, *Martin and Malcolm and America: A Dream or a Nightmare* (Maryknoll, N.Y.: Orbis Books, 1993), 22.
29. King, *Stride toward Freedom: The Montgomery Story* (New York: Harper and Row, 1958), 21; Farris, "Young Martin," 57; Cone, *Martin and Malcolm and America*, 23.
30. Cone, *Martin and Malcolm and America*, 24; King, *Daddy King: An Autobiography*, ed. Clayton Riley (New York: William Morrow, 1980), 108.
31. Stephen Oates, *Let the Trumpet Sound: The Life of Martin Luther King, Jr.* (New York: Harper and Row, 1982), 12.
32. Berry and Blassingame, *Long Memory*, 77–82.
33. Oates, *Let the Trumpet Sound*, 8.
34. Coles, *Children of Crisis: A Study of Courage and Fear* (1964; rpt., Boston: Little, Brown, 1967), 66.
35. King Sr., *Daddy King*, 94.
36. Cone, *My Soul Looks Back* (Nashville, Tenn.: Abingdon Press, 1982), 19.
37. "An Autobiography of Religious Development" (12 September–22 November 1950), in *The Papers of Martin Luther King, Jr.*, vol. 1: *Called to Serve*, ed. Clayborne Carson et al. (Berkeley: University of California Press, 1992), 360. On black extended families, see Carol Stack, *All Our Kin: Strategies for Survival in a Black Community* (New York: Harper and Row, 1974); Elmer P. Martin and Joanne Mitchell Martin, *The Black Extended Family* (Chicago: University of Chicago Press, 1978).
38. King, "Autobiography of Religious Development."
39. Farris, "Young Martin," 56.
40. Baldwin, *There Is a Balm in Gilead*, 109–110. See also Ella Mitchell, "Black Nurture," in *Black Church Life-Styles*, ed. Emmanuel McCall (Nashville, Tenn.: Abingdon Press, 1986), 45–67.
41. Collins, "Black Women and Motherhood," in *Re-Thinking the Family: Some Feminist Questions*, ed. Barrie Thorne with Marilyn Yalom (Boston: Northeastern University Press, 1992), 223.
42. Len Davis, quoted in Bob Blauner, *Black Lives, White Lives: Three Decades of Race Relations in America* (Berkeley: University of California Press, 1989), 30.
43. Proctor, *My Moral Odyssey* (Valley Forge, Pa.: Judson Press, 1989), 20, 25.
44. Willie, *A New Look at Black Families* (Bay Side, N.Y.: General Hall, 1976), 5–6.
45. Roberts, *Roots of a Black Future: Family and Church*, 86.
46. Thurman, *With Head and Heart: The Autobiography of Howard Thurman* (New York: Harcourt Brace Jovanovich, 1979), 19–20. See also Harold Carter, *The Prayer Tradition of Black People* (Valley Forge, Pa.: Judson Press, 1976), 75–79.
47. O. Richard Bowyer, Betty L. Hart, and Charlotte A. Meade, *Prayer in the Black Tradition* (Nashville, Tenn.: Upper Room, 1986), 62.
48. The quotation is from Franklin's sermon on "Hannah, the Ideal Mother," preached in the late 1950s, from Jeff Todd Tilton, ed., *Give Me This Mountain: Life Story and Selected Sermons* (Urbana: University of Illinois Press, 1989), 147.
49. Thurman, *With Head and Heart*, 16.
50. Cone, *God of the Oppressed* (New York: Seabury Press, 1975), 13.
51. Proctor, *My Moral Odyssey*, 25.
52. Dulin, "Social Contexts for Black Christian Education," *Spectrum* 47 (July–August 1971): 20–21. See also Bonita Pope Curry, "The Role of the Church in the Educational Development of Black Children," in *The Black Family: Past, Present, and Future*, ed. Lee N. June (Grand Rapids, Mich.: Zondervan, 1991), 116.

53. Martin Luther King Jr., "The Christian Way of Life in Human Relations," *A.M.E. Church Review* 73 (January–March 1958): 36.
54. Penny Marler, "Lost in the Fifties: The Changing Family and the Nostalgic Church," in *Work, Family, and Religion in Contemporary Society*, ed. Nancy Tatom Ammerman and Wade Clark Roof (New York: Routledge, 1995), 23–60.
55. Nevin, "Educational Religion," *Weekly Messenger of the German Reformed Church*, 7 July 1847.

Index

Abbott, Jacob, 23
Abbott, Lyman, 52
Abingdon Religious Education Text
  series, 72
Abington v. Schempp, 124
abortion, 2, 132, 133, 134, 136
Adam's sin, federal theory of, 26
A.D. magazine, 120
adolescents: delinquency of, 93, 102;
  evangelical, 140–141; and
  intergenerational conflict, 128–130;
  sexuality of, 130–133, 139–140; in
  work force, 93
Adorno, Theodor W., 109
African American family: child rearing in,
  149–152, 153–154, 155–156; extended, 153; family devotions in, 154–
  155; and home mission movement,
  47–48; influences on religion, 145;
  problems in, 150, 153; Reconstruction
  policy on, 46–47
age: of church membership, 123; at
  marriage, 100
agnosticism, parental, 83–85
Allport, Gordon, 109
altar. *See* family altar/devotions
American Baptist Home Missionary
  Society, 47
American Family Forum, 134
American Woman's Home, The (Beecher
  and Stowe), 43, 44 (fig.)
Ames, Edward Scribner, 83

anger: in African American family, 153;
  repression of, 33–34
architecture. *See* home design
attachment theory, 96

baby boomers, 100–101, 129
Baby and Child Care (Spock), 102
Baker, Ray Stannard, 54
baptism, 35
Baptist Missionary Training School, 49
Baptists: membership decline of, 121; in
  mission movement, 47–48, 49
Beecher, Catherine, 43, 44–45
Bellah, Robert, 131
Berger, Peter, 108, 116, 119
Berrigan, Daniel, 150
Betts, Anna Freelove, 72
Betts, George, 72
Bible, family values in, 125
Bible reading, 51, 52, 54, 84, 101, 111
Bible story books, 72
birthrate, 17, 100–101, 121
Blackwell, Henry, 18
Board of Christian Education (Presbyte-
  rian), 91, 113, 114, 128
Boardman, H.A., 14, 40
*Bobbed Hair, Bossy Wives, and Women
  Preachers* (Rice), 137
Boston Missionary Training School, 56
Bower, William Clayton, 90–91
Bowlby, John, 96
Bringing Home the New Born Calf, 72

About the Author

Margaret Lamberts Bendroth is professor of history at Calvin College, Grand Rapids, Michigan. She is author of *Fundamentalism and Gender, 1875 to the Present*, as well as numerous articles and reviews on religion and family life. She has served as an editor for the Living Theological Heritage series of the United Church of Christ. She is a clergy spouse and, with her husband, Norman, the parent of two children, Nathan and Anna.